OCS Study
MMS 2001-077

Coastal Marine Institute

Across-Shelf Larval, Postlarval, and Juvenile Fish Collected at Offshore Oil and Gas Platforms and a Coastal Rock Jetty West of the Mississippi River Delta

MMS U.S. Department of the Interior
Minerals Management Service
Gulf of Mexico OCS Region

Cooperative Agreement
Coastal Marine Institute
Louisiana State University

OCS Study
MMS 2001-077

Coastal Marine Institute

Across-Shelf Larval, Postlarval, and Juvenile Fish Collected at Offshore Oil and Gas Platforms and a Coastal Rock Jetty West of the Mississippi River Delta

Authors

Frank J. Hernandez, Jr.
Richard F. Shaw
Joseph S. Cope
James G. Ditty
Mark C. Benfield
Talat Farooqi

September 2001

Prepared under MMS Contract
14-35-0001-30660-19926
by
Coastal Fisheries Institute
Louisiana State University
Baton Rouge, Louisiana 70803

Published by

U.S. Department of the Interior
Minerals Management Service
Gulf of Mexico OCS Region

Cooperative Agreement
Coastal Marine Institute
Louisiana State University

DISCLAIMER

REPORT AVAILABILITY

Extra copies of the report may be obtained from the Public Information Office (Mail Stop 5034) at the following address:

> U.S. Department of the Interior
> Minerals Management Service
> Gulf of Mexico OCS Region
> Public Information Office (MS 5034)
> 1201 Elmwood Boulevard
> New Orleans, Louisiana 70123-2394

> Telephone: (504) 736-2519 or
>   1-800-200-GULF

CITATION

Suggested Citation:

Hernandez, F.J., Jr., R.F. Shaw, J.C Cope, J.G. Ditty, M.C. Benfield and T. Farooqi. 2001. Across-shelf Larval, Postlarval, and Juvenile Fish Communities Collected at Offshore Oil and Gas Platforms and a Coastal Rock Jetty West of the Mississippi River Delta. OCS Study MMS 2001-077. Prepared by the Coastal Fisheries Institute, Louisiana State University. U.S. Department of the Interior, Minerals Management Service, Gulf of Mexico OCS Region, New Orleans, LA. 144 pp.

ACKNOWLEDGMENTS

We gratefully acknowledge funding by the Minerals Management Service-Louisiana State University-Coastal Marine Institute (Contract Number 14-75-0001-30660, Task Order Number 19926) and by the Louisiana Sea Grant Program, part of the National Sea Grant College Program maintained by the National Oceanic and Atmospheric Administration. We thank David Bunch, Nathan Craig, Heather Haas, Robin Hargroder, Ross Horton, Sean Keenan, Gregory Lavergne, David Lindquist, Bradley McDonald, Cory New, Nick Ortega, John Plunkett, and Christopher Whatley for assistance in the field and laboratory. We gratefully acknowledge the assistance of Drs. Charles A. Wilson and David R. Stanley. We are further indebted to Exxon USA, Inc. and Mobil USA Exploration and Production, Inc. for access to their offshore oil and gas platforms and logistical support, and to the crews of Mobil's West Cameron 352, West Cameron 71D, Green Canyon 18, and Grand Isle 94 and Exxon's South Timbalier 54 platforms.

EXECUTIVE SUMMARY

The introduction and proliferation of offshore oil and gas structures in the northern Gulf has undoubtedly affected the marine ecosystem. The central and western Gulf is dominated by a mud/silt/sand bottom with only an estimated 2780 km^2 of natural available reef. There are approximately 4,000 oil and gas structures in the federal waters of the Gulf, accounting for approximately 11.7 km^2 (or 4.0%) of the total "reef" habitat in the northern Gulf. The fact that platforms represent vertical artificial substrate that extends from the bottom to the surface (photic zone), regardless of location and depth, increases their significance. Since fish populations are usually limited by available energy, recruitment, or habitat, it is important to determine if platforms: 1) provide critical habitat for early life history stages; 2) serve as new or additional spawning habitat; and 3) influence energy flow through the ecosystem by aggregating prey.

The adult fish communities around natural and artificial reefs are fairly well known and the fisheries aggregation value and enhanced biodiversity of oil and gas structures is well-recognized. Despite research efforts, however, biologists still disagree over the paradigm of whether these artificial reefs (e.g., platforms) contribute significantly to new fish production or simply attract and concentrate existing fish biomass. Since the central and western Gulf has little natural reef habitat, we believe that the contribution of artificial reefs to existing reef habitat has enhanced reef fish populations, but the overall or net impact of this augmentation is not known, especially when corrected for increased commercial and recreational fishing mortality associated with platforms.

Few studies have attempted to compare the ichthyofaunal assemblages collected at oil and gas platforms in the northcentral Gulf across wide depth zones, and the information that is available primarily concerns adult fishes and not their early life history stages. This study focused on three main objectives. The first was to respond to specific requests for more basic biological information on reef fish, e.g., larval, postlarval, and juvenile taxonomy, seasonality, lunar periodicity, distribution (vertical and across shelf), and relative abundance. Secondly, we wished to provide much needed information on the role that oil and gas platforms (hard substrate habitat) may play as nursery/recruitment grounds and/or refugia for postlarval and juvenile fish, which could contribute to fish production. Finally, as a long-term objective, we wished to evaluate the ecological significance that this artificial habitat building, which has occurred on an unprecedented scale in the northcentral Gulf, may have had on the early life history stages of fish.

Ichthyoplankton and juvenile fish assemblages were sampled at three petroleum platforms and a coastal rock jetty which served as a low salinity, artificial habitat end-member. Mobil's Green Canyon (GC) 18, which lies in about 230 m of water on the shelf slope (27°56'37"N, 91°01'45"W), was sampled monthly during new moon phases over a 2-3 night period during July 1995-June 1996. Mobil's Grand Isle (GI) 94B, which lies in approximately 60 m of water at mid-shelf (28°30'57"N, 90°07'23"W), was sampled twice monthly during new and full moon phases over a three night period during April-August 1996. Exxon's South Timbalier (ST) 54G, which lies in approximately 20 m of water on the inner shelf (28°50'01"N, 90°25'00"W), was sampled twice monthly during new and full moon periods during April-September 1997. All platforms had very similar structural complexity. The stone rubble jetties

(2-3 m depth) at the terminus of Belle Pass near Fourchon, Louisiana (N 29 03.90, W 90 13.80), were also sampled over a two night period in 1997 simultaneously with the sampling of ST 54. At the platforms, fish larvae and juveniles were collected within the platform structure using passive plankton nets and light-traps fished at depth (approximately 20 m) and near-surface, and about 20 m downstream of the platforms with a light-trap floated downstream at surface. At Belle Pass, fish larvae and juveniles were collected with light-traps deployed at the surface within two meters of the rock walls and with a bow-mounted plankton pushnet fished along the length of each jetty.

Overall family richness was highest at GC 18 (52), followed by GI 94 (43), ST 54 (42), and Belle Pass (41). At the genus level, richness was highest at Belle Pass (127), followed by GI 94 (114), ST 54 (86), and GC 18 (82). At all sites clupeiforms dominated samples, comprising 59-97% of the total catch. Reef-associated (e.g., scombrids, carangids, lutjanids, gobiids) and reef-dependent (e.g., blenniids, chaetodontids, pomacentrids) taxa were relatively rare in our collections compared to pelagic and demersal taxa. At GC 18, reef-associated and reef-dependent taxa (identified at least to the genus level) comprised 18% and 32% of the total number of fish collected with plankton nets and light-traps, respectively. At GI 94 these taxa comprised 10% of the plankton net catch and 17% of the light-trap catch. At ST 54, these fishes comprised less than 1% of the total number of fish collected with plankton nets and only 8% of the fish collected with light-traps. At the Belle Pass jetties, reef-associated and reef-dependent fishes comprised approximately 15% and 2% of plankton pushnet and light-trap catches, respectively.

Distributional differences were observed for many species within and around the platforms. Few taxa were found only in off-platform samples (4 at GC 18, 6 at GI 94, and 12 at ST 54). Some pelagic species, e.g., *Caranx crysos* and *C. hippos/latus* (GC 18) and *Euthynnus alletteratus* (GI 94 and ST54) generally had higher catch-per-unit-efforts (CPUEs) in surface waters downstream from the platforms. Several species were collected only at depth, particularly mesopelagic and benthic taxa, e.g., *Chlorophthalmus agassizi* (GC 18), *Robia legula* (GI 94), and *Ophidion robinsi* (ST 54). Other taxa predominantly found at depth included *Mugil cephalus* (GC 18), *Symphurus* spp. (GI 94), and *Ariomma* spp. (ST 54). Few differences were observed between Shannon-Weiner diversity indices calculated by gear and location, with the exception of sub-surface light-trap samples, which were significantly lower in diversity at the inner shelf and shelf slope platforms. Significant differences in mean total plankton net densities and mean total light-trap CPUEs were found between new vs. full moon phases. Plankton net densities were significantly higher during new moon sampling periods at GI 94, ST 54 and the Belle Pass jetties. Light-trap CPUEs were significantly higher during new moon periods at GI 94 and the jetties, but there was no significant difference observed at ST 54. These differences in lunar periodicities occurred in spite of the potential for competitive interference by the platforms' large ambient light-fields which could confound any lunar effect or sampling efficiency.

Between sites, the ichthyoplankton and juvenile fish assemblages sampled were relatively dissimilar, based on Schoener's Index of Similarity (0-1 scale; clupeiforms excluded), with the highest index value for any two sites being 0.45 for GI 94 and ST 54 . No significant difference was observed between mean Shannon-Weiner diversity indices calculated for plankton net samples at each site. For light-trap samples, however, diversity was lowest at GC 18, significantly higher at GI 94, and then decreased inshore. Canonical correlation analyses indicated that temperature and salinity explained most of the variation in larval abundance for some dominant taxa at the platforms, while at Belle Pass, dissolved oxygen and turbidity were also important environmental variables.

Gear comparisons demonstrated that plankton nets collected individuals from more families than light-traps at two platforms (plankton net vs. light-trap: 45 vs. 37 on the shelf slope; 40 vs. 37 on the mid-shelf; and 34 vs. 34 on the inner shelf), but only collected more taxa (genus level) than light-traps at one platform (plankton net vs. light-trap: 64 vs. 59 on the shelf slope; 83 vs. 90 on the mid-shelf; and 59 vs. 65 on the inner shelf). At the jetty, the pushnet collected more families (41 vs. 21) and taxa (85 vs. 42) than the light-trap. Results of Kolmogorov-Smirnov length-frequency comparisons of fish collected in plankton nets vs. light-traps indicated light-traps generally collected significantly larger individuals. At the jetty, greater overlap in size distributions was observed for comparisons of the pushnet and light-trap. Schoener's Similarity Indices for light-trap and plankton net samples indicated low similarity between gears at the inner shelf and shelf slope platforms (0.32-0.38), but higher similarity (0.63) at the inner shelf platform which was most dominated by clupeiforms. At the jetty, pushnet and light-trap samples had relatively high taxonomic similarity (0.61). Few significant differences were detected between Shannon-Weiner Diversity Indices for platform light-trap and plankton net samples, while at the jetty, pushnet samples had significantly higher diversity than light-trap samples.

While reef-associated and reef-dependent taxa were collected at all sites, taxonomic richness and diversity of these taxa were highest at GI 94. At this mid-shelf site, the intermediate location, depth and proximity to a high density of surrounding platforms may have created generally favorable conditions for the recruitment of reef taxa. The presence and proximity of upstream reefs and spawning habitats, therefore, may play an important role in the eventual makeup of the pre-adult assemblages. The fact that reef-dependent and reef-associated postlarvae and juveniles were rare is not surprising. Mortality rates for pelagic larvae prior to settlement approach 100%, resulting in relatively few postlarvae and juveniles surviving to settlement. Secondly, predation pressures can be high at the time of settlement with no shortage of potential predators of all sizes, as indicated by relatively high abundances of juvenile, piscivorous scombrids and synodontids. Finally, while oil and gas platforms may be suitable habitat for adults, the physical structure may not afford enough protection for juvenile fishes. Smaller reef structures have been shown to support more settlers, in part due to their greater edge effect, lower vertical relief, and greater availability of small shelter holes, i.e., porosity and rugosity. Petroleum platforms, in contrast, are larger reefs characterized as having a higher profile, less complexity, and lower porosity than natural reefs.

Other potential effects of oil and gas platforms may be an increase in available habitat for adult nesting or spawning. Since preflexion, reef-dependent larvae were often collected, it is likely that they were locally spawned upstream at either natural or artificial habitats nearby. With the limited amount of hard-substrate habitat available in the northcentral Gulf of Mexico, the addition of artificial habitats (platforms) may increase the chances of finding suitable spawning habitat. Another important consideration is the degree to which organisms associated with the reef structure interact with pelagic species and contribute to adjacent off-reef production. Pelagic, but often structure-associated taxa, such as scombrids and carangid juveniles, are competent swimmers, highly predatory and often piscivorous. If these juveniles, which were relatively abundant in our collections, are actively feeding in association with the platforms, then they, and similar taxa could serve as important trophic links between the reef and pelagic environments. Relatively little is known about the relationship between offshore petroleum platforms and the early life history stages of fishes anywhere in the world. Our findings, therefore, represent an important first step towards this aspect of artificial reef research.

TABLE OF CONTENTS

LIST OF FIGURES

LIST OF TABLES

Introduction

The Gulf of Mexico (Gulf) yields about 40% of the commercial fish landings (NOAA/NMFS 1993) in the United States and supports 33% of the country's recreational fishery (Essig et al. 1991; Van Voorhies et al. 1992). The region also possesses the vast majority of the nation's coastal wetlands. Louisiana alone has over 3.8 million acres (>40% of the nation's total wetlands), but these areas are disappearing at an alarming rate, i.e., Louisiana land loss represents 60-80% of the nation's total annual coastal wetland loss (Boesch et al. 1994). The continual loss of Gulf estuarine and wetland habitats that serve as the nursery grounds for a large number of our commercially- and recreationally-important fisheries makes knowledge of the potential nursery function of other habitats critical. Habitat issues have received increased attention lately, in part due to the Essential Fish Habitat Provisions added to the Federal Sustainable Fisheries Act of 1996 that facilitate the long-term protection of waters and substrate necessary to fish for spawning, breeding, feeding or growth to maturity (USDOC 1996).

The introduction and proliferation of offshore oil and gas structures in the northern Gulf has undoubtedly affected the marine ecosystem. There are approximately 4,000 oil and gas structures in the federal waters of the Gulf (Stanley and Wilson 2000). The central and western Gulf is dominated by a mud/silt/sand bottom with little relief or hard bottom habitat. Parker et al. (1983) reported only 2780 km^2 of natural available reef in the central and western Gulf. Although Gallaway (1998) calculated that oil and gas platforms in the northern Gulf provided 11.7 km^2 (or 4.0%) of the total "reef" habitat, the fact that platforms represent vertical artificial substrate that extends from the bottom to the surface (photic zone), regardless of location and depth, increases their significance. Since fish populations are usually limited by available energy, recruitment, or habitat, it is important to determine if platforms: 1) provide critical habitat for early life history stages; 2) serve as new or additional spawning habitat; and 3) influence energy flow through the ecosystem by aggregating prey.

Oil and gas platforms can enhance fisheries by providing attachment substrate for habitat-limited sessile invertebrates, thereby creating food and habitat for reef-dependent species that are trophically-dependent on sessile and motile invertebrates associated with reefs (Gallaway 1981; Bohnsak and Sutherland 1985; Stephan et al. 1990; Bohnsak 1991). Since reef fish assemblages are among the most diverse and taxonomically rich in the aquatic biosphere (Sale 1991), platform communities may significantly enhance biodiversity. In addition, oil and gas structures may offer refugia for species which are trophically-independent of the biofouling community (i.e., reef-associated species; Choat and Bellwood 1991), but are ecologically-important resident, seasonal, or transient members of the hard substrate fish community (Gallaway et al. 1980). The extensive range (latitudinally and longitudinally) of this artificial substrate may also serve as migratory routes for tropical and subtropical species.

The adult fish communities around natural and artificial reefs are fairly well known (Seaman and Sprague 1992; Rooker et al. 1997; Stanley and Wilson 2000) and the fisheries aggregation value of oil and gas structures is well-recognized in the Gulf (CDOP 1985). Despite research efforts, however, biologists still disagree over the paradigm of whether these artificial reefs (e.g., platforms) contribute significantly to new fish production or simply attract and concentrate existing fish biomass (Pickering and Whitmarsh 1997; Bortone 1998). Existing data on adult fishes support both sides of the debate (Stone et al. 1979; Alevizon et al. 1985). Bohnsak (1989) theorized that reef effects fall along a continuum between attraction of existing organisms and production, with increased productivity occurring for reef-dependent species in areas of limited hard substrate habitat. Since the central and western Gulf has little natural reef habitat, we believe that the contribution of artificial reefs to existing reef habitat has enhanced reef fish populations, but the overall or net impact of this augmentation is not known, especially when corrected for increased fishing mortality associated with platforms (Stanley and Wilson 1990).

Few baseline ecological ichthyoplankton studies within the oil field have been published (Finucane et al. 1979a; Finucane et al., 1979b; Bedinger et al. 1980), and none have been published that focus upon platform infrastructure. The Southeastern Area Monitoring and Assessment Program's (SEAMAP) and the National Marine Fisheries Service's (NMFS) Gulf-wide fisheries surveys, and the Minerals Management Service Louisiana-Texas (MMS LATEX) Physical Oceanography Program have historically not sampled in the immediate vicinity of oil and gas platforms because of the conservative navigation/safety requirements of their ships. Thus, fisheries-independent assessment of the abundance of fish life stages within and immediately around these platforms and the role they might play as essential fisheries habitat has not been adequately addressed in federal waters where such structures exist. Clearly additional information is needed on the early life history stages of fishes associated with petroleum platforms.

Across-Shelf Ichthyofaunal Zonation

Gallaway et al. (1980) and Gallaway (1981) reviewed previous descriptions of invertebrate and vertebrate faunal assemblages from the northcentral Gulf's continental shelf and characterized differences largely upon different bottom types (fluvial/terrigenous sediments west of the Mississippi River Delta and carbonaceous sediments to the east), circulation patterns, and related hydrographic conditions. Climatic differences were also acknowledged as having an important role in determining marine faunal distributions, since the inner shelf waters of the northern Gulf are warm and subtropical in the eastern Gulf and along the southwestern coast near the Mexican border, but are warm-temperate from just east of the Mississippi River Delta to Matagorda Bay, Texas (Parker 1960). Reef fish fauna are generally less tolerant of the lower water temperatures that can occur in the more inshore areas during winter in the northern Gulf (Chittenden and McEachran 1976). Along with temperature, topographical relief is another major factor contributing to the distribution of reef fish. Although topographical relief is described as extensive throughout the Gulf (Bright et al. 1974), it is also disjunctly distributed, thus potentially isolating reef fish populations. Several authors have attempted to classify shelf ichthyofaunal assemblages based on depth zones and invertebrate distributions. Defenbaugh (1976), for example, used macroinvertebrate data from trawls to describe three primary depth zones (4-20 m, 20-60 m, and 60-120 m). In his review, however, Gallaway (1981) adopted the zonation description of Chittenden and McEachran (1976) who observed that the distribution of major shrimp species (white shrimp grounds, 3-22 m depth and brown shrimp grounds, 22-110 m depth) matched quite closely the distribution of sediment types and used this information, along with bathymetry, to divide demersal fish assemblages into three different zones characterized primarily by depth.

Table 1 summarizes reef or structure-associated fish for Gallaway's (1981) analysis of previous studies that addressed demersal and pelagic adult fish off Texas (Chittenden and McEachran 1976) and adult reef species off Louisiana, including both artificial and natural reefs (George and Thomas 1974; Gallaway et al. 1979; Shinn 1974; Sonnier et al. 1976). Distinct transitions in species assemblages can be seen in the reef species when analyzed across depths. Overall, the outer shelf (>60 m depth) reefs appear to be more speciose, followed by the mid-shelf (20-60 m) and then the inner shelf (3-20 m). More tropical taxa are present on the outer shelf reefs, such as haemulids, labrids, and scarids, and similar taxa occurred on both natural and artificial reefs. There was some overlap between reef species on the outer shelf and mid-shelf (chaetodontids, pomacanthids, and pomacentrids), but the previously mentioned tropical taxa are replaced by more temperate reef species, such as serranids, *Archosargus probatocephalus*, pomatomids, and rachycentrids. Also, taxa that are common on artificial reefs on the mid-shelf are generally common on the inner shelf as well. In general, *Caranx crysos* and other jacks were noted as being relatively common reef-associated species in each zone.

Few studies have attempted to compare the ichthyofaunal assemblages collected at oil and gas platforms in the northcentral Gulf across wide depth zones, and the information that is available primarily concerns adult fishes and not their early life history stages. Sonnier et al. (1976) surveyed oil and gas platforms (18-55 m depth) as well as inshore (37-59 m) and offshore (110-155 m) reefs off Louisiana and described the offshore reefs as being more speciose than inshore reefs or platforms. This greater offshore reef species richness was primarily due to the presence of southern Gulf-Caribbean taxa (e.g., butterflyfishes, parrotfishes, and cleaning gobies) and taxa common to reefs in the northwestern Gulf off Texas. The authors suggested that the lower temperatures that occur at the inshore reefs and platforms are a limiting factor in the number of species, particularly tropicals, which inhabit inshore reef habitats. As one progressed inshore, the tropical fauna was replaced by more temperate reef fish species, including *Archosargus probatocephalus*, *Selene vomer*, and *Lutjanus griseus* (Sonnier et al. 1976). Twelve species, including tropicals such as *Cantherhines macrocerus*, *Melichthys niger*, and *Diodon holocanthus*, were found only at the platform sites.

Ichthyoplankton Collected at Oil and Gas Platforms

We are aware of only one study that investigated the ichthyoplankton community found in proximity to petroleum platforms. Finucane et al. (1979b), using bongo and neuston nets, sampled within 30-90 m of two oil platforms and two satellite (well) jackets in 17 m of water within the Buccaneer Oil Field, approximately 50 km south southeast of Galveston, Texas. Two far-field, control sites were also sampled for comparison. Three, 2-day cruises (13-14 July,1977; 13-14 October, 1977; and 20 and 22 February, 1978) collected 15,711 fish larvae, primarily engraulids, sciaenids, and bothids. Analyses were limited, but species richness was found to be greatest at the platform sites in July and October and at the satellite structures in February. Overall, of the 68 taxa identified to genus, 38 were associated exclusively with at least one of the structure sites, while another 29 were found near both structure sites and control sites. Dominant taxa at the platform sites included unidentified engraulids (26.1%), *Anchoa* spp. (8.8%), *Cynoscion* spp. (7.3%), and *Syacium* spp. (5.9%). Dominant taxa at the satellite stations were once again unidentified engraulids (32.5%) and *Anchoa* spp. (13.4%), along with *Micropogonias*

Table 1. Summary of the commonly observed adult fish assemblage associated with reefs or platforms by depth as reported in Gallaway et al. (1980) and subsequently modified by Gallaway (1981). Taxa were reported from these depth zones as being affiliated with natural reefs (N) or artificial reefs (A).

		Ichthyofaunal Assemblage		
Taxa	Gallaway et al. (1980)	Coastal (3-27 m)	Offshore (27-64 m)	Blue Water or Tropical (>64 m)
	Gallaway (1981)	Inner Shelf (White Shrimp Ground) (3-20 m)	Intermediate Shelf (Brown Shrimp Ground) (20-60 m)	Outer Shelf (Tropical) (>60 m)
Serranidae				
Epinephelus spp. (grouper spp.)				N
Epinephelus itajara (jewfish)			A	
Epinephelus nigritus (warsaw grouper)			A	
Mycteroperca spp. (grouper spp.)				N
Paranthias furcifer (creole-fish)				N, A
Pomatomidae				
Pomatomus saltatrix (bluefish)		A	A	
Rachycentridae				
Rachycentron canadum (cobia)			A	
Carangidae				
Caranx crysos (blue runner)		A	A	R
Caranx hippos (crevalle jack)			A	
carangid spp. (jack spp.)		A	A	N
Selene setapinnis (moonfish)			A	
Selene vomer (lookdown)		A	A	
Seriola rivoliana (almaco jack)				N, A
Lutjanidae				
Lutjanus campechanus (red snapper)			A	N
Lutjanus synagris (lane snapper)		A	A	
Rhomboplites aurorubens (vermilion snapper)				N
Haeumulidae				
Haeumulon melanurum (cottonwick)				N
Sparidae				
Archosargus probatocephalus (sheepshead)		A	A	
Kyphosidae				
Kyphosus sectatrix (Bermuda chub)			A	
Ephippidae				
Chaetodipterus faber (Atlantic spadefish)		A	A	
Chaetodontidae				
butterflyfish spp.			A	N
Pomacanthidae				
Holacanthus tricolor (rock beauty)				A

Table 1. (continued)

Taxa		Ichthyofaunal Assemblage		
	Gallaway et al. (1980)	Coastal (3-27 m)	Offshore (27-64 m)	Blue Water or Tropical (>64 m)
	Gallaway (1981)	Inner Shelf (White Shrimp Ground) (3-20 m)	Intermediate Shelf (Brown Shrimp Ground) (20-60 m)	Outer Shelf (Tropical) (>60 m)
pomacanthid spp. (angelfish spp.)			A	N, A
Pomacentridae damselfish spp.			A	N, A
Cirrhitidae *Amblycirrhitus pinos* (redspotted hawkfish)				A
Sphyraenidae *Sphyraena barracuda* (great barracuda)			A	A
Labridae *Bodianus rufus* (Spanish hogfish)				A
Decodon puellaris (red hogfish)				A
Clepticus parrai (creole wrasse)				N, A
Scaridae parrotfish spp.				N
Blenniidae blenny spp.			A	
Acanthuridae surgeonfish/tang spp.			A	A
Balistidae *Balistes capriscus* (gray triggerfish)			A	A

undulatus (11.2%), *Cynoscion* spp. (5.5%), and unidentified clupeids (5.4%). No dominant taxa list was reported for the far-field stations. Based on eggs and larval abundance, the petroleum field was determined to be an active spawning area for anguilliforms, callionymids, clupeids, sciaenids, scombrids and soleids, but reef fish eggs and larvae were not abundant. Noteworthy reef or structure-associated taxa collected during the survey include *Etelis oculatus*, *Lutjanus campechanus*, *Centropristis* spp., *Diplectrum* spp., and *Serraniculus pumilio*, although *Etelis oculatus* and *Diplectrum* spp. were also collected in the far-field control sites.

While the Buccaneer Oil Field study did attempt to address larval fish assemblages near petroleum structures, all of the sites with structure were within a 5 km radius from each other, and all sites, including the controls, were in 17 m of water, not allowing for any comparisons of different community regimes across depth zones or large geographic areas. Also, sampling in the oil field study was limited to only three, 2-day cruises. While our study presently has no replicate platforms within the Gallaway's (1981) depth zones, all three zones were sampled intensively, allowing for at least a preliminary characterization of ichthyoplankton assemblages collected within these artificial habitats across the continental shelf.

Objectives

This study focused on three main objectives. The first was to provide much needed information on the role that oil and gas platforms (hard substrate habitat) may play as nursery/recruitment grounds and/or refugia for postlarval and juvenile fish, which could contribute to fish production. Secondly, we wished to respond to specific requests for more basic biological information on reef fish, e.g., larval, postlarval, and juvenile taxonomy, seasonality, lunar periodicity, distribution (vertical and across shelf), and relative abundance. Finally, as a long-term objective, we wished to evaluate the ecological significance that this artificial habitat building, which has occurred on an unprecedented scale in the northcentral Gulf, may have had on the early life history stages of fish. These objectives were accomplished by collecting a wide variety of taxa and sizes utilizing two sampling techniques, light-trap methodology and more traditional techniques (i.e., passive horizontal and hauled vertical plankton net collections). These methodologies complemented each other, since nets effectively sample yolk-sac, larval, and some postlarval fishes, whereas light-traps sample photopositive species at overlapping and larger sizes to give us more complete estimates of sizes (cohorts or inferred ages) and developmental/early life history stages present (Gregory and Powles 1988; Choat et al. 1993). The plankton net samples were envisioned as providing estimates of the larval fish supply to the platforms while the light-trap collections (and the larger postlarvae/early juveniles collected within the nets) were envisioned as providing estimates of settlement-sized fish that would represent potential recruits to the platforms. An integral part of this study, therefore, was the development of an effective sampling strategy and its subsequent evaluation for collecting larval fish for the first time within and immediately around platform infrastructure.

Data collection and analyses focused on three offshore oil and gas platforms in the northcentral Gulf west of the Mississippi River Delta and at a low-salinity, coastal rock jetty environment, which provided a far-field, non-platform site, end-member that was equally complex structurally and represented another artificial, reef-like, hard-substrate habitat. The jetty site was also added in an effort to collect juvenile reef fish (lutjanids, serranids, etc.) that may be utilizing such inshore complex habitats as refuge. The resultant analyses and synthesis of these efforts and on-going sampling efforts east of the Delta (Figure 1) are intended to build a practical characterization and synthesis leading to a much broader understanding of platform ecology and pertinent environment issues over a larger geographic region.

Materials and Methods

Study Areas

Two pilot studies at oil and gas platforms off the Louisiana-Texas border were conducted, one at Mobil's West Cameron (WC) 352 during November 1991-August 1992 and the other at Mobil's WC 71D in July 1994 (Figure 1). West Cameron 352 is located along the Louisiana/Texas border (28°59'35"N, 93°30'15"W) in about 20 m of water. West Cameron 71D is located off western Louisiana (29°37.30' N, 93°10.54' W) in approximately 12 m of water. These exploratory studies were followed by sampling along a transect west of the Mississippi River Delta with site selection for platforms based upon the work of Gallaway et al. (1980), Gallaway (1981), and Continental Shelf Associates (1982) who reported that nekton communities around platforms could be categorized by water depth in the northern Gulf. Three communities were characterized: a coastal assemblage, an offshore assemblage, and a bluewater/tropical assemblage. The platforms selected and the jetty site encompass all three zones. Mobil's Green Canyon (GC) 18, which lies in about 230 m of water on the shelf slope (27°56'37"N, 91°01'45"W), was sampled monthly during new moon phases over a 2-3 night period during July 1995-June 1996. Mobil's Grand Isle (GI) 94B, which lies in approximately 60 m of water at mid-shelf (28°30'57"N, 90°07'23"W), was sampled twice monthly during new and full moon phases over a three night period during April-August 1996. In addition, during May extra samples during the first quarter and third quarter moon phases were collected, but due to inclement weather, full moon collections were cancelled. Exxon's South Timbalier (ST) 54G, which lies in approximately 20 m of water on the inner shelf (28°50'01"N, 90°25'00"W), was sampled twice monthly during new and full moon periods in during April-September 1997. All platforms had very similar structural complexity. GC 18 is a very large six pile (column or leg) production platform, while GI 94 and ST 54 are eight pile production platforms. The stone rubble jetties (2-3 m depth) at the terminus of Belle Pass, a major shipping channel near Fourchon, Louisiana (N 29 03.90, W 90 13.80), were also sampled over a two night period in 1997 simultaneously with the sampling of ST 54. The two jetties are approximately 91 m apart and run in a general north-south direction. The east jetty is approximately 335 m long and the west jetty is approximately 305 m long.

Sampling Procedure

Collections were made at WC 352 within the platform structure during seven sample periods between November 1991 and August 1992. All sampling commenced and terminated at least one hour after sunset and before sunrise, respectively. Each sample was obtained by deploying a modified quatrefoil light-trap for 10 to 15 minutes, although two 35-minute samples were also collected. Sample depths included 1 m (surface) and 18 m (February through May 1992 only). When a subsurface sample was taken, a surface sample was concurrently collected. Surface samples were obtained by lowering a trap with floatation into the water. Subsurface

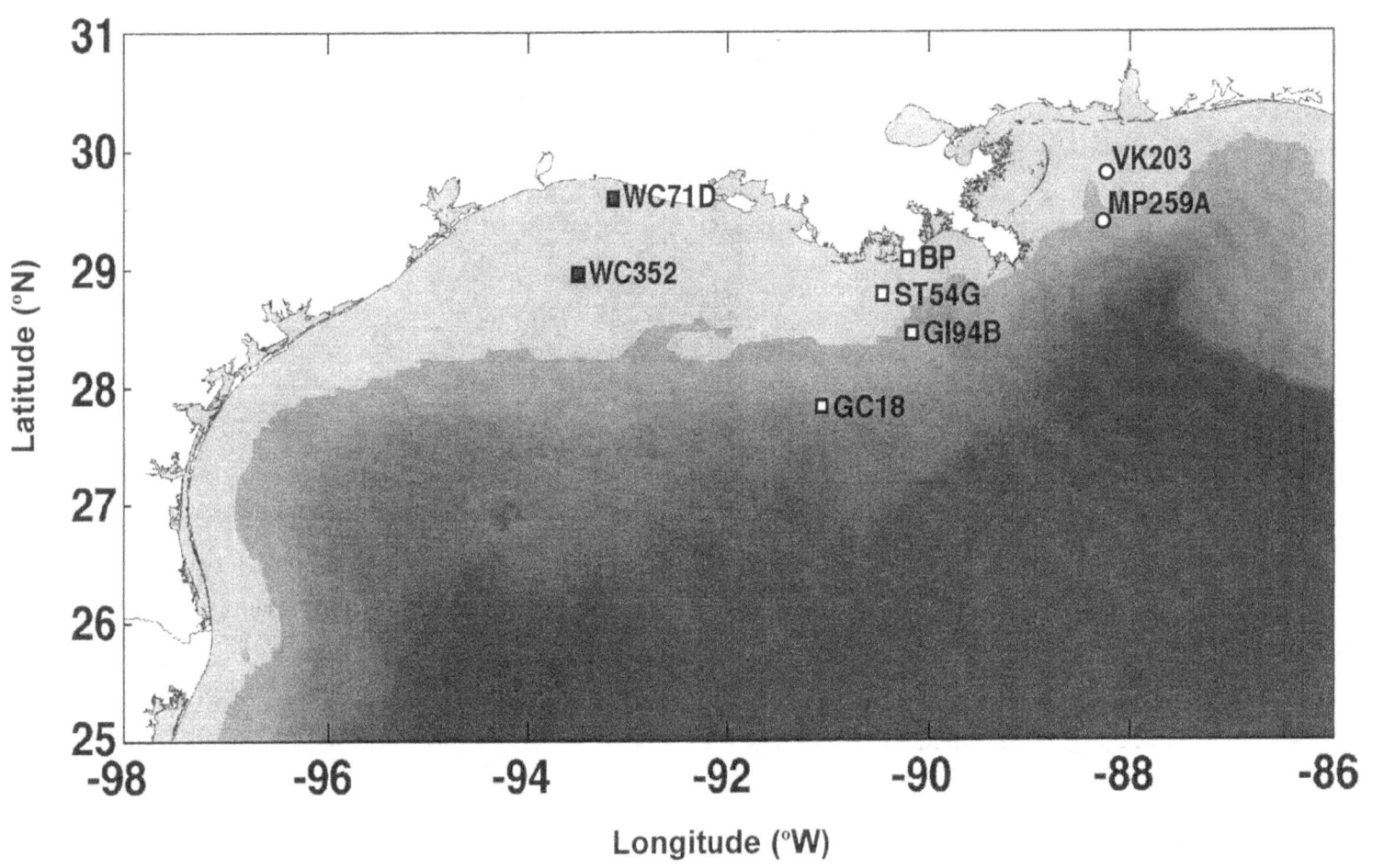

Figure 1. Open squares are sites of the oil and gas platforms and coastal jetty sampled during the course of this study. Solid squares represent sites sampled previously during pilot studies. Open circles represent sites of ongoing sampling for future comparisons.

samples were collected by lowering a trap without floatation along a stainless steel cable guideline tethered to the bottom.

The quatrefoil light-trap (Figure 2) used at this and subsequent locations was modified from Floyd et al. (1984) and Secor et al. (1993). The main modifications are described as follows. The acrylic tubes in the main body of the trap were enlarged to 15.24 cm (6") outer diameter. The collection assembly at the bottom of the trap was replaced with short conical plankton-net and cod-end assembly. Four, vertical stainless steel bars were added to the corners of the trap for additional support. The light source was a Brinkman Starfire II 12-volt halogen fishing light (250,000 candlepower). For surface samples, power was supplied through an umbilical cord by a 12-volt marine battery located on the lower deck of the platform. A submersible battery pack which consisted of 10 NiCad D cells encased in PVC tubing powered the light during subsurface collections at the West Cameron sites. For the remaining sites, either an umbilical cord connected to a 12-volt battery or a different submersible battery was used. This battery was made by placing a 7.0 amp/h rechargeable sealed lead battery in a 1/4" thick PVC tube with a watertight connector on one end and a complimentary pig-tail on the end of the cable supplying power to the light.

Samples were collected at WC 71D over three consecutive nights (July 21-24, 1994). All sampling commenced or terminated at least one hour after sunset and before sunrise, respectively. Three light-trap designs, a modified quatrefoil, a Doherty trap (Doherty 1987), and a cylindrical design (an acrylic model modified from Riley & Holt (1993), were deployed off a stainless steel cable guideline within the platform structure. Sampling depths included 1 m (surface) and 8.5 m (Night 3 only). In addition, six vertical plankton tow samples (202-μm mesh, 60-cm diameter net) were collected during Night 2. The net, mounted on rigid frame and attached to the central cable, was lowered to the bottom (effective depth = 8.5 m) and raised at approximately 1 m/s after a five minute time interval to allow the water column to re-stabilize. A set of samples included one sample by each of the three light traps, and there were 6 sets made each night, except for Night 3 where 4 sets were made near the surface and 4 sets were at depth. On Night 2 only, a vertical net tow was added to each set. The order of the trap (or vertical net tows) collections was randomized within each set as was the case with all subsequent platform sampling.

Sampling protocols for GC 18, GI 94, and ST 54 were similar. At GC 18, eleven monthly sampling trips were taken over a 3-night period coinciding with new moon phases from July 1995-June 1996, with the exception of the month of December (adverse weather). New moon phases were targeted at this platform because they have been associated with the peak recruitment periods of many reef-dependent fishes (Johannes 1978; Robertson et al. 1988). All sampling began one hour after sunset and was completed one hour before sunrise. The major sampling station for each platform was located in the internal central region along a stainless steel, small diameter guidewire (monorail) tethered to the first set of the platform's underwater, cross-member, support structures. At this central station, replicate trap collections (N = 2) were taken three times each night at near-surface and at a depth between 15 and 23m, depending upon the individual platform's underwater configuration of the first set of cross-member supports. Subsurface samples were collected by lowering a trap without floatation. Light-traps were deployed for 10 minute periods. Passive, horizontal plankton net collections were taken three

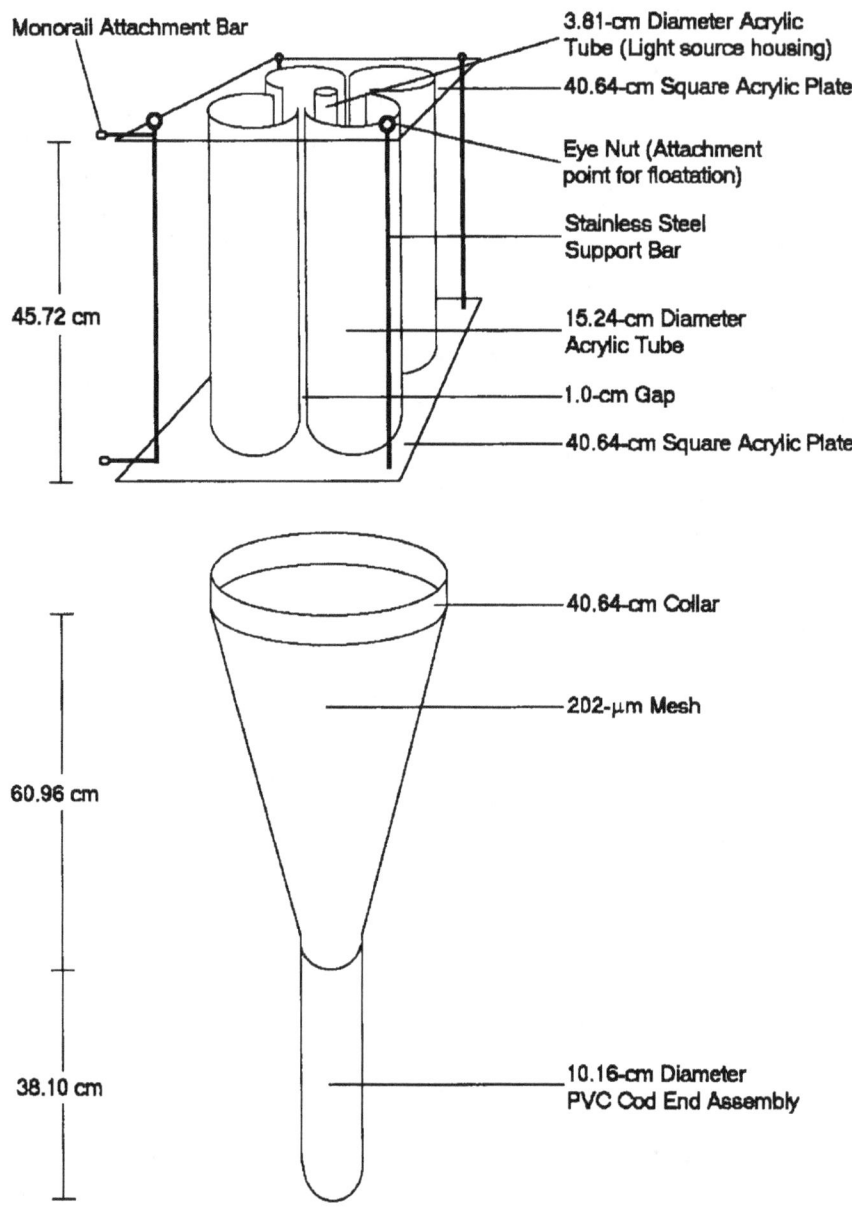

Figure 2. Specifications for the modified quatrefoil light-trap used in this study.

times at both depths during each night at the central station using a metered (General Oceanics flowmeter model 2030 with slow velocity rotor), 60-cm diameter, 333μm mesh net dyed dark green. The nets had a vane (to help orient into the current) which was fixed to a gimbled attachment on the net ring, which allowed the net to be set and retrieved closed for the at depth deployment. In addition, 3 collections each night were made with a floating light-trap which was tethered and free drifted away (off-platform) from the platform (approximately 20 m) on the down current side of the platform. For light-traps sampled at depth or off-platform, the trap was deployed with the light off, fished with the light on, and then retrieved with the light off.

Temperature (°C) and salinity (ppt), turbidity (NTU), and current speed and direction were determined during each set using either a Data Sonde 3 Hydrolab or an Inter Ocean S4 Current Meter. During each set, a vertical plankton net (20-cm diameter, 63-μm mesh) which was held rigidly to the guidewire, was lowered codend first to the bottom of the monorail, left at depth for 5 minutes for water column restabilization, and then hauled to the surface at approximately 1m/s to ascertain zooplankton biomass as a measure of food availability. The samples were returned to the lab where they were dried in an oven for 24 h at 60°C and then weighed to determine the dry weight biomass (g/m^3). Also, surface water samples were collected during each set in order to determine total suspended sediments, an estimate of turbidity. Water samples were later filtered in the lab through a pre-weighed, microfiber filter (1.2 μm), dried in an oven for 24 h at 60°C, and weighed to determine the suspended sediment load (g/L). Both the macrozooplankton biomass and suspended sediment (turbidity) estimates were used in the canonical correlation analyses (see below).

At GI 94, a total of 11 sampling trips were taken, and samples were collected twice monthly during new and full moons for 3 consecutive nights from April-August 1996 (the peak recruitment period for most reef-associated species in the northern Gulf). Sampling at GC 18 and GI 94, therefore, overlapped monthly from April-June 1996. At ST 54 sampling also occurred twice monthly from April-September 1997 (8 trips total), during new and full moon periods. Sampling effort was modified at GI 94 and ST 54 to obtain one (rather than two) subsurface, surface, and off-platform light-trap collection per set.

Samples were collected twice monthly (new and full moon phases) over 2-night periods at Belle Pass from April-September 1997 (11 trips total) simultaneously with the sampling of ST 54. For sampling purposes, the sides of the two, channel jetties were labeled as East Exterior (EE), East Interior (EI), West Interior (WI), and West Exterior (WE). A total of four sampling stations, one on each side of each jetty, were located approximately at the jetty mid-points and were identified during sampling by distinct rock outcroppings that were sprayed with fluorescent paint. Two sets of samples were taken each night. A set included a light-trap and a bow-mounted, pushnet sample at each of the four stations. The order of stations sampled within each set was chosen using a random number table. Light-traps were equipped with a submersible battery that was secured to the top of the light-trap with bungee cords. At each station, a buoyed mooring was used to suspend the light-trap approximately 1 m below the surface as close to the jetty as possible, which was usually within 2 m of the surface-exposed rocks. Light-traps were allowed to fish for 10 minutes. A bow-mounted pushnet (1 m x 1 m, 1000 μm mesh net dyed green) was pushed by an 18 foot boat at approximately 1 m/sec just below the surface along the edge of the jetty for 3-5 minutes, depending upon the density of plankton. A General Oceanics flowmeter (large rotor) was used to determine the volume of water filtered. Salinity (ppt), temperature (°C), dissolved oxygen (% saturation and mg/l), and turbidity (NTU) were measured at each station during each set using a DataSonde 3 Hydrolab and Multiprobe Logger.

All samples collected at WC 352 and WC 71D were preserved in 5% formalin and later changed over to ethanol. Samples collected at GC 18 and GI 94 were preserved in ethanol and had the ethanol changed over again within 12-18 hours. Samples collected at ST 54 and Belle Pass were fixed in 4% buffered formaldehyde and changed over to ethanol within 8-12 hours. Fish were removed from all samples, enumerated, and measured under a dissecting microscope with the aid of an ocular micrometer, and identified to the lowest taxonomic level possible using primarily the taxonomic classification of Robins et al. (1991). Large samples were split using a Folsom plankton splitter (Van Guelpen et al. 1982). In the event that the number of fish in a sample or a split was greater than 50 for any single species, the largest, smallest and a random subsample of 50 individuals were measured. Preflexion larvae were measured to the end of the notochord (NL) and all postflexion larvae, juveniles, and adults were measured to the posterior end of the vertebral column (SL). Light-trap samples were standardized to a catch-per-unit-effort (CPUE) of fish per 10 min. Plankton net and pushnet samples were standardized to the number of fish per 100 m^3 (density). This core sampling sequence formed the basis of our sampling protocols at all other platforms. Sea states, adverse weather, transportation delays, and platform safety concerns often forced us to suspend some sample collections. Only 7 subsurface plankton net collections were taken at ST 54 (April 7-8) because of problems with the monorail rigging. Similar gear problems reduced the number of subsurface net samples collected at GC 18. Table 2 summarizes the number of samples collected by trip, gear type, and depth/location for the WC 352 and WC 71D pilot studies and for GC 18, GI 94, ST 54, and Belle Pass.

Analyses of Data

Data collected at GC 18, GI 94, ST 54, and Belle Pass were used in all analyses where possible. Data collected in the pilot studies (WC 352 and WC 71D) are included here only in community structure analyses. Also, due to the very large numbers of clupeiform (Clupeidae and Engraulidae) fishes collected, particularly in light-trap samples, some analyses were run with and without these taxa, since these fish are seldom the taxa of interest in studies of hard substrate habitats and their abundances tend to overwhelm the trends of other taxa (Choat et al. 1993). All ANOVA, Tukey's Studentized Range Tests, Student's t-tests, and canonical correlations were run with SAS version 6.12 (SAS 1989).

Studentized t-tests (α=0.05) were used to compare overall plankton net densities between locations (subsurface and surface) within the GC 18, GI 94, and ST 54 sites. Light-trap CPUEs were compared between locations (subsurface, surface, and off-platform) within each of the platform sites using an ANOVA model with gear as a main effect. Tukey's Studentized Range tests were used to determine which light-trap collections were significantly different. Before testing, plankton net densities were log transformed ($\log_{10}(x+1)$) in an effort to conform to normality and homogeneity of variances. Analyses on light-trap CPUEs were run on ranked-transformed data. These tests were run both with and without clupeiform fishes. The same analyses were also run on some of dominant taxa (top three taxa identified at least to the level of genus for each gear location/depth) collected at each of the sites.

12

Table 2. Number of samples collected at each site by date, gear type, and depth/location. (Lunar phases: N, new moon; F, full moon; 1, first quarter; 3, last quarter)

	Vertical Net	Subsurface Net	Surface Net	Subsurface Light-trap	Surface Light-trap	Off-platform Light-trap	Pushnet
West Cameron 352							
(1991-1992)							
Nov 21-22 (F)					23		
Dec 16 (1)				1	5		
Feb 7-9 (1)				8	12		
Mar 24-25 (3)				4	12		
Apr 9-10 (1)				7	13		
May 26-27 (3)				9	13		
August 4-6 (1)					15		
Totals				**29**	**93**		
West Cameron 71D							
(1994)							
Jul 21-23 (F)	6			12	48		
Totals	**6**			**12**	**48**		
Green Canyon 18							
(1995-1996)							
Jul 26-29 (N)		0	9	18	18	5	
Aug 25-28 (N)		0	12	18	18	9	
Sep 24-25 (N)		0	12	12	12	6	
Oct 23-25 (N)		9	9	18	18	9	
Nov 21-23 (N)		9	9	18	17	9	
Jan 19 (N)		3	3	6	6	3	
Feb 17-18 (N)		5	5	10	6	4	
Apr 15-18 (N)		0	0	0	0	15	
May 17-20 (N)		2	9	5	5	18	
Jun 18-21 (N)		13	16	14	13	9	
Totals		**41**	**84**	**119**	**113**	**87**	
Grand Isle 94							
(1996)							
Apr 16-18 (N)		6	6	4	8	8	
Apr 26-29 (1)		18	18	18	18	18	
May 10-12 (3)		10	12	12	12	12	
May 17-20 (N)		18	18	18	18	18	
May 24-26 (1)		12	13	12	13	11	
Jun 14-17 (N)		18	18	18	18	18	
Jun 28-Jul 1 (F)		17	17	13	12	13	
Jul 12-15 (N)		17	17	15	13	16	
Jul 29-Aug 1 (F)		11	13	11	12	12	
Aug 12-15 (N)		16	17	15	17	17	
Aug 26-29 (F)		18	19	18	18	18	
Totals		**161**	**168**	**154**	**159**	**161**	
South Timbalier 54							
(1997)							
Apr 7-8 (N)		7	7	5	6	8	
May 5-8 (N)		0	15	0	16	12	
May 20-23 (F)		0	18	12	18	10	
Jun 4-5 (N)		0	6	6	6	5	
Jun 20-21 (F)		0	8	6	9	9	
Jul 3-5 (N)		0	5	7	7	3	
Aug 17-20 (F)		0	13	4	12	14	
Sep 3-5 (N)		0	10	9	10	0	
Totals		**7**	**82**	**49**	**84**	**61**	

Table 2. (continued)

	Vertical Net	Subsurface Net	Surface Net	Subsurface Light-trap	Surface Light-trap	Off-platform Light-trap	Pushnet
Bell Pass							
(1997)							
Apr 4-7 (N)					9		9
Apr 21-23 (F)					8		8
May 5-7 (N)					16		16
May 20-22 (F)					16		16
Jun 3-5 (N)					16		16
Jun 20-21 (F)					8		8
Jul 3-5 (N)					16		15
Jul 19-21 (F)					12		15
Aug 1-3 (N)					15		14
Aug 18-20 (F)					16		16
Aug 31-Sep 2 (N)					16		16
Totals					**148**		**149**

Kolmogorov-Smirnov (K-S) length-frequency analyses ($\alpha=0.05$) were performed for selected species from GC 18, GI 94, ST 54, and Belle Pass to determine if there were any significant differences between the size distributions of fish collected with light-traps vs. plankton nets (Sokal and Rohlf 1981). Taxa from each platform site and Belle Pass were chosen for these analyses if at least 10 individuals were collected by each gear type. All K-S analyses were performed using SYSTAT version 4 (SPSS 1999).

Lunar periodicity (full and new moon) was examined for plankton net and light-trap samples collected at GI 94, ST 54, and Belle Pass using Student's t-tests ($\alpha=0.05$). An ANOVA model and Tukey's Studentized Range tests were used to analyze the CPUEs and densities of samples collected in May of 1996 at GI 94 (1/4, 3/4, and new moon periods). Also customized comparisons were made using contrast statements in the SAS statistical package to test for differences between different combinations of the jetty stations at Belle Pass, e.g., east stations vs. west or internal vs. external stations. Log-transformed pushnet densities were analyzed using the same ANOVA design. These analyses were performed both with and without clupeiform fishes.

Schoener's index of niche overlap (Schoener 1970) was calculated for all sites by combining fish collected by all gears within each site as an indication of the community similarity between sites. Only fish identified to at least the genus level were used in the analyses. Since this type of analysis can be heavily influenced by large abundances of a single species, it was done both with and without the most dominant taxa included at each site. At times, the sampling efforts differed temporally between sites, so the samples used for comparisons were limited to only those months where samples were collected for both sites in a pairing. For example, all comparisons with WC 71D were done using only July samples from the other sites. Comparisons between the WC 352 and the three across shelf sites (GI 94, ST 54, and Belle Pass) were done using only April and May samples. Comparisons with WC 352 and GC 18 were done using samples from November, December, April, and May. Only April-August samples were used to compare GC 18 to GI 94, ST 54, and Belle Pass. Full data sets were used in comparisons between GI 94, ST 54, and Belle Pass. For GC 18, GI 94, and ST 54, indices were calculated for comparisons of fish collections within the platform structure (surface net and surface light-trap) and far-field collections (off-platform light-trap) and total net collections vs. total light-trap collections. This same gear analysis was performed to compare the similarity of light-trap and pushnet collections at Belle Pass. Shannon-Weiner diversity indices (Magurran 1988) were calculated for each sample collected at GC 18, GI 94, ST 54, and Belle Pass. Differences in diversity between gear types at each site were analyzed with ANOVA models using gear as a main effect. Post-ANOVA tests (Tukey's Studentized Range, $\alpha=0.05$) were used to determine which gear types where significantly different. Only fish identified at least to the level of genus were included in these analyses. Similarly, diversity indices were also compared between sites for each gear type. Also, since the intent of the similarity and diversity indices was to characterize the taxonomic assemblages sampled by each gear type, clupeiform fishes were included in these analyses.

Canonical correlations were used to determine relationships at each site between plankton net or pushnet densities or light-trap CPUEs for dominant taxa and environmental variables. For GC 18 and GI 94, log-transformed densities of the top 15 taxa (excluding clupeiforms) collected in subsurface and surface plankton nets combined were analyzed along with temperature, salinity, zooplankton biomass, and total suspended sediments (turbidity). The same analyses were performed for log-transformed CPUEs of the top 15 taxa collected in subsurface and surface light-traps. Occasionally more than 15 taxa were analyzed for light-trap data due to ties in the ranking of CPUEs. For ST54, the same analyses were performed, but only surface plankton net data were used because there were very few subsurface plankton net samples collected at this site (Table 2). For Belle Pass, the same analyses were performed, but included Hydrolab measurements of turbidity and dissolved oxygen, and did not include total suspended sediments and zooplankton biomass estimates since these data were not collected at this site. The importance of an environmental variable was based on the magnitude of its correlation with the environmental variate, with the sign of the correlation indicating if the variable was directly (positively) or inversely (negative) related with the variate. A species was considered to be related to the variate if the absolute value of the interset correlation was greater than 0.387 (i.e., the variate predicted 15% or more of the species variation within the model).

Results

Environmental Characterization of Sampling Sites

Mean temperatures varied seasonally at all platforms and at the jetty site and were similar between sites for the late spring and summer months (Figure 3). At GC 18, the only platform sampled during all seasons, mean temperatures peaked at 31.8 °C in July 1995 and steadily decreased to a mean of 19.2 °C in January 1996. Mean temperatures rose throughout the spring to 29.1 °C by the end of our sampling in June 1996. Mean temperatures for the late spring and summer months (April-September), the same months sampled at the other sites, ranged from 21.5-31.8 °C. At GI 94, temperatures ranged from a mean low of 20.8 °C in April to a mean high of 30.7 °C in July. At ST 54, mean temperatures ranged from 22.3 °C in May to 31.6 °C in August. Similarly at the Belle Pass jetties temperatures ranged from a mean low of 20.2 °C in April to a mean high of 32.8 °C in August.

Mean surface salinities at GC 18 (outer shelf) were relatively stable ranging from 34.8-36.6 ppt for most of the sampling trips (Figure 4). However, surface salinity means during June and August 1995 were relatively low (24.3-28.4 ppt) for offshore waters. These low salinity values were associated with a visibly "green" water mass that pulsed through the area. This water mass was further characterized by high abundances of cnidarians, ctenophores, and patches of *Sargassum*. Similarly, mean salinity values for GI 94 (mid-shelf) ranged from 35.2-36.0 ppt for much of the sampling season, but also experienced pulses of relatively low salinity water. Lower mean surface salinities were recorded for ST 54 (inner shelf) and Belle Pass (coastal) and ranged from 22.7-28.5 ppt and 18.0-26.2 ppt, respectively.

Mean zooplankton biomass estimates were generally low, with little variation within each platform site (Figure 5). At GC 18, estimates ranged between 0.03-0.29 g/m³, with a peak in July 1995. Even less variation was observed at GI 94, where macrozooplankton biomass estimates ranged from 0.03-0.10 g/m³. The greatest variation in macrozooplankton biomass was observed at ST 54 where estimates generally ranged from 0.11-0.17 g/m³, with the exception of

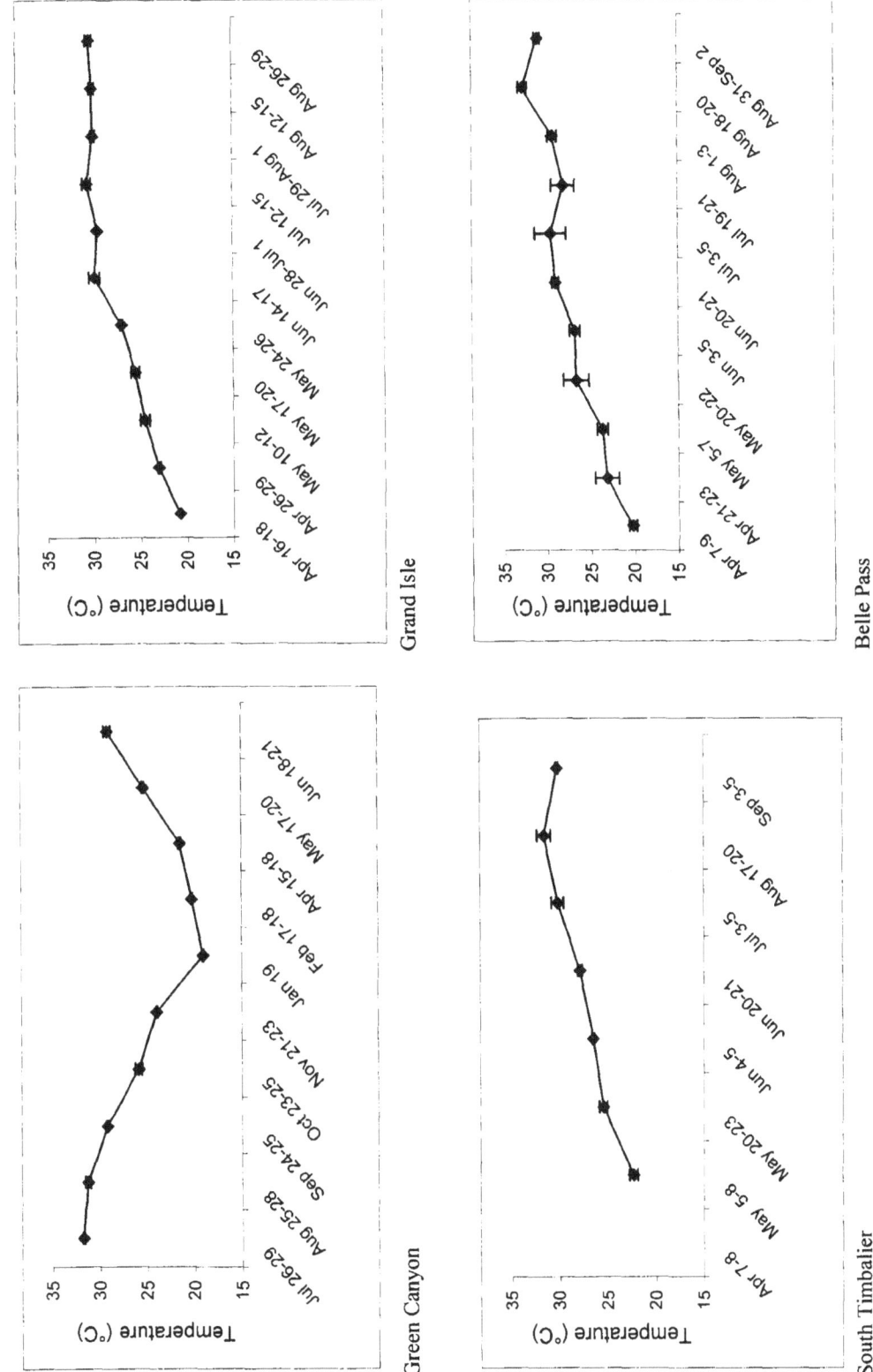

Figure 3. Mean surface temperatures (and standard errors) for each sampling site.

17

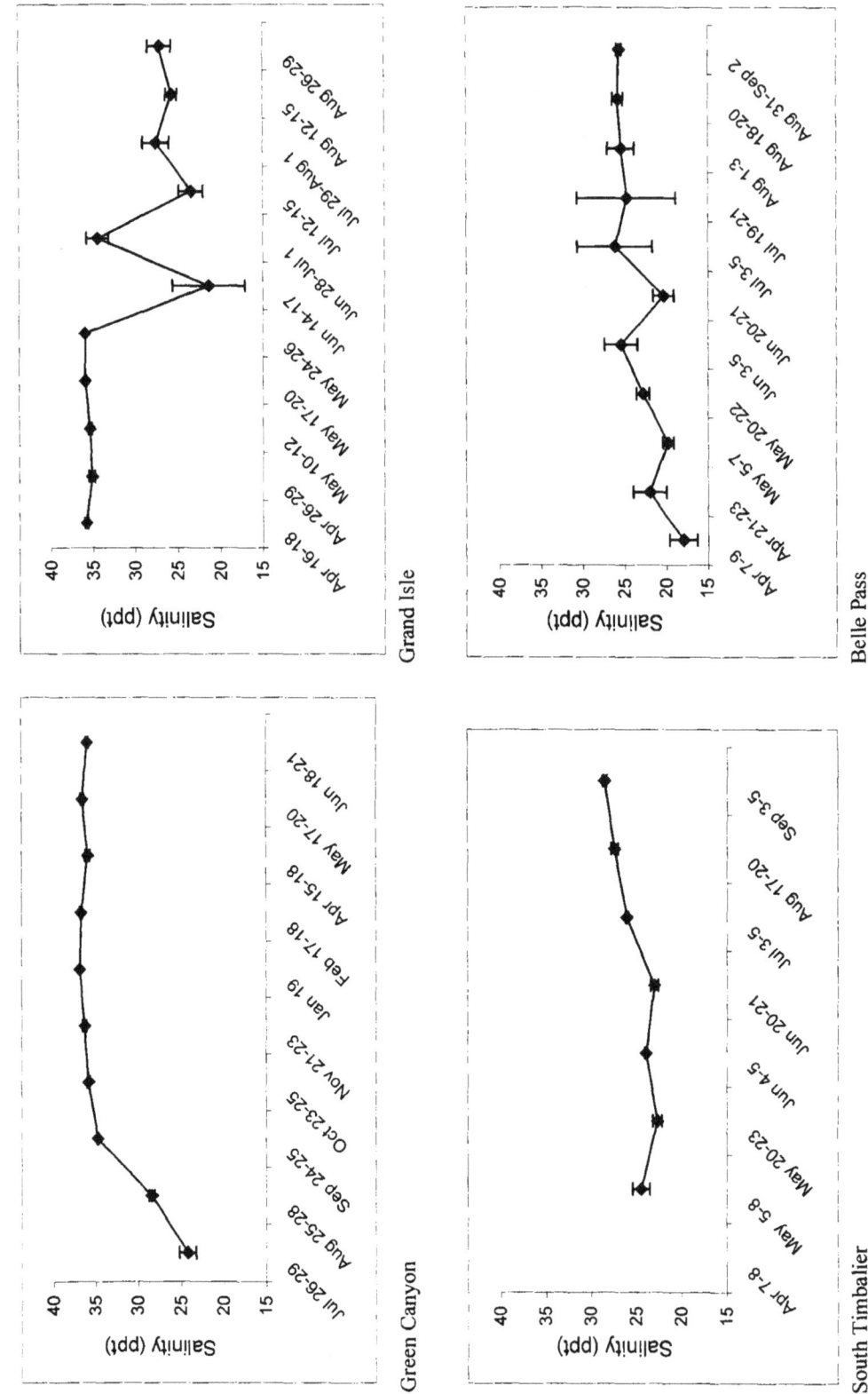

Figure 4. Mean surface salinities (and standard errors) for each sampling site.

18

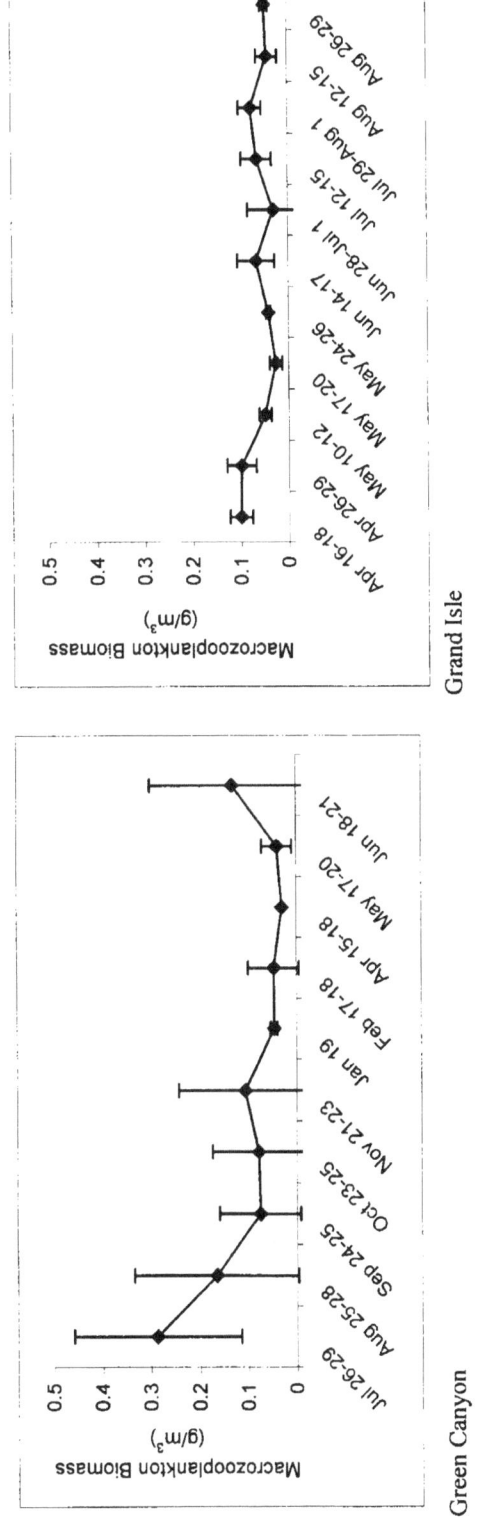

Grand Isle

Green Canyon

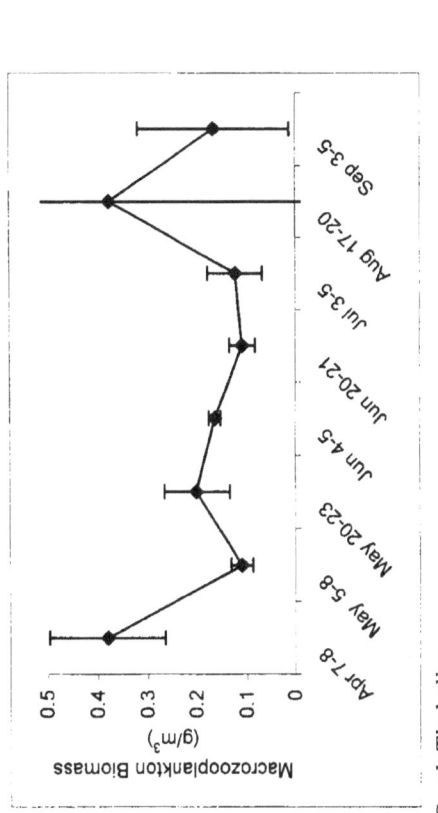

South Timbalier

Figure 5. Mean Macrozooplankton biomass (and standard errors) for each platform site.

19

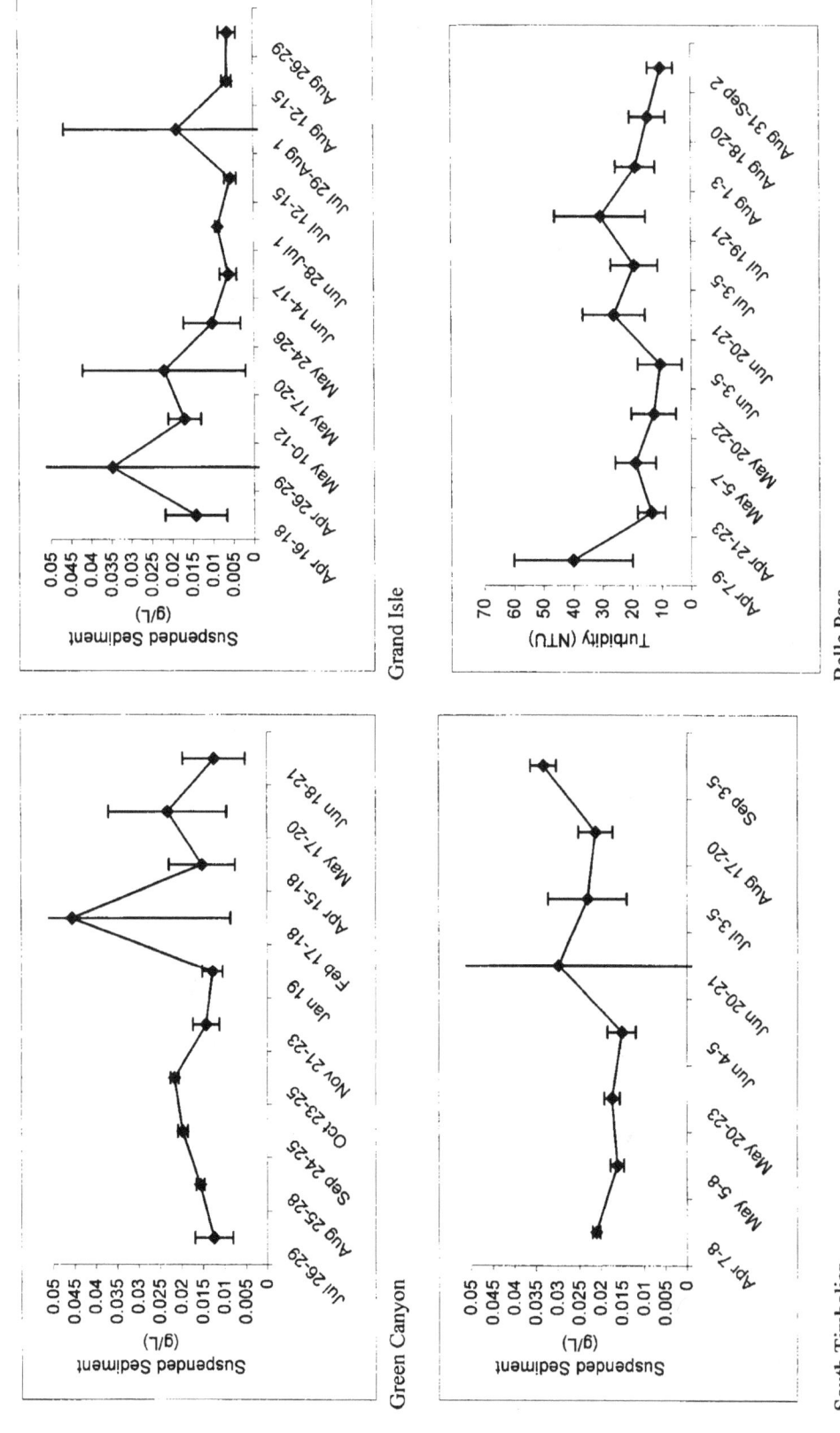

Figure 6. Mean suspended sediments (and standard errors) for each platform site and mean surface turbidity (and standard errors) for the Belle Pass jetty site.

20

two peaks of 0.38 g/m^3 in April and August. Macrozooplankton biomass samples were not collected for the Belle Pass jetty site.

Mean suspended sediment values (turbidity estimates) did not vary greatly either within sites or between sites (Figure 6). At GC 18, mean suspended sediments concentrations ranged from approximately 0.01-0.02 g/L, with the exception of a peak of approximately 0.05 g/L in February. At GI 94 and ST 54, mean suspended sediment concentrations fluctuated slightly throughout the sampling season but only ranged from approximately 0.01-0.03 g/L. At the Belle Pass jetties, mean turbidity measurements (NTU) ranged from 10.4-19.0 NTU, with the exception of a large turbidity peak in April (40.0 NTU) and two smaller peaks in June (26.2 NTU) and July (30.8 NTU).

Overall Abundances and Seasonality

A total of 67 families were represented in our plankton net and light-trap collections from the three platform sites (Tables 3-6). The number of families represented in passive plankton net collections decreased from 45 at GC 18 (shelf slope) to 40 at GI 94 (mid-shelf) and 34 at ST 54 (inner shelf). In contrast, the number of families represented in light-trap collections was fairly consistent, from 37 at GC 18 and GI 94 to 34 at ST 54.

A total of 5,057 fish were collected at GC 18 over the course of the year. Light-traps and plankton nets collected 1,114 and 3,943 fish, respectively. Plankton nets collected fish from 45 different families, 15 of which were not collected with light-traps (Table 3). Light-traps collected fish from 37 different families, 7 of which were only collected with light-traps. Plankton nets collected fish from 64 taxa (identified at least to genus level), 25 of which were not collected with light-traps, while light-traps collected fish from 59 taxa with 18 being unique to light-trap collections. Clupeiform fishes, primarily unidentified engraulids, *Opisthonema oglinum*, *Anchoa nasuta/hepsetus*, and *Engraulis eurystole* dominated the total catch for both gear types, particularly the plankton nets where these fishes comprised 65% and 71% of the total numerical catch for subsurface and surface plankton net collections, respectively. Gobies and *Mugil cephalus* were among the most common non-clupeiform fishes in the plankton net collections. Preflexion *Sciaenops ocellatus* individuals, commonly found along the inner shelf and coastal waters, were also collected in plankton nets in September. While the subsurface light-trap collections were also dominated by clupeiforms (72%), other coastal pelagic taxa such as *Caranx crysos*, *C. hippos/latus*, *Euthynnus alletteratus*, and *Auxis* spp. were common in the surface and off-platform collections.

At GC 18, summer peaks in CPUEs were observed with the highest values occurring during both June and July sampling trips (Figure 7a). Mean CPUEs ranged from 0-20.6 fish/10 min. While there was a CPUE trend for the within-platform light-traps to decrease during the fall and winter, the decrease was not as evident in the off-platform collections. In general, either the surface or off-platform light-trap had the highest CPUE during each trip and, with the exception of the August trip, the subsurface light-trap always had the lowest CPUE. The same seasonal and vertical trends were evident once the clupeiform fishes were removed from the data set (Figure 7b), which decreased the mean CPUEs to between 0-12.2 fish/10 min. There was a bimodal pattern in mean plankton net density with peaks in the summer and winter (Figure

Table 3. Total plankton net density (fish/100 m³) and light-trap CPUE (fish/10 min) for fish collected at Green Canyon 18 with standard error (SE), rank, percent of total catch (%), and months collected for each taxa. (N) indicates taxa collected only with plankton nets. (L) indicates taxa collected only with light-traps. For ranks, tied values received the mean of the corresponding ranks. ‡ indicates a value <1.00%.

Taxa	Months Collected	Surface Net Density (SE) Rank (%)	Bottom Net Density (SE) Rank (%)	Bottom Light-trap CPUE (SE) Rank (%)	Surface Light-trap CPUE (SE) Rank (%)	Off-platform Light-trap CPUE (SE) Rank (%)
Osteichthyes						
Unidentified	Feb, Apr, Jun, Jul, Aug, Sep, Oct, Nov	0.85 (0.39) 23 ‡	4.93 (2.73) 6 (1.54)	0.08 (0.04) 7 (3.27)	0.02 (0.01) 41.5 ‡	0.26 (0.16) 4 (8.36)
Elopiformes						
Elopidae						
Elops saurus (N) (ladyfish)	Oct	0 (0)	0.35 (0.35) 35 ‡	0 (0)	0 (0)	0 (0)
Anguilliformes						
Unidentified (eel)	Jul, Oct, Nov	1.57 (0.72) 13 ‡	4.32 (2.46) 9 ‡	<0.01 (0.01) 28.5 ‡	0.02 (0.01) 41.5 ‡	0.01 (0.01) 40.5 ‡
Moringuidae						
Neoconger mucronatus (ridged eel)	Oct	0.21 (0.21) 52 ‡	0 (0)	0 (0)	<0.01 (0.01) 55 ‡	0 (0)
Muraenidae						
Unidentified (moray eel)	Jun, Jul, Aug, Sep, Oct	0.02 (0.02) 85 ‡	0 (0)	<0.01 (0.01) 28.5 ‡	0.03 (0.02) 33 ‡	0.02 (0.02) 25 ‡
Ophichthidae						
Unidentified (snake eel)	Jul, Oct, Nov	1.09 (0.71) 19 ‡	2.87 (1.27) 11 ‡	0 (0)	0.05 (0.02) 22 (1.06)	0 (0)
Myrophis punctatus (L) (speckled worm eel)	Feb	0 (0)	0 (0)	0 (0)	<0.01 (0.01) 55 ‡	0 (0)
Ophichthus gomesi (L) (shrimp eel)	Jul	0 (0)	0 (0)	<0.01 (0.01) 28.5 ‡	0.03 (0.03) 33 ‡	0 (0)
Congridae						
Unidentified (L) (conger eel)	Jul	0 (0)	0 (0)	0 (0)	0.03 (0.02) 33 ‡	0 (0)
Clupeiformes						
Unidentified (herring/anchovy)	Jul, Sep	1.08 (0.92) 20 (1.08)	0 (0)	0 (0)	0 (0)	0.01 (0.01) 40.5 ‡
Clupeidae						
Brevoortia patronus (gulf menhaden)	Jan, Feb, Nov	1.12 (0.55) 18 ‡	2.44 (1.21) 12 ‡	0 (0)	0.03 (0.02) 33 ‡	0.02 (0.02) 25 ‡
Etrumeus teres (N) (round herring)	Jan, Feb	1.16 (1.05) 16 ‡	0.19 (0.19) 42.5 ‡	0 (0)	0 (0)	0 (0)

Table 3. (continued)

Taxa	Months Collected	Surface Net Density (SE) Rank (%)	Bottom Net Density (SE) Rank (%)	Bottom Light-trap CPUE (SE) Rank (%)	Surface Light-trap CPUE (SE) Rank (%)	Off-platform Light-trap CPUE (SE) Rank (%)
Harengula jaguana (scaled sardine)	Jul, Aug	0.06 (0.04) 71 ‡	0 (0)	<0.01 (0.01) 28.5 ‡	0.15 (0.06) 11.5 (3.01)	0 (0)
Opisthonema oglinum (Atlantic thread herring)	Jul, Aug, Sep	39.41 (16.26) 1 (38.40)	0 (0)	0.11 (0.06) 4 (4.73)	0.42 (0.11) 3 (8.51)	0.28 (0.11) 2.5 (8.73)
Engraulidae						
Unidentified (anchovy)	Feb, Jun, Jul, Aug, Sep Oct, Nov	39.21 (12.21) 2 (24.32)	57.18 (26.10) 1 (53.90)	0.46 (0.11) 2 (20.00)	0.51 (0.15) 1 (10.28)	0.28 (0.13) 2.5 (8.73)
Anchoa spp. (L) (anchovy spp.)	Jul	0 (0)	0 (0)	0.07 (0.07) 8 (2.91)	0 (0)	0 (0)
Anchoa mitchilli (bay anchovy)	Jul	0.03 (0.03) 79 ‡	0 (0)	0 (0)	0.15 (0.12) 11.5 (3.01)	0 (0)
Anchoa nasuta/hepsetus (L) (longnose/striped anchovy)	Jul, Aug, Sep, Nov	0 (0)	0 (0)	0.80 (0.31) 1 (34.91)	0.22 (0.12) 8 (4.43)	0.16 (0.10) 8 (5.09)
Engraulis eurystole (silver anchovy)	Jun, Jul, Aug, Sep, Oct	0.34 (0.30) 42 ‡	8.63 (8.63) 5 (9.45)	0.15 (0.04) 3 (6.55)	0.25 (0.11) 5 (5.14)	0.02 (0.02) 25 ‡
Stomiiformes						
Gonostomatidae						
Cyclothone braueri	Jan, May, Jun, Jul, Oct, Nov	1.01 (0.65) 21 ‡	3.05 (1.55) 10 ‡	0 (0)	0.23 (0.21) 7 (4.61)	0 (0)
Diplophos taenia (N)	Nov	0.29 (0.29) 44.5 ‡	0.41 (0.41) 31 ‡	0 (0)	0 (0)	0 (0)
Aulopiformes						
Chlorophthalmidae						
Chlorophthalmus agassizi (N) (shortnose greeneye)	Jun, Nov	0 (0)	0.70 (0.61) 24 ‡	0 (0)	0 (0)	0 (0)
Scopelarchidae						
Scopelarchoides spp. (N) (pearleye spp.)	Jan	0.03 (0.03) 80 ‡	0 (0)	0 (0)	0 (0)	0 (0)
Synodontidae						
Unidentified (lizardfish)	Jan, May, Jul, Oct	0.27 (0.16) 46 ‡	0.61 (0.61) 26 ‡	<0.01 (0.01) 28.5 ‡	<0.01 (0.01) 55 ‡	0 (0)
Saurida brasiliensis (largescale lizardfish)		<0.01 (<0.01) 92 ‡	0 (0)	0.03 (0.02) 12.5 (1.09)	0.20 (0.14) 9 (4.08)	0 (0)
Synodus synodus (red lizardfish)	Jun	0.29 (0.29) 44.5 ‡	0 (0)	0 (0)	0.03 (0.02) 33 ‡	0 (0)

23

Table 3. (continued)

Taxa	Months Collected	Surface Net Density (SE) Rank (%)	Bottom Net Density (SE) Rank (%)	Bottom Light-trap CPUE (SE) Rank (%)	Surface Light-trap CPUE (SE) Rank (%)	Off-platform Light-trap CPUE (SE) Rank (%)
Trachinocephalus myops (snakefish)	Sep, Oct	0.10 (0.10) 63 ‡	0 (0)	0 (0)	0.04 (0.02) 25 ‡	0.03 (0.02) 19 (1.09)
Paralepidae Unidentified (N) (barracudina)	Nov	0.26 (0.26) 47 ‡	0.41 (0.41) 31 ‡	0 (0)	0 (0)	0 (0)
Paralepis atlantica (L) (duckbill barracudina)	Jul	0 (0)	0 (0)	0.02 (0.01) 18 ‡	0 (0)	0 (0)
Lestrolepis intermedia (L)	Jul	0 (0)	0 (0)	0.02 (0.02) 18 ‡	0 (0)	0 (0)
Myctophiformes Myctophidae Unidentified (lanternfish)	Jan, Feb, Apr, May, Jun, Jul, Sep, Nov	0.83 (0.45) 24 ‡	0.31 (0.22) 36 ‡	0.03 (0.02) 12.5 (1.09)	0.04 (0.02) 27.5 ‡	0.17 (0.06) 7 (5.45)
Gadiformes Unidentified (N)	Sep, Oct	0.19 (0.15) 55 ‡	0 (0)	0 (0)	0 (0)	0 (0)
Bregmacerotidae *Bregmaceros cantori* (codlet)	Jan, May, Aug, Sep, Oct	1.80 (0.88) 11 (1.08)	2.42 (1.21) 13 ‡	0.03 (0.02) 11 (1.45)	<0.01 (0.01) 55 ‡	0.05 (0.02) 15.5 (1.45)
Merluccidae Unidentified (L) (whiting)	Nov	0 (0)	0 (0)	0 (0)	<0.01 (0.01) 55 ‡	0 (0)
Ophidiidae Unidentified (N) (cuskeel)	May	<0.01 (<0.01) 89.5 ‡	0 (0)	0 (0)	0 (0)	0 (0)
Lepophidium spp. (cusk-eel spp.)	Aug, Sep, Oct	0.43 (0.27) 37 ‡	1.30 (0.94) 17 ‡	0.02 (0.01) 18 ‡	0 (0)	0.01 (0.01) 40.5 ‡
Bythitidae Unidentified (brotula)	Oct, Nov	0.33 (0.23) 43 ‡	0.41 (0.41) 31 ‡	<0.01 (0.01) 28.5 ‡	<0.01 (0.01) 55 ‡	0.01 (0.01) 40.5 ‡
Lophiiformes Unidentified	May, Aug	<0.01 (<0.01) 92 ‡	0 (0)	0 (0)	<0.01 (0.01) 55 ‡	0 (0)
Gobiesociformes Gobiesocidae						

24

Table 3. (continued)

Taxa	Months Collected	Surface Net Density (SE) Rank (%)	Bottom Net Density (SE) Rank (%)	Bottom Light-trap CPUE (SE) Rank (%)	Surface Light-trap CPUE (SE) Rank (%)	Off-platform Light-trap CPUE (SE) Rank (%)
Gobiesox strumosus (L) (skilletfish)	Jul	0 (0)	0 (0)	0 (0)	0.08 (0.08) 16 (1.60)	0 (0)
Atheriniformes						
Exocoetidae						
Unidentified (flyingfish)	Jun, Aug, Sep	0.63 (0.40) 31 ‡	0.27 (0.20) 38 ‡	0 (0)	0 (0)	0.01 (0.01) 40.5 ‡
Cypselurus cyanopterus (L) (margined flyingfish)	Jul	0 (0)	0 (0)	0 (0)	<0.01 (0.01) 55 ‡	0 (0)
Cypselurus furcatus/heterurus (L) (spotfin/Atlantic flyingfish)	May	0 (0)	0 (0)	0 (0)	0 (0)	0.01 (0.01) 40.5 ‡
Parexocoetus brachypterus (L) (sailfin flyingfish)	Jul	0 (0)	0 (0)	0 (0)	0.04 (0.02) 27.5 ‡	0 (0)
Beryciformes						
Holocentridae						
Holocentrus spp. (squirrelfish)	Jun	0.18 (0.10) 56 ‡	0 (0)	0 (0)	0.07 (0.04) 18 (1.42)	0.11 (0.05) 11 (3.64)
Melamphaidae						
Melamphaes spp. (N)	Jan, Jun	0.05 (0.04) 73 ‡	0 (0)	0 (0)	0 (0)	0 (0)
Scorpaeniformes						
Unidentified (N)	Oct	0.24 (0.17) 48 ‡	0 (0)	0 (0)	0 (0)	0 (0)
Scorpaenidae						
Unidentified (N) (scorpionfish)	Oct	0.08 (0.08) 68 ‡	0 (0)	0 (0)	0 (0)	0 (0)
Scorpaena spp. (N) (scorpionfish spp.)	Jun, Aug	0.09 (0.07) 67 ‡	0 (0)	0 (0)	0 (0)	0 (0)
Triglidae						
Prionotus spp. (N) (searobin)	May	0.01 (0.01) 87.5 ‡	0 (0)	0 (0)	0 (0)	0 (0)
Perciformes						
Unidentified	Jan, May, Jun, Jul, Aug, Sep, Oct	2.60 (1.27) 9 (1.11)	1.48 (0.64) 16 (1.23)	0.09 (0.05) 5.5 (4.00)	0.03 (0.02) 33 ‡	0.02 (0.02) 25 ‡
Serranidae						
Unidentified (sea bass/grouper)	Jan, Jun, Oct, Nov	0.22 (0.14) 50 ‡	1.86 (1.28) 15 ‡	0 (0)	<0.01 (0.01) 55 ‡	0 (0)

25

Table 3. (continued)

Taxa	Months Collected	Surface Net Density (SE) Rank (%)	Bottom Net Density (SE) Rank (%)	Bottom Light-trap CPUE (SE) Rank (%)	Surface Light-trap CPUE (SE) Rank (%)	Off-platform Light-trap CPUE (SE) Rank (%)
Anthinae (sea perch)	Apr, May, Jun, Nov	0.46 (0.19) 34‡	0.38 (0.23) 33‡	0 (0)	<0.01 (0.01) 55‡	0.02 (0.02) 25‡
Epinephelinae (N) (grouper)	May, Jun	0.41 (0.23) 38‡	0.23 (0.13) 39‡	0 (0)	0 (0)	0 (0)
Grammistinae (N)	Jun	0 (0)	0.14 (0.10) 48‡	0 (0)	0 (0)	0 (0)
Priacanthidae Unidentified (N) (bigeye)	May, Jun	0.10 (0.07) 64‡	0.08 (0.08) 53‡	0 (0)	0 (0)	0 (0)
Priacanthus spp. (L) (bigeye/glasseye spp.)	Jun	0 (0)	0 (0)	0 (0)	<0.01 (0.01) 55‡	0 (0)
Apogonidae Unidentified (N) (cardinalfish)	May	<0.01 (<0.01) 89.5‡	0 (0)	0 (0)	0 (0)	0 (0)
Apogon spp. (N) (cardinalfish spp.)	May	<0.01 (<0.01) 92‡	0 (0)	0 (0)	0 (0)	0 (0)
Pomatomidae Pomatomus saltatrix (L) (bluefish)	Sep, Oct	0 (0)	0 (0)	0 (0)	0 (0)	0.05 (0.03) 15.5 (1.45)
Echeneidae Unidentified (N) (remora)	Jun	0.14 (0.10) 59.5‡	0 (0)	0 (0)	0 (0)	0 (0)
Carangidae Unidentified (N) (jack)	May, Jun, Jul	0.41 (0.28) 39‡	0.23 (0.16) 40‡	0 (0)	0 (0)	0 (0)
Caranx spp. (jack spp.)	May, Jun	0 (0)	0.07 (0.07) 56‡	0 (0)	0 (0)	0.01 (0.01) 40.5‡
Caranx crysos (blue runner)	Jun, Jul, Aug, Sep	2.75 (1.30) 8‡	0.56 (0.49) 27‡	<0.01 (0.01) 28.5‡	0.24 (0.08) 6 (4.79)	0.30 (0.10) 1 (9.45)
Caranx hippos/latus (crevalle/horse-eye jack)	May, Jun, Jul, Aug, Oct	1.89 (0.65) 10 (1.85)	4.45 (1.62) 8 (4.31)	<0.01 (0.01) 28.5‡	0.08 (0.03) 16 (1.60)	0.22 (0.06) 5 (6.91)
Chloroscombrus chrysurus (Atlantic bumper)	Jun, Jul, Aug, Sep	0.57 (0.24) 33‡	0 (0)	0 (0)	0.03 (0.02) 33‡	0 (0)
Decapterus punctatus (round scad)	Jun, Jul	0.03 (0.03) 77.5‡	0 (0)	<0.01 (0.01) 28.5‡	<0.01 (0.01) 55‡	0 (0)

26

Table 3. (continued)

Taxa	Months Collected	Surface Net Density (SE) Rank (%)	Bottom Net Density (SE) Rank (%)	Bottom Light-trap CPUE (SE) Rank (%)	Surface Light-trap CPUE (SE) Rank (%)	Off-platform Light-trap CPUE (SE) Rank (%)
Elagatis bipinnulata (rainbow runner)	May	0.19 (0.12) 54‡	0 (0)	0 (0)	0 (0)	0.01 (0.01) 40.5‡
Selar crumenophthalmus (N) (bigeye scad)	May, Jun	0.02 (0.02) 86‡	0.19 (0.19) 42.5‡	0 (0)	0 (0)	0 (0)
Selene vomer (N) (lookdown)	Sep	0.24 (0.24) 49‡	0 (0)	0 (0)	0 (0)	0 (0)
Seriola spp. (jack spp.)	May, Jun, Aug, Oct	0.11 (0.06) 62‡	0.44 (0.36) 28‡	0 (0)	<0.01 (0.01) 55‡	0 (0)
Trachurus lathami (rough scad)	Jan, Feb, Apr, May	0.12 (0.07) 61‡	0.19 (0.19) 42.5‡	0 (0)	<0.01 (0.01) 55‡	0.02 (0.02) 25‡
Coryphaenidae						
Coryphaena equiselis (N) (pompano dolphin)	May	0.01 (0.01) 87.5‡	0 (0)	0 (0)	0 (0)	0 (0)
Coryphaena hippurus (N) (dolphin)	Jun, Sep	0.09 (0.07) 65‡	0.09 (0.09) 51‡	0 (0)	0 (0)	0 (0)
Lutjanidae						
Unidentified (snapper)	Feb, May	0.04 (0.04) 76‡	0.03 (0.03) 58‡	0 (0)	0 (0)	0.01 (0.01) 40.5‡
Lutjanus spp. (snapper spp.)	Jun	0.14 (0.10) 59.5‡	0.19 (0.19) 42.5‡	0 (0)	<0.01 (0.01) 55‡	0 (0)
Lutjanus apodus/vivanus (L) (schoolmaster/silk snapper)	Jul	0 (0)	0 (0)	0 (0)	0.02 (0.01) 41.5‡	0 (0)
Lutjanus campechanus (L) (red snapper)	Sep	0 (0)	0 (0)	0 (0)	0.02 (0.02) 41.5‡	0 (0)
Pristipomoides aquilonaris (N) (wenchman)	Jun, Oct	0.91 (0.71) 22‡	1.95 (0.88) 14 (2.16)	0 (0)	0 (0)	0 (0)
Rhomboplites aurorubens (N) (vermillion snapper)	Jul	0.05 (0.05) 72‡	0 (0)	0 (0)	0 (0)	0 (0)
Gerreidae						
Eucinostomus spp. (L) (jenny/mojarra spp.)	Jun, Jul, Sep	0 (0)	0 (0)	0 (0)	0.05 (0.02) 22 (1.06)	0.10 (0.07) 12 (3.27)
Sparidae						
Unidentified (N) (porgy)	May	0 (0)	0.07 (0.07) 56‡	0 (0)	0 (0)	0 (0)
Lagodon rhomboides (N) (pinfish)	Jan	0.17 (0.14) 57‡	0.38 (0.38) 34‡	0 (0)	0 (0)	0 (0)

Table 3. (continued)

Taxa	Months Collected	Surface Net Density (SE) Rank (%)	Bottom Net Density (SE) Rank (%)	Bottom Light-trap CPUE (SE) Rank (%)	Surface Light-trap CPUE (SE) Rank (%)	Off-platform Light-trap CPUE (SE) Rank (%)
Sciaenidae						
Cynoscion arenarius (sand seatrout)	Jul, Aug	1.51 (0.66) 14 (2.09)	0 (0)	0 (0)	0.04 (0.02) 25 ‡	0 (0)
Leiostomus xanthurus (spot)	Jan	0 (0)	0 (0)	0 (0)	0 (0)	0.01 (0.01) 40.5 ‡
Micropogonias undulatus (Atlantic croaker)	Oct	0.45 (0.23) 35 ‡	0.30 (0.30) 37 ‡	0.02 (0.01) 18 ‡	<0.01 (0.01) 55 ‡	0.02 (0.02) 25 ‡
Sciaenops ocellatus (red drum)	Sep	4.11 (1.92) 5 (3.70)	0 (0)	0 (0)	<0.01 (0.01) 55 ‡	0 (0)
Mullidae						
Unidentified (L) (goatfish)	Jun	0 (0)	0 (0)	0 (0)	0 (0)	0.01 (0.01) 40.5 ‡
Upeneus parvus (L) (dwarf goatfish)	Apr	0 (0)	0 (0)	0 (0)	0 (0)	0.01 (0.01) 40.5 ‡
Ephippidae						
Chaetodipterus faber (N) (Atlantic spadefish)	May, Jul	0.05 (0.04) 74 ‡	0 (0)	0 (0)	0 (0)	0 (0)
Chaetodontidae						
Unidentified (N) (butterfly fish)	Jun	0.03 (0.03) 77.5 ‡	0 (0)	0 (0)	0 (0)	0 (0)
Pomacentridae						
Pomacentrus spp. (L) (damselfish spp.)	Jun, Jul	0 (0)	0 (0)	0.02 (0.01) 18 ‡	0.14 (0.08) 13 (2.84)	0.03 (0.03) 19 (1.09)
Mugilidae						
Mugil cephalus (striped mullet)	Jan, Feb, Oct, Nov	8.27 (4.58) 3 ‡	32.05 (15.62) 2 (5.54)	0 (0)	0.04 (0.02) 25 ‡	0.14 (0.06) 9.5 (4.36)
Sphyraenidae						
Sphyraena guachancho (guaguanche)	Jun, Jul	0.44 (0.39) 36 ‡	0.08 (0.08) 53 ‡	0 (0)	0.03 (0.03) 33 ‡	0.01 (0.01) 40.5 ‡
Scaridae						
Unidentified (parrotfish)	Aug, Oct, Nov	3.01 (1.35) 7 ‡	16.31 (5.64) 3 (3.08)	<0.01 (0.01) 28.5 ‡	0.06 (0.03) 19.5 (1.24)	0 (0)
Blenniidae						
Unidentified (blenny)	May, Jun, Jul, Sep, Oct	0.34 (0.19) 41 ‡	0.98 (0.98) 19 ‡	0.06 (0.06) 9.5 (2.55)	0.17 (0.15) 10 (3.37)	0.01 (0.01) 40.5 ‡

Table 3. (continued)

Taxa	Months Collected	Surface Net Density (SE) Rank (%)	Bottom Net Density (SE) Rank (%)	Bottom Light-trap CPUE (SE) Rank (%)	Surface Light-trap CPUE (SE) Rank (%)	Off-platform Light-trap CPUE (SE) Rank (%)
Hypsoblennius invemar (tessellated blenny)	Jun, Oct	0 (0)	0.08 (0.08) 53‡	0 (0)	0 (0)	0.01 (0.01) 40.5‡
Ophioblennius atlanticus (redlip blenny)	Jun, Oct	0.65 (0.47) 29‡	0 (0)	0 (0)	<0.01 (0.01) 55‡	0.01 (0.01) 40.5‡
Callionymidae						
Foetorepus agassizi (N) (spotfin dragonet)	Aug	0.05 (0.03) 75‡	0 (0)	0 (0)	0 (0)	0 (0)
Paradiplogramus bairdi (N) (lancer dragonet)	Aug	0.03 (0.02) 84‡	0 (0)	0 (0)	0 (0)	0 (0)
Gobiidae						
Unidentified (goby)	Jan, Feb, Apr, Jun, Jul, Aug, Oct Nov	4.63 (1.78) 4 (2.02)	11.08 (3.87) 4 (4.41)	0.09 (0.04) 5.5 (4.00)	0.44 (0.40) 2 (8.87)	0.05 (0.02) 15.5 (1.45)
Microdesmidae						
Microdesmus spp. (N) (wormfish spp.)	Jun, Aug	0.03 (0.03) 83‡	0.75 (0.52) 23‡	0 (0)	0 (0)	0 (0)
Microdesmus lanceolatus (N) (lancetail wormfish)	Jun, Jul, Aug	0.65 (0.41) 28‡	0.15 (0.11) 47‡	0 (0)	0 (0)	0 (0)
Microdesmus longipinnis (pink wormfish)	Jul	0.04 (0.06) 70‡	0 (0)	0 (0)	0.05 (0.03) 22 (1.06)	0.02 (0.02) 25‡
Scombridae						
Unidentified (mackerel)	May, Jun, Jul, Aug, Sep	1.75 (1.01) 12 (2.73)	0.75 (0.75) 22‡	0 (0)	0.01 (0.01) 41.5‡	0.02 (0.01) 40.5‡
Acanthocybium solandri (wahoo)	Jun	0 (0)	0.09 (0.09) 49.5‡	0 (0)	0 (0)	0 (0)
Auxis spp. (mackerel spp.)	May, Jun, Aug, Sep, Oct	1.41 (0.42) 15 (1.99)	0.94 (0.50) 20‡	0.02 (0.01) 18‡	0.40 (0.13) 4 (8.16)	0.14 (0.04) 9.5 (4.36)
Euthynnus alletteratus (little tunny)	May, Jun, Jul, Aug, Sep, Oct	0.65 (0.25) 30‡	0.09 (0.09) 49.5‡	0 (0)	0.06 (0.02) 19.5 (1.24)	0.18 (0.08) 6 (5.82)
Scomberomorus cavalla (king mackerel)	Aug	0.09 (0.07) 66‡	0 (0)	(<0.01) (0.01) 28.5‡	0.02 (0.02) 41.5‡	0.03 (0.03) 19 (1.09)
Scomberomorus maculatus (Spanish mackerel)	Jul, Aug	0.75 (0.42) 26‡	0 (0)	0 (0)	0.02 (0.01) 41.5‡	0 (0)
Thunnus spp. (tuna spp.)	May, Jun	0.01 (0.02) 82‡	0.17 (0.12) 46‡	0 (0)	0.02 (0.01) 41.5‡	0.03 (0.01) 40.5‡
Thunnus thynnus (N) (bluefin tuna)	Jun	0.06 (0.07) 69‡	0.18 (0.18) 45‡	0 (0)	0 (0)	0 (0)

29

Table 3. (continued)

Taxa	Months Collected	Surface Net Density (SE) Rank (%)	Bottom Net Density (SE) Rank (%)	Bottom Light-trap CPUE (SE) Rank (%)	Surface Light-trap CPUE (SE) Rank (%)	Off-platform Light-trap CPUE (SE) Rank (%)
Stromateidae						
Ariomma spp. (driftfish spp.)	Apr, May	0.77 (0.52) 25 (2.16)	0.44 (0.36) 29 ‡	0 (0)	0 (0)	0.02 (0.02) 25 ‡
Nomeidae						
Cubiceps pauciradiatus (N) (bigeye cigarfish)	May	0.03 (0.03) 81 ‡	0 (0)	0 (0)	0 (0)	0 (0)
Peprilus burti (gulf butterfish)	Jan, Jun, Aug, Oct, Nov	0.72 (0.34) 27 ‡	1.05 (0.64) 18 ‡	0.02 (0.01) 18 ‡	0.03 (0.02) 33 ‡	0.05 (0.03) 15.5 (1.45)
Tetragonuridae						
Tetragonurus atlanticus (N) (bigeye squaretail)	Nov	0.20 (0.20) 53 ‡	0 (0)	0 (0)	0 (0)	0 (0)
Pleuronectiformes						
Bothidae						
Unidentified (lefteye flounder)	Jul, Oct, Nov	0.59 (0.59) 32 ‡	0.81 (0.81) 21 ‡	<0.01 (0.01) 28.5 ‡	0 (0)	0 (0)
Bothus spp. (flounder spp.)	May, Sep, Oct, Nov	0.17 (0.17) 58 ‡	0 (0)	0.02 (0.01) 18 ‡	0 (0)	0.01 (0.01) 40.5 ‡
Citharichthys spilopterus (baywhiff)	Feb, Oct, Nov	1.14 (0.92) 17 ‡	4.85 (1.98) 7 (1.44)	0 (0)	<0.01 (0.01) 55 ‡	0 (0)
Etropus crossotus (fringed flounder)	Aug, Nov	0.39 (0.39) 40 ‡	0 (0)	0 (0)	0 (0)	0.01 (0.01) 40.5 ‡
Monolene sessilicauda (L) (deepwater flounder)	Feb	0 (0)	0 (0)	0 (0)	0 (0)	0.02 (0.01) 40.5 ‡
Syacium spp. (flounder spp.)	Jul, Aug, Sep	0.22 (0.12) 51 ‡	0 (0)	0.02 (0.01) 18 ‡	0.08 (0.05) 16 (1.60)	0.01 (0.01) 40.5 ‡
Soleidae						
Sympharus spp. (tonguefish spp.)	Feb, Jul, Aug, Sep, Oct	3.03 (1.16) 6 (2.02)	0.70 (0.70) 25 ‡	0.06 (0.05) 9.5 (2.55)	0.10 (0.04) 14 (1.95)	0.07 (0.03) 13 (2.18)
Tetraodontiformes						
Tetraodontidae						
Sphoeroides spp. (N) (puffer spp.)	May	0 (0)	0.07 (0.07) 56 ‡	(0)	0 (0)	0 (0)

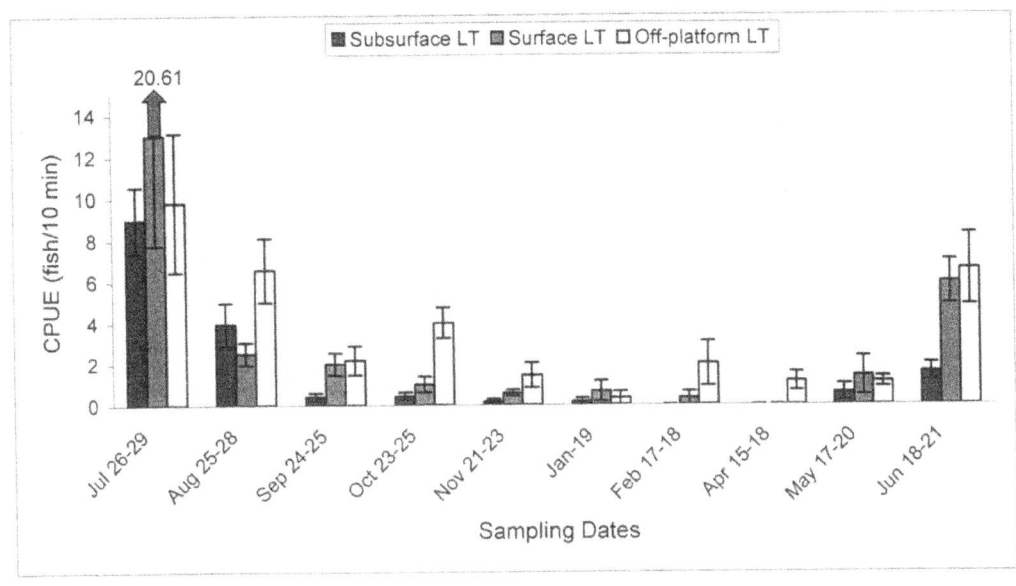

With clupeiform fishes

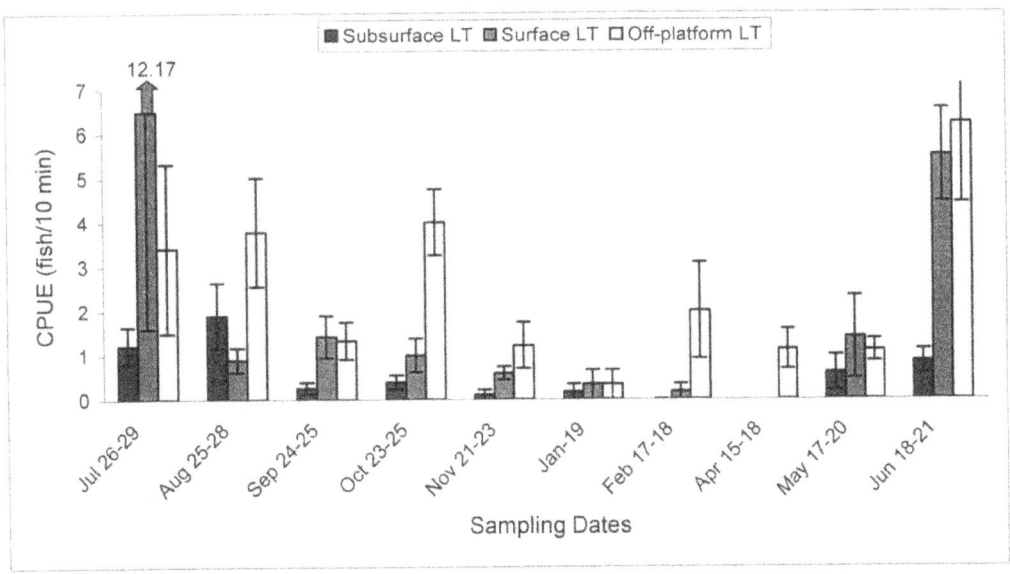

Without clupeiform fishes

Figure 7. Mean light-trap CPUEs and standard errors for data with and without clupeiform fishes included for each sampling trip at Green Canyon 18 (1995-1996). Arrows above each bar point toward the mean for that gear. No surface or subsurface light-trap samples were taken during April 15-18. No fish were present in subsurface light-trap samples (n=10) during February 17-18.

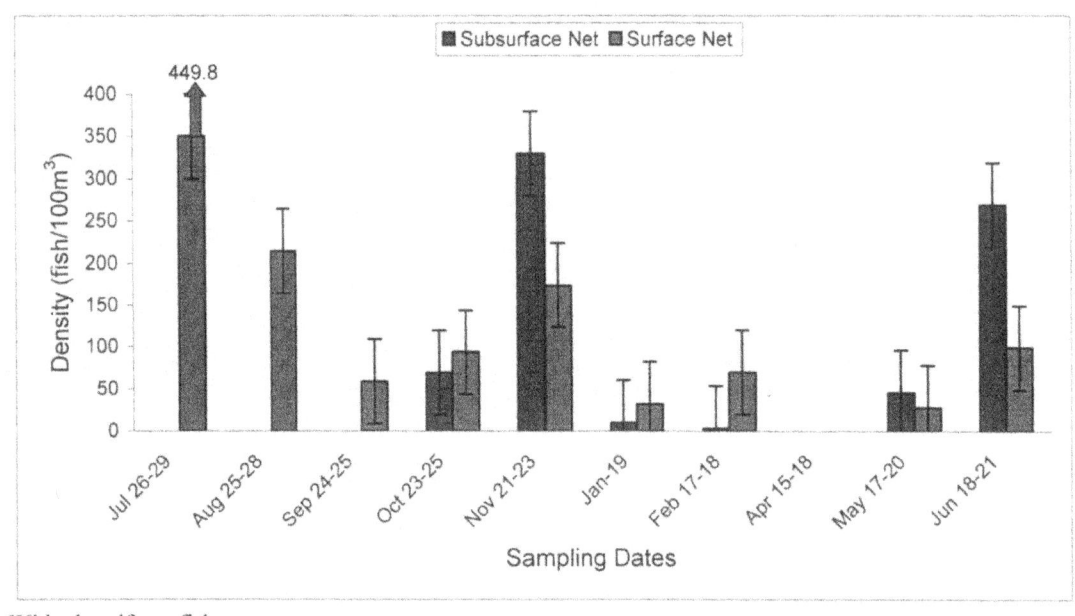

With clupeiform fishes

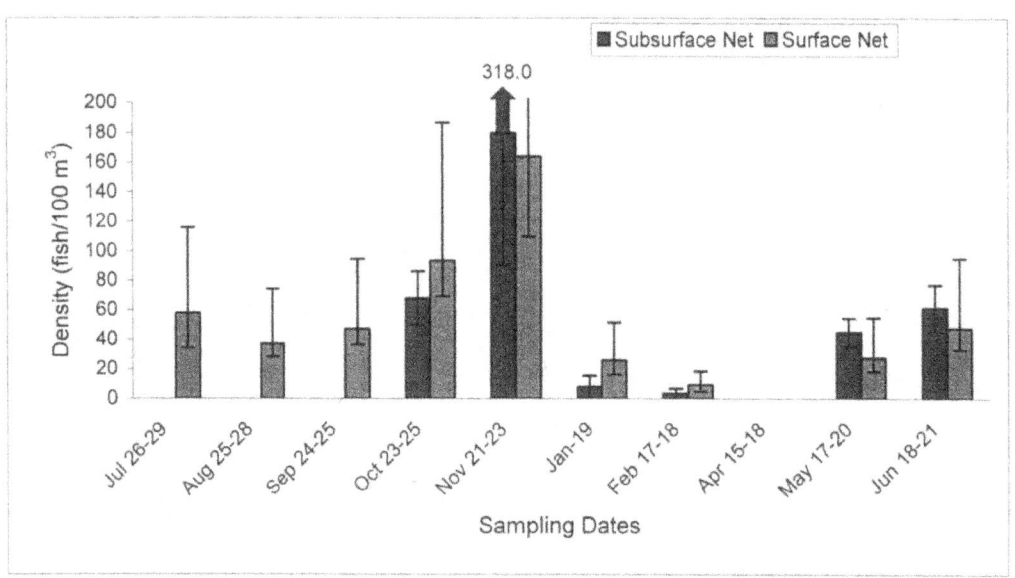

Without clupeiform fishes

Figure 8. Mean plankton net densities and standard errors for data with and without clupeiform fishes included for each sampling trip at Green Canyon 18 (1995-96). No subsurface plankton net samples were taken during June 26-29, August 25-28, September 24-25, and April 15-18. No surface net samples were taken during April 15-18.

8a). Plankton net mean densities ranged from 3.3-449.8 fish/100 m³. Once clupeiform fishes were removed, the mean densities ranged from 3.3-318.0 fish/100 m³ and a single dominant peak was observed in November (Figure 8b).

At GI 94, a total of 45,754 fish were collected with light-traps collecting 31,353 fish and plankton nets collecting 14,401 fish. Plankton nets collected individuals from 40 different families, 6 of which were not collected by light-traps (Table 4). Light-traps sampled fish from 37 families, only 3 of which were not sampled by plankton nets. Plankton nets collected fish from 83 taxa (identified at least to the level of genus), 26 of which were not collected in light-traps, while light-traps collected fish from 90 taxa, 31 of which were not sampled with plankton nets. Clupeiforms dominated the total catch (66%). The most common taxa collected included *Anchoa* spp., *A. nasuta*, *Engraulis eurystole*, and *Opisthonema oglinum*. Among the most common non-clupeiform fishes were synodontids (primarily *Synodus foetens* and *S. poeyi*), blenniids (*Hypsoblennius invemar* and *Parablennius marmoreus*), and scombrids (*Auxis* spp. and *Euthynnus alletteratus*).

At GI 94, mean CPUE values ranged from 1.4-506.7 fish/10 min for all gear types, with the largest peak occurring in late August in surface light-trap collections (Figure 9a). In general, the surface light-trap was more effective in collecting fishes throughout the sampling season. Catches in off-platform light-traps were generally higher than those of subsurface light-traps during the early part of the sampling season, but mean subsurface CPUEs were generally higher than off-platform CPUEs in July and August. Once clupeiform fishes were removed, mean CPUEs ranged from 1.2-197.1 fish/10 min (Figure 9b). Surface light-trap collections were relatively high in April and May and all light-trap collections were relatively low between June and August. Mean plankton net densities at GI 94 ranged from 19.5-1651.7 fish/100 m³ (Figure 10a), with relatively high surface net collections occurring from late May through August. Though the densities were much lower, subsurface net collections were generally higher than surface net collections during April and early May. Once clupeiforms were removed, the mean densities decreased to between 16.6-201.0 fish/100 m³ (Figure 10b). Subsurface catches were more prominent and generally collected more fish than the surface nets, particularly early (April-early May) and late (July-August) in the sampling season.

At ST 54, a total of 97,697 fish were collected, with light-traps collecting 6,116 fish and plankton nets collecting 91,583 fish (Table 5). Due to problems with the deploying the subsurface net at this site (Table 1), the plankton net catch is almost exclusively from the surface. The plankton nets collected fish from 34 families, 8 of which were not present in light-trap collections. Light-traps also collected fish from a total of 34 families, 8 of which were not collected with plankton nets. The plankton nets caught fish from 59 taxa (identified to genus), 19 of which were not in light-trap samples. Light-traps caught fish from 65 taxa, 27 of which were not in plankton net collections. Overall, clupeiforms, primarily clupeids, dominated the collections at ST 54, comprising 97% of the total catch for both gear types combined. The only gear and location not dominated by clupeiforms was the subsurface light-traps, in which *Synodus foetens* was the most common taxon. Of the non-clupeiform fishes collected, sciaenids, synodontids, carangids, and scombrids were dominant.

Table 4. Total plankton net density (fish/100 m³) and light-trap CPUE (fish/10 min) for fish collected at Grand Isle 94 with standard error (SE), rank, percent of total catch (%), and months collected for each taxa. (N) indicates taxa collected only with plankton nets. (L) indicates taxa collected only with light-traps. For ranks, tied values received the mean of the corresponding ranks. ‡ indicates a value <1.00%.

Taxa	Months Collected	Surface Net Density (SE) Rank (%)	Bottom Net Density (SE) Rank (%)	Bottom Light-trap CPUE (SE) Rank (%)	Surface Light-trap CPUE (SE) Rank (%)	Off-platform Light-trap CPUE (SE) Rank (%)
Osteichthyes Unidentified	Apr, May, Jun, July, Aug	0.92 (0.60) 19 ‡	0.78 (0.41) 23 (1.31)	0.28 (0.26) 10 (1.13)	0.13 (0.10) 22 ‡	1.12 (0.94) 9 (4.55)
Anguilliformes Unidentified (N) (eel)	Jun	0.07 (0.07) 69 ‡	0 (0)	0 (0)	0 (0)	0 (0)
Muraenidae Unidentified (moray eel)	May, Jun, Jul	0.07 (0.05) 71 ‡	0.44 (0.23) 33 ‡	<0.01 (<0.01) 49 ‡	0 (0)	0 (0)
Ophichthidae Unidentified (snake eel)	Jun, Jul, Aug	0.10 (0.05) 55 ‡	0.69 (0.35) 26 ‡	0.04 (0.02) 26.5 ‡	0.02 (0.01) 51 ‡	0 (0)
Ophichthus spp. (snake eel)	Aug	0 (0)	0 (0)	0 (0)	0.03 (0.02) 46.5 ‡	0 (0)
Ophichthus gomesi (N) (shrimp eel)	Jun	0.01 (0.01) 98 ‡	0 (0)	0 (0)	0 (0)	0 (0)
Nettastomatidae Hoplunnis macrurus (L) (freckled-pike conger)	May	0 (0)	0 (0)	0 (0)	0.01 (<0.01) 61.5 ‡	0 (0)
Clupeiformes Unidentified (herring/anchovy)	Apr, May, Jun, Jul, Aug	2.38 (2.14) 12 ‡	0.05 (0.04) 69 ‡	<0.01 (<0.01) 58 ‡	<0.01 (<0.01) 81.5 ‡	0 (0)
Clupeidae Unidentified (herring)	Apr, May, Aug	0 (0)	0.52 (0.37) 30 ‡	0 (0)	0.01 (<0.01) 61.5 ‡	0 (0)
Brevoortia patronus (L) (gulf menhaden)	Apr	0 (0)	0 (0)	<0.01 (<0.01) 49 ‡	0 (0)	0 (0)
Etrumeus teres (round herring)	Apr	0.08 (0.06) 66 ‡	0.23 (0.16) 44 ‡	0.02 (0.01) 32 ‡	0.03 (0.02) 46.5 ‡	0.01 (<0.01) 51.5 ‡
Harengula jaguana (scaled sardine)	Apr, Jun, Jul, Aug	0.61 (0.27) 25 ‡	0.31 (0.31) 38.5 ‡	0.06 (0.02) 21 ‡	0.69 (0.18) 18 ‡	0.68 (0.15) 11 (2.76)
Opisthonema oglinum (Atlantic thread herring)	Apr, Jun, Jul, Aug	70.99 (35.34) 2 (15.81)	4.81 (1.97) 5 (2.20)	1.26 (0.85) 6 (4.99)	6.04 (1.23) 8 (4.07)	4.11 (1.11) 1 (16.66)
Sardinella aurita (Spanish sardine)	Apr, Jul, Aug	0.08 (0.06) 67 ‡	0.16 (0.16) 54 ‡	0 (0)	0.04 (0.02) 41.5 ‡	0 (0)

Table 4. (continued)

Taxa	Months Collected	Surface Net Density (SE) Rank (%)	Bottom Net Density (SE) Rank (%)	Bottom Light-trap CPUE (SE) Rank (%)	Surface Light-trap CPUE (SE) Rank (%)	Off-platform Light-trap CPUE (SE) Rank (%)
Engraulidae						
Unidentified (anchovy)	Apr, May, Jun, Jul, Aug	232.66 (44.32) 1 (62.01)	66.92 (17.27) 1 (24.74)	0.41 (0.09) 7 (1.64)	0.55 (0.12) 20 ‡	0.96 (0.17) 10 (3.92)
Anchoa spp. (anchovy spp.)	Apr, May, Jun, Jul, Aug	14.23 (8.25) 3 (3.55)	1.21 (0.73) 21 ‡	0.18 (0.17) 15 ‡	0.02 (0.01) 51 ‡	<0.01 (<0.01) 64 ‡
Anchoa hepsetus (striped anchovy)	Aug	0 (0)	0 (0)	0.10 (0.08) 16.5 ‡	0.70 (0.49) 16 ‡	0.50 (0.47) 12 (2.04)
Anchoa mitchilli (bay anchovy)	Jun, Jul, Aug	6.24 (2.37) 6 (1.89)	2.70 (1.03) 11 ‡	0.37 (0.18) 8 (1.46)	1.89 (0.83) 10 (1.27)	0.47 (0.23) 14 (1.91)
Anchoa nasuta (longnose anchovy)	Aug	0 (0)	0 (0)	7.80 (6.15) 1 (30.96)	11.10 (5.93) 4 (7.47)	1.31 (0.70) 6 (5.30)
Anchoa nasuta/hepsetus (longnose/striped anchovy)	Apr, May, Jun, Jul, Aug	5.64 (2.80) 8 (1.87)	4.59 (1.69) 7 (3.14)	2.73 (0.52) 3 (10.88)	30.11 (12.33) 2 (20.27)	1.45 (0.53) 5 (5.86)
Anchoviella perfasciata (flat anchovy)	Aug	0 (0)	0 (0)	0 (0)	0.07 (0.07) 33.5 ‡	0.09 (0.09) 24 ‡
Engraulis eurystole (silver anchovy)	Apr, May, Jun, Jul, Aug	1.93 (1.90) 13 ‡	2.43 (1.12) 12 (1.15)	5.72 (1.41) 2 (22.79)	38.79 (13.81) 1 (26.12)	1.25 (0.48) 7 (5.08)
Stomiiformes						
Gonostomatidae						
Cyclothone braueri (N)	Apr, Jul	0.02 (0.02) 94 ‡	0.11 (0.08) 60 ‡	0 (0)	0 (0)	0 (0)
Vinciguerria nimbaria (L)	Apr	0 (0)	0 (0)	0 (0)	<0.01 (<0.01) 81.5 ‡	0 (0)
Aulopiformes						
Synodontidae						
Unidentified	Apr, May, Jun, Jul, Aug	0.22 (0.08) 40 ‡	2.11 (0.56) 15 (1.05)	0.10 (0.03) 16.5 ‡	0.90 (0.39) 14 ‡	0.12 (0.06) 21 ‡
Saurida brasiliensis (largescale lizardfish)	Apr, May, Jun, Jul, Aug	0.81 (0.22) 21 ‡	4.77 (1.26) 6 (4.86)	1.97 (0.42) 5 (7.84)	3.35 (0.51) 9 (2.27)	0.50 (0.14) 13 (2.01)
Saurida normani (L) (shortjaw lizardfish)	Apr, May	0 (0)	0 (0)	0 (0)	0.01 (<0.01) 61.5 ‡	0 (0)
Saurida normani/brasiliensis (L) (shortjaw/largescale lizardfish)	May	0 (0)	0 (0)	0 (0)	<0.01 (<0.01) 81.5 ‡	0 (0)
Saurida suspicio (L)	May	0 (0)	0 (0)	0 (0)	<0.01 (<0.01) 81.5 ‡	0 (0)

35

Table 4. (continued)

Taxa	Months Collected	Surface Net Density (SE) Rank (%)	Bottom Net Density (SE) Rank (%)	Bottom Light-trap CPUE (SE) Rank (%)	Surface Light-trap CPUE (SE) Rank (%)	Off-platform Light-trap CPUE (SE) Rank (%)
Synodus spp. (lizardfish spp.)	May, Jun	0 (0)	0.03 (0.03) 72.5 ‡	<0.01 (<0.01) 49 ‡	0.06 (0.06) 37.5 ‡	0.04 (0.03) 35.5 ‡
Synodus foetens (inshore lizardfish)	Apr, May, Jun, Jul, Aug	0.64 (0.26) 24 ‡	2.12 (0.77) 14 (1.20)	0.20 (0.06) 12 ‡	22.11 (5.24) 3 (14.92)	0.20 (0.05) 19 ‡
Synodus poeyi (offshore lizardfish)	Apr, May, Jun, Jul, Aug	0.17 (0.13) 47 ‡	1.35 (0.44) 17 ‡	0.34 (0.09) 9 (1.36)	9.98 (1.78) 5 (6.74)	0.13 (0.28) 8 (4.57)
Synodus synodus (L) (red lizardfish)	May	0 (0)	0 (0)	0 (0)	0.01 (<0.01) 61.5 ‡	0 (0)
Trachinocephalus myops (L) (snakefish)	Apr, May, Jun, Aug	0 (0)	0 (0)	0 (0)	0.08 (0.03) 30.5 ‡	<0.01 (<0.01) 64 ‡
Paralepidae Unidentified (N) (barracudina)	May	0.03 (0.03) 88 ‡	0 (0)	0 (0)	0 (0)	0 (0)
Lestrolepis intermedia	May, Jun, Aug	0 (0)	0.15 (0.11) 56 ‡	0.02 (0.01) 32 ‡	<0.01 (<0.01) 81.5 ‡	0 (0)
Lestrolepis spp. (L) (barracudina spp.)	Aug	0 (0)	0 (0)	<0.01 (<0.01) 49 ‡	0 (0)	0 (0)
Myctophiformes Unidentified (N)	Jun	0 (0)	0.21 (0.21) 48 ‡	0 (0)	0 (0)	0 (0)
Myctophidae Unidentified (lanternfish)	Apr, May, Jun, Jul, Aug	0.09 (0.05) 60 ‡	0.75 (0.41) 25 ‡	0.03 (0.02) 28 ‡	0.05 (0.02) 40 ‡	0.06 (0.02) 29.5 ‡
Gadiformes Bregmacerotidae *Bregmaceros cantori*	Apr, May, Jun, Jul, Aug	1.59 (0.42) 16 ‡	16.67 (3.00) 3 (15.06)	2.18 (1.02) 4 (8.68)	0.06 (0.02) 35.5 ‡	0.03 (0.02) 38.5 ‡
Ophidiiformes Ophidiidae Unidentified (cusk-eel)	May, Jun, Jul	0.31 (0.13) 35 ‡	0.21 (0.21) 48 ‡	0 (0)	<0.01 (<0.01) 81.5 ‡	0 (0)
Lepophidium spp. (N) (cusk-eel spp.)	Jul	0 (0)	0.13 (0.13) 58.5 ‡	0 (0)	0 (0)	0 (0)
Lepophidium profundorum (N) (fawn cusk-eel)	Jun	0.03 (0.02) 84 ‡	0.23 (0.21) 45 ‡	0 (0)	0 (0)	0 (0)
Lepophidium staurophor (N)	May, Jun, Aug	0.09 (0.06) 59 ‡	0 (0)	0 (0)	0 (0)	0 (0)

Table 4. (continued)

Taxa	Months Collected	Surface Net	Bottom Net	Bottom Light-trap	Surface Light-trap	Off-platform Light-trap
		Density (SE) Rank (%)	Density (SE) Rank (%)	CPUE (SE) Rank (%)	CPUE (SE) Rank (%)	CPUE (SE) Rank (%)
Ophidiinae Type A (N) (cusk-eel spp.)	Jun	0 (0)	0.02 (0.02) 80 ‡	0 (0)	0 (0)	0 (0)
Ophidion nocomis	May, Jun	0 (0)	0.05 (0.05) 68 ‡	0.01 (<0.01) 37 ‡	0 (0)	0 (0)
Ophidion nocomis/selenops (cusk-eel spp.)	May	0.09 (0.06) 63 ‡	0.31 (0.23) 38.5 ‡	0 (0)	<0.01 (<0.01) 81.5 ‡	0 (0)
Ophidion selenops (N) (mooneye cusk-eel)	May, Jun	0 (0)	0.19 (0.14) 50 ‡	0 (0)	0 (0)	0 (0)
Lophiiformes						
Caulophrynidae						
Robia legula (N)	Jul	0 (0)	0.09 (0.08) 61 ‡	0 (0)	0 (0)	0 (0)
Atheriniformes						
Exocoetidae						
Unidentified (flyingfish)	Jun	0.14 (0.07) 51 ‡	0.07 (0.07) 64.5 ‡	0 (0)	0 (0)	0 (0)
Cypselurus spp. (flyingfish spp.)	May, Jun	0 (0)	0.07 (0.07) 64.5 ‡	0 (0)	<0.01 (<0.01) 81.5 ‡	<0.01 (<0.01) 64 ‡
Cypselurus cyanopterus (L) (margined flyingfish)	Jul	0 (0)	0 (0)	0 (0)	<0.01 (<0.01) 81.5 ‡	0 (0)
Beryciformes						
Holocentridae						
Holocentrus spp. (squirrelfish spp.)	May, Jun, Jul	0.18 (0.08) 44 ‡	0 (0)	0.01 (<0.01) 40 ‡	0 (0)	<0.01 (<0.01) 64 ‡
Scorpaeniformes						
Scorpaenidae						
Unidentified (N) (scorpionfish)	May, Jun	0.01 (0.01) 95 ‡	0.16 (0.16) 54 ‡	0 (0)	0 (0)	0 (0)
Scorpaena spp. (scorpionfish spp.)	May, Jul, Aug	0 (0)	0.45 (0.34) 32 ‡	0 (0)	0.01 (<0.01) 61.5 ‡	0 (0)
Triglidae						
Unidentified (N) (searobin)	Jul	0.01 (0.01) 99 ‡	0 (0)	0 (0)	0 (0)	0 (0)
Prionotus spp. (searobin spp.)	Apr	0.21 (0.11) 42 ‡	0.09 (0.09) 62 ‡	0 (0)	<0.01 (<0.01) 81.5 ‡	0 (0)
Perciformes						

37

Table 4. (continued)

Taxa	Months Collected	Surface Net Density (SE) Rank (%)	Bottom Net Density (SE) Rank (%)	Bottom Light-trap CPUE (SE) Rank (%)	Surface Light-trap CPUE (SE) Rank (%)	Off-platform Light-trap CPUE (SE) Rank (%)
Unidentified	Apr, May, Jun, Jul, Aug	1.74 (0.69) 15‡	2.22 (0.76) 13 (1.41)	0.05 (0.02) 24.5‡	0.09 (0.05) 27‡	0.04 (0.02) 34‡
Serranidae						
Unidentified (N) (seabass/grouper)	Apr, May, Jun	0.08 (0.05) 68‡	0.16 (0.13) 52‡	0 (0)	0 (0)	0 (0)
Anthinae (sea perch)	May	0.17 (0.09) 46‡	0.35 (0.24) 36‡	0 (0)	0.01 (<0.01) 61.5‡	0 (0)
Epinephelinae (grouper)	May, Jun	0.07 (0.04) 72‡	0 (0)	0 (0)	0.03 (0.01) 43‡	0 (0)
Grammistinae (N)	Jun, Jul	0.04 (0.03) 80‡	0.01 (0.01) 81‡	0 (0)	0 (0)	0 (0)
Serraninae (sea bass)	Apr, May, Jun, Aug	0.36 (0.14) 31‡	0.95 (0.33) 22‡	<0.01 (<0.01) 49‡	0.08 (0.03) 30.5‡	0 (0)
Priacanthidae						
Priacanthus spp. (N) (bigeye/glasseye spp.)	May	0 (0)	0.03 (0.03) 74.5‡	0 (0)	0 (0)	0 (0)
Pomatomidae						
Pomatomus saltatrix (bluefish)	Apr, May	0.08 (0.06) 65‡	0 (0)	0 (0)	0.01 (<0.01) 61.5‡	0 (0)
Rachycentridae						
Rachycentron canadum (N) (cobia)	May, Jun, Jul	0.14 (0.07) 52‡	0.02 (0.02) 78‡	0 (0)	0 (0)	0 (0)
Carangidae						
Unidentified (jack)	Jun, Jul	0.17 (0.11) 45‡	0.03 (0.03) 72.5‡	0 (0)	0 (0)	<0.01 (<0.01) 64‡
Caranx spp. (N) (jack spp.)	Jun	0.16 (0.09) 49‡	0 (0)	0 (0)	0 (0)	0 (0)
Caranx crysos (blue runner)	Jun, Jul, Aug	1.14 (0.41) 17‡	0.62 (0.43) 28‡	0.04 (0.03) 26.5‡	0.08 (0.03) 30.5‡	0.08 (0.02) 25‡
Caranx hippos/latus (crevalle/horse-eye jack)	May, Jun, Jul, Aug	0.50 (0.31) 27‡	0 (0)	<0.01 (<0.01) 49‡	0.11 (0.03) 24‡	0.09 (0.03) 23‡
Chloroscombrus chrysurus (Atlantic bumper)	Jul, Aug	1.00 (0.34) 18‡	0.29 (0.18) 40‡	<0.01 (<0.01) 49‡	0.01 (<0.01) 61.5‡	0.02 (0.01) 44.5‡
Decapterus punctatus (L) (round scad)	Apr, May, Jul, Aug	0 (0)	0 (0)	0 (0)	0.06 (0.02) 35.5‡	<0.01 (<0.01) 64‡
Oligoplites saurus (N) (leatherjack)	Jul	0.16 (0.12) 48‡	0 (0)	0 (0)	0 (0)	0 (0)

Table 4. (continued)

Taxa	Months Collected	Surface Net Density (SE) Rank (%)	Bottom Net Density (SE) Rank (%)	Bottom Light-trap CPUE (SE) Rank (%)	Surface Light-trap CPUE (SE) Rank (%)	Off-platform Light-trap CPUE (SE) Rank (%)
Selar crumenophthalmus (N) (bigeye scad)	Jun, Jul	0.34 (0.15) 34‡	0.13 (0.13) 58.5‡	0 (0)	0 (0)	0 (0)
Selene vomer (N) (lookdown)	Jun, Jul	0.01 (0.01) 96‡	0.05 (0.03) 70‡	0 (0)	0 (0)	0 (0)
Seriola spp. (N) (jack spp.)	May	0.03 (0.03) 85‡	0 (0)	0 (0)	0 (0)	0 (0)
Seriola dumerili/rivoliana (L) (greater amberjack/almaco jack)	May, Jun	0 (0)	0 (0)	<0.01 (<0.01) 49‡	0 (0)	0.02 (0.01) 44.5‡
Seriola fasciata (L) (lesser amberjack)	May	0 (0)	0 (0)	0 (0)	<0.01 (<0.01) 93‡	0 (0)
Trachinotus carolinus (L) (Florida pompano)	Jun	0 (0)	0 (0)	0 (0)	0 (0)	0.01 (<0.01) 51.5‡
Trachinotus falcatus/goodei (L) (permit/palometa)	May	0 (0)	0 (0)	0 (0)	0.03 (0.02) 46.5‡	0 (0)
Trachurus lathami (rough scad)	Apr, May	0.04 (0.04) 82‡	0.15 (0.10) 57‡	0.02 (0.01) 32‡	0.06 (0.03) 37.5‡	0.01 (<0.01) 51.5‡
Coryphaenidae *Coryphaena equiselis* (L) (pompano dolphin)	May	0 (0)	0 (0)	0 (0)	0 (0)	<0.01 (<0.01) 64‡
Coryphaena hippurus (dolphin)	May, Jul	0.03 (0.03) 86.5‡	0 (0)	0 (0)	0 (0)	<0.01 (<0.01) 64‡
Lutjanidae Unidentified (snapper)	May, Jun, Jul	0.09 (0.05) 61‡	0.06 (0.06) 67‡	<0.01 (<0.01) 49‡	<0.01 (<0.01) 81.5‡	0 (0)
Lutjanus spp. (snapper spp.)	May, Jun, Jul	0.67 (0.24) 22‡	0.02 (0.02) 78‡	0 (0)	0.01 (<0.01) 61.5‡	0.01 (0.01) 51.5‡
Lutjanus campechanus (red snapper)	May, Jun, Jul	0.02 (0.02) 93‡	0 (0)	0 (0)	0.02 (0.02) 49‡	0 (0)
Rhomboplites aurorubens (vermilion snapper)	May, Jun, Jul	0.40 (0.25) 30‡	0.37 (0.21) 35‡	0.20 (0.06) 13‡	0.07 (0.03) 33.5‡	<0.01 (<0.01) 64‡
Gerreidae *Eucinostomus* spp. (jenny/mojarra spp.)	May, Jun, Jul, Aug	0 (0)	0 (0)	<0.01 (<0.01) 49‡	<0.01 (<0.01) 81.5‡	0.02 (0.01) 41‡
Sparidae Unidentified (porgy)	Apr, May	0.04 (0.04) 83‡	0 (0)	0 (0)	0.01 (<0.01) 61.5‡	0.02 (0.01) 44.5‡

Table 4. (continued)

Taxa	Months Collected	Surface Net Density (SE) Rank (%)	Bottom Net Density (SE) Rank (%)	Bottom Light-trap CPUE (SE) Rank (%)	Surface Light-trap CPUE (SE) Rank (%)	Off-platform Light-trap CPUE (SE) Rank (%)
Calamus spp. (L) (porgy spp.))	May	0 (0)	0 (0)	0 (0)	<0.01 (<0.01) 81.5 ‡	0 (0)
Sciaenidae						
Unidentified (N) (drum spp.)	Aug	<0.01 (<0.01) 100 ‡	0 (0)	0 (0)	0 (0)	0 (0)
Cynoscion arenarius (sand seatrout)	Apr, May, Jul, Aug	3.12 (1.11) 11 ‡	1.25 (0.88) 19 ‡	<0.01 (<0.01) 49 ‡	0 (0)	0.01 (<0.01) 51.5 ‡
Menticirrhus spp. (N) (kingfish spp.)	Aug	0.15 (0.11) 50 ‡	0.63 (0.63) 27 ‡	0 (0)	0 (0)	0 (0)
Stellifer lanceolatus (N) (star drum)	Aug	0.09 (0.09) 64 ‡	0 (0)	0 (0)	0 (0)	0 (0)
Mullidae						
Unidentified (goatfish)	Apr, May, Jul	0.25 (0.14) 38 ‡	0 (0)	<0.01 (<0.01) 49 ‡	<0.01 (<0.01) 81.5 ‡	0.05 (0.02) 32 ‡
Mullus auratus (L) (red goatfish)	Apr, May	0 (0)	0 (0)	0 (0)	0 (0)	0.06 (0.02) 27 ‡
Pseudupeneus maculatus (L) (spotted goatfish)	Apr, May	0 (0)	0 (0)	0 (0)	0 (0)	0.06 (0.03) 28 ‡
Upeneus parvus (L) (dwarf goatfish)	May, Jun	0 (0)	0 (0)	0 (0)	0.01 (<0.01) 61.5 ‡	0.38 (0.09) 15 (1.58)
Chaetodontidae						
Unidentified (N) (butterflyfish)	May	0.02 (0.02) 91 ‡	0 (0)	0 (0)	0 (0)	0 (0)
Pomacentridae						
Unidentified (L) (damselfish)	May, Jun	0 (0)	0 (0)	<0.01 (<0.01) 49 ‡	0.01 (<0.01) 61.5 ‡	0.01 (0.01) 51.5 ‡
Abudefduf saxatilis (L) (sergeant major)	May, Jun, Aug	0 (0)	0 (0)	0 (0)	0 (0)	0.03 (0.02) 38.5 ‡
Abudefduf taurus (L) (night sergeant)	May	0 (0)	0 (0)	0 (0)	0.01 (<0.01) 61.5 ‡	0 (0)
Chromis spp. (chromis spp.)	May, Jun	0.29 (0.29) 37 ‡	0 (0)	0.01 (<0.01) 37 ‡	0.37 (0.13) 21 ‡	0.06 (0.02) 31 ‡
Pomacentrus spp. (damselfish spp.)	May, Jun, Jul, Aug	0.09 (0.05) 62 ‡	0.03 (0.03) 74.5 ‡	0.07 (0.02) 20 ‡	0.12 (0.03) 23 ‡	0.30 (0.14) 16 (1.28)
Mugilidae						
Mugil curema (L) (white mullet)	May, Jun	0 (0)	0 (0)	0 (0)	0.01 (<0.01) 61.5 ‡	0.02 (0.01) 41 ‡

40

Table 4. (continued)

Taxa	Months Collected	Surface Net Density (SE) Rank (%)	Bottom Net Density (SE) Rank (%)	Bottom Light-trap CPUE (SE) Rank (%)	Surface Light-trap CPUE (SE) Rank (%)	Off-platform Light-trap CPUE (SE) Rank (%)
Sphyraenidae						
Sphyraena borealis (L) (northern sennet)	May	0 (0)	0 (0)	0 (0)	0.01 (<0.01) 61.5‡	0 (0)
Sphyraena guachancho (guaguanche)	Jun, July, Aug	1.83 (0.60) 14‡	0 (0)	0 (0)	0.01 (<0.01) 61.5‡	0.01 (<0.01) 57‡
Labridae						
Unidentified (wrasse)	May, Aug	0.05 (0.05) 78‡	0.16 (0.16) 54‡	0 (0)	<0.01 (<0.01) 81.5‡	0 (0)
Opisthognathidae						
Unidentified (jawfish)	Apr, May, Jun	0.46 (0.14) 28‡	0.48 (0.33) 31‡	0 (0)	0.63 (0.20) 19‡	0.06 (0.02) 29.5‡
Opisthognathus spp. (N) (jawfish spp.)	May	0.05 (0.05) 77‡	0 (0)	0 (0)	0 (0)	0 (0)
Opisthognathus aurifrons (yellowhead jawfish)	May	0.06 (0.06) 76‡	0 (0)	0 (0)	0.03 (0.02) 44‡	0 (0)
Opisthognathus lonchurus (N) (moustache jawfish)	May	0.10 (0.10) 58‡	0 (0)	0 (0)	0 (0)	0 (0)
Blenniidae						
Unidentified (blenny)	Apr, May, Jun, Jul, Aug	4.73 (3.95) 9 (1.53)	1.22 (0.69) 20‡	0.05 (0.04) 24.5‡	0.69 (0.21) 17‡	0.04 (0.03) 33‡
Hypsoblennius hentz/ionthas (L) (feather/freckled blenny)	May, Jun, Jul	0 (0)	0 (0)	0.02 (0.01) 29‡	1.76 (0.57) 11 (1.21)	0.04 (0.01) 37‡
Hypsoblennius invemar (tessellated blenny)	Apr, May, Jun, Jul	0.04 (0.04) 81‡	0 (0)	0.08 (0.03) 18‡	6.33 (1.77) 7 (4.32)	3.58 (0.67) 2 (14.55)
Ophioblennius atlanticus (N) (redlip blenny)	Aug	0.42 (0.42) 29‡	0 (0)	0 (0)	0 (0)	0 (0)
Parablennius marmoreus (seaweed blenny)	Apr, May, Jun	0.02 (0.02) 92‡	0 (0)	0.19 (0.04) 14‡	7.20 (1.06) 6 (4.87)	1.62 (0.35) 4 (6.61)
Scartella/Hypleurochilus (blenny spp.)	Apr, May, Jun, Jul	0.06 (0.04) 74.5‡	0.21 (0.15) 46‡	<0.01 (<0.01) 49‡	1.14 (0.24) 12‡	0.11 (0.03) 22‡
Callionymidae						
Unidentified (N) (dragonet)	Jul	0.03 (0.03) 86.5‡	0 (0)	0 (0)	0 (0)	0 (0)
Gobiidae						
Unidentified	Apr, May, Jun, Jul, Aug	5.75 (0.80) 7 (1.77)	10.73 (1.76) 4 (8.53)	0.21 (0.06) 11‡	0.05 (0.02) 39‡	0.01 (<0.01) 51.5‡

41

Table 4. (continued)

Taxa	Months Collected	Surface Net Density (SE) Rank (%)	Bottom Net Density (SE) Rank (%)	Bottom Light-trap CPUE (SE) Rank (%)	Surface Light-trap CPUE (SE) Rank (%)	Off-platform Light-trap CPUE (SE) Rank (%)
Bollmannia communis (L) (ragged goby)	Jun	0 (0)	0 (0)	0.01 (0.01) 37 ‡	0 (0)	0 (0)
Gobionellus oceanicus (highfin goby)	Jun, Aug	0.03 (0.03) 89 ‡	0 (0)	0 (0)	<0.01 (<0.01) 81.5 ‡	0 (0)
Microdesmidae						
Microdesmus spp. (N) (wormfish spp.)	Apr, May, Jun, Jul	0.30 (0.11) 36 ‡	0 (0)	0 (0)	0 (0)	0 (0)
Microdesmus lanceolatus (lancetail wormfish)	Apr, May, Jun, Jul, Aug	0.89 (0.18) 20 ‡	0.77 (0.31) 24 ‡	0.02 (0.01) 32 ‡	<0.01 (<0.01) 81.5 ‡	0.01 (<0.01) 51.5 ‡
Microdesmus longipinnis (N) (pink wormfish)	Apr, May, Jul	0.53 (0.18) 26 ‡	0 (0)	0 (0)	0 (0)	0 (0)
Trichiuridae						
Gempylus spp. (N) (snake mackerel spp.)	Jul	0 (0)	0.02 (0.02) 78 ‡	0 (0)	0 (0)	0 (0)
Trichiurus lepturus (Atlantic cutlassfish)	Apr, May, Jun, Jul, Aug	0.35 (0.13) 33 ‡	0.26 (0.13) 43 ‡	0.05 (0.02) 22.5 ‡	0.01 (0.01) 61.5 ‡	<0.01 (<0.01) 64 ‡
Scombridae						
Unidentified (mackerel)	May, Jun, Jul, Aug	0.10 (0.06) 56 ‡	0.43 (0.29) 34 ‡	0.01 (<0.01) 37 ‡	0.10 (0.08) 25 ‡	0.04 (0.01) 35.5 ‡
Auxis spp. (mackerel spp.)	Apr, May, Jun, Jul, Aug	6.61 (2.32) 5 (1.69)	1.26 (0.79) 18 ‡	0.02 (0.01) 32 ‡	0.76 (0.19) 15 ‡	0.24 (0.06) 18 ‡
Euthynnus alletteratus (little tunny)	May, Jun, Jul, Aug	4.55 (1.05) 10 (1.39)	4.10 (1.06) 8 (3.09)	0.08 (0.03) 19 ‡	0.92 (0.17) 13 ‡	2.83 (0.62) 3 (11.54)
Katsuwonus pelamis (skipjack tuna)	May	0.06 (0.04) 74.5 ‡	0 (0)	0 (0)	0.08 (0.03) 30.5 ‡	0 (0)
Scomber japonicus (L) (chub mackeral)	Apr	0 (0)	0 (0)	0 (0)	0 (0)	0.02 (0.02) 44.5 ‡
Scomberomorus cavalla (king mackerel)	May, Jun, Jul, Aug	0.13 (0.06) 54 ‡	0.07 (0.04) 66 ‡	<0.01 (<0.01) 49 ‡	0.09 (0.03) 26 ‡	0.27 (0.11) 17 (1.11)
Scomberomorus maculatus (Spanish mackerel)	Jun, Jul, Aug	0.36 (0.14) 32 ‡	0.21 (0.21) 48 ‡	0 (0)	0.04 (0.02) 41.5 ‡	0.17 (0.05) 20 ‡
Thunnus spp. (L) (tuna spp.)	Aug	0 (0)	0 (0)	0 (0)	0 (0)	0.01 (0.01) 51.5 ‡
Thunnus thynnus (L) (bluefin tuna)	May	0 (0)	0 (0)	0 (0)	0.01 (0.01) 61.5 ‡	0.01 (0.01) 51.5 ‡
Stromateidae						

Table 4. (continued)

Taxa	Months Collected	Surface Net — Density (SE) Rank (%)	Bottom Net — Density (SE) Rank (%)	Bottom Light-trap — CPUE (SE) Rank (%)	Surface Light-trap — CPUE (SE) Rank (%)	Off-platform Light-trap — CPUE (SE) Rank (%)
Ariomma regulus (L) (spotted driftfish)	Aug	0 (0)	0 (0)	0 (0)	<0.01 (<0.01) 81.5 ‡	0 (0)
Centrolophus medusophagus (brown ruff)	Apr	0 (0)	0.32 (0.26) 37 ‡	0 (0)	<0.01 (<0.01) 81.5 ‡	<0.01 (<0.01) 64 ‡
Peprilus burti (gulf butterfish)	Apr, May	0.07 (0.05) 70 ‡	0.04 (0.04) 71 ‡	<0.01 (<0.01) 49 ‡	0.03 (0.02) 46.5 ‡	0.02 (0.01) 41 ‡
Peprilus alepidotus (N) (harvestfish)	May, Jul, Aug	0.21 (0.11) 43 ‡	2.79 (1.72) 10 ‡	0 (0)	0 (0)	0 (0)
Pleuronectiformes						
Unidentified (N) (flounder)	Aug	0.01 (0.01) 97 ‡	0.08 (0.08) 63 ‡	0 (0)	0 (0)	0 (0)
Bothidae						
Unidentified (lefteye flounder)	Apr, May, Jul	0.06 (0.05) 73 ‡	0.17 (0.13) 51 ‡	<0.01 (<0.01) 49 ‡	0 (0)	0 (0)
Bothus spp. (L) (flounder spp.)	May	0 (0)	0 (0)	0 (0)	<0.01 (<0.01) 81.5 ‡	0 (0)
Citharichthys spilopterus (bay whiff)	Apr, May, Jul	0.05 (0.04) 79 ‡	0.28 (0.20) 41 ‡	0 (0)	0 (0)	<0.01 (<0.01) 64 ‡
Cyclopsetta spp. (N) (flounder spp.)	Jun, Jul	0.10 (0.08) 57 ‡	0.53 (0.47) 29 ‡	0 (0)	0 (0)	0 (0)
Engyophrys senta (N) (spiny flounder)	Jul	0 (0)	0.02 (0.02) 76 ‡	0 (0)	0 (0)	0 (0)
Etropus crossotus (fringed flounder)	Apr, May, Jun, Jul, Aug	0.65 (0.19) 23 ‡	1.79 (0.54) 16 ‡	0.01 (<0.01) 37 ‡	<0.01 (<0.01) 81.5 ‡	0.01 (<0.01) 51.5 ‡
Syacium spp. (flounder spp.)	Apr, Jun, Jul, Aug	0.25 (0.12) 39 ‡	3.78 (1.14) 9 (2.82)	0 (0)	0.02 (0.01) 51 ‡	<0.01 (<0.01) 64 ‡
Soleidae						
Achirus lineatus (N) (lined sole)	Jun, Jul	0.21 (0.08) 41 ‡	0 (0)	0 (0)	0 (0)	0 (0)
Symphurus spp. (tonguefish spp.)	Apr, May, Jun, Jul, Aug	6.79 (1.18) 4 (1.69)	17.00 (3.82) 2 (14.49)	0.05 (0.02) 22.5 ‡	0.08 (0.02) 28 ‡	0.07 (0.03) 26 ‡
Tetraodontiformes						
Balistidae						
Unidentified (N) (leatherjacket)	Jul	0.03 (0.03) 90 ‡	0 (0)			
Tetraodontiformes						
Tetraodontidae						

43

Table 4. (continued)

Taxa	Months Collected	Surface Net Density (SE) Rank (%)	Bottom Net Density (SE) Rank (%)	Bottom Light-trap CPUE (SE) Rank (%)	Surface Light-trap CPUE (SE) Rank (%)	Off-platform Light-trap CPUE (SE) Rank (%)
Sphoeroides spp. (puffer spp.)	Apr, May, Jun, Jul	0.14 (0.07) 53 ‡	0.28 (0.22) 42 ‡	0 (0)	<0.01 (<0.01) 81.5 ‡	0 (0)

44

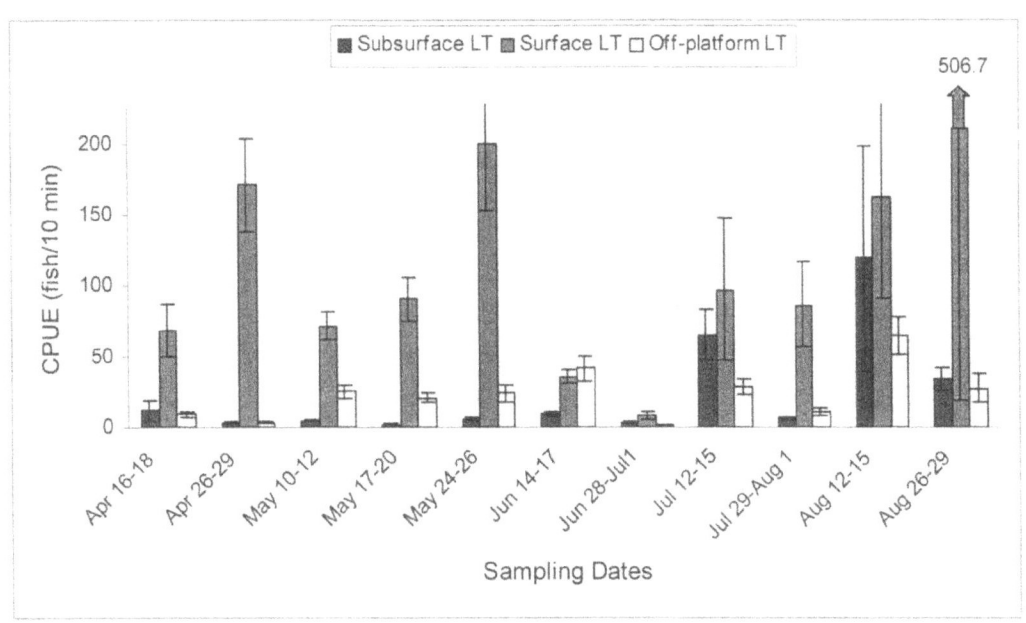

With clupeiform fishes

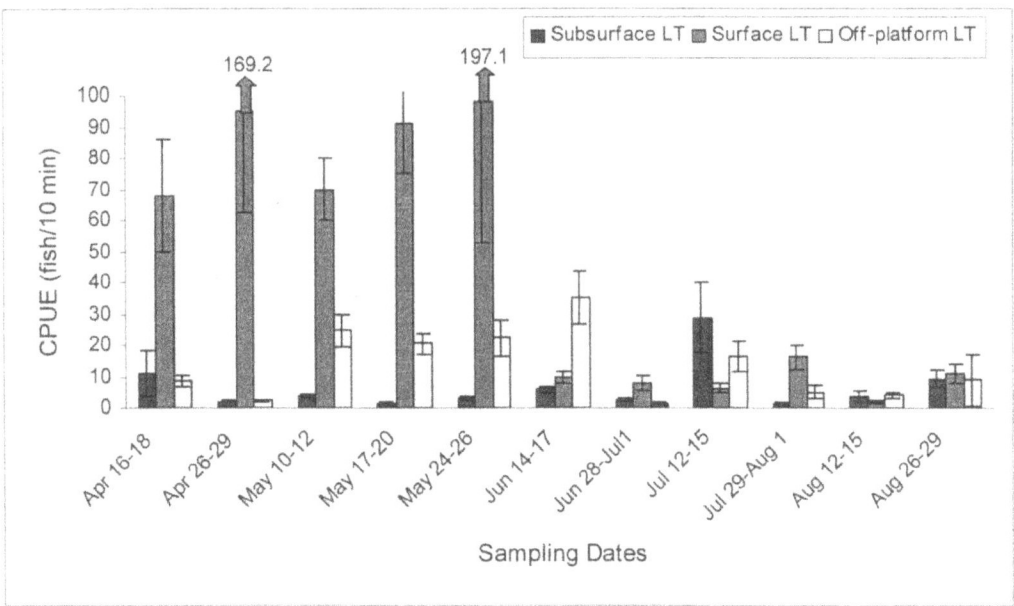

Without clupeiform fishes

Figure 9. Mean light-trap CPUEs and standard errors for data with and without clupeiform fishes included for each sampling trip at Grand Isle 94 (1996). Arrows above bars point toward the mean for that gear.

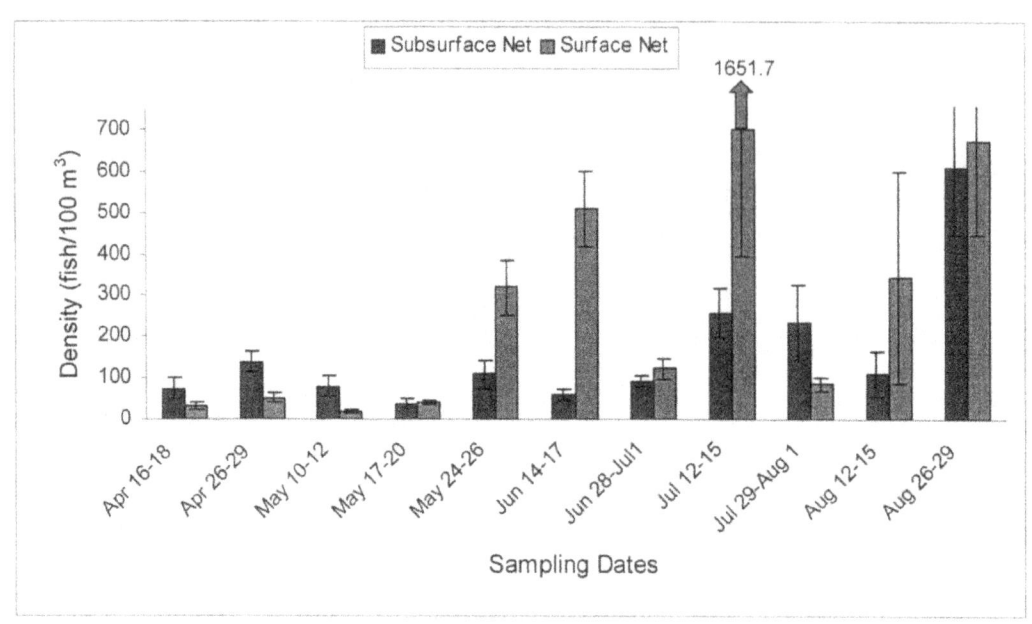

With clupeiform fishes

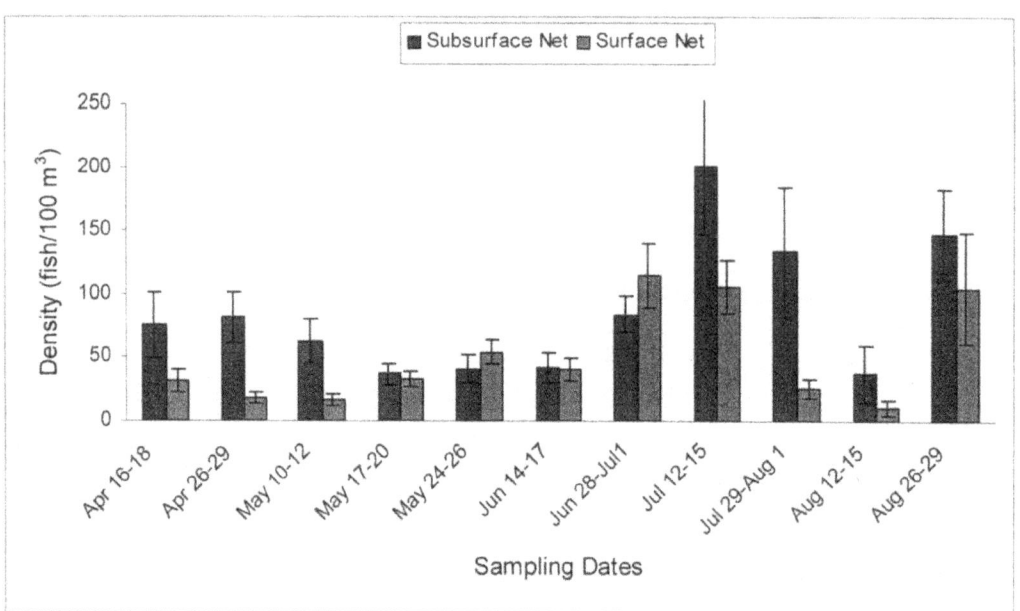

Without clupeiform fishes

Figure 10. Mean plankton net densities and standard errors for data with and without clupeiform fishes included for each trip at Grand Isle 94 (1996). Arrows above bars point toward the mean for that gear.

At ST 54, peaks in surface light-trap catches occurred during late May, June, and August (Figure 11a). Mean CPUEs ranged from 0.6-127.1 fish/10 min. The fewest fish were generally collected with the subsurface light-trap during each trip. When clupeiform fishes were removed, the mean CPUEs ranged from 0-18 fish/10 min (Figure 11b). Subsurface light-trap collections were generally still the lowest, with the exception of a peak during May 20-23. Overall mean plankton densities ranged from 42.3-23,136 fish/100 m^3 (Figure 12a). Subsurface plankton nets were only collected during the first trip and mean density was approximately equal to that of the surface net. The largest peaks in surface net densities occurred during early June and July, and mid-August. Once clupeiform fishes were removed, the mean densities ranged from 15.7-809.7 fish/100 m^3 (Figure 12b). Peaks in surface net densities occurred in early June, July, and September.

At Belle Pass, the light-trap and pushnet collected 17,949 fish and 111,854 fish, respectively. Catches by both gear types were dominated by clupeiform fishes that comprised 95.3% of the light-trap total catch and 68.3% of the total pushnet catch (Table 6). The pushnet collected fish from 41 families with 85 taxa identifiable to at least genus. Non-clupeiform taxa collected by the pushnet that comprised over 1% of the total catch included *Gobiosoma bosc*, *Cynoscion arenarius*, *Gobionellus oceanicus*, *Citharichthys* spp., *Symphurus* spp., and *Microgobius* spp. Overall, the light-trap collected fish from 21 families with 42 taxa identifiable to at least the genus level. Only one non-clupeiform species, *Membras martinica*, comprised over 1% of the total light-trap catch. The pushnet collected fish from 20 families and 44 taxa unique to this gear type. All families and all but three taxa that were sampled with the light-trap were also collected by the pushnet.

Mean light-trap CPUEs for each trip ranged from 2.4-29.9 fish/10 min (Figure 13a). Peaks in mean CPUE occurred during early June, July, and September. Once clupeiform fishes were removed, mean CPUEs decreased with a range from 0-9.7 fish/10 min (Figure 13b). Non-clupeiform CPUEs were highest from mid-May through early July. No non-clupeiform fish were collected with light-traps during July 19-21. Mean pushnet densities for each trip ranged from 132.7-978.7 fish/100 m^3 (Figure 14a). Peak mean densities occurred during May 5-7, June 20-21, and August 31-September 2. Once clupeiform fishes were removed, mean densities decreased with a range from 18.7-288.7 fish/100 m^3 (Figure 14b). Non-clupeiform density peaks were recorded during early May and August.

Reef-dependent and reef-associated fish (Choat and Bellwood, 1991) made up a relatively small percentage of the total plankton net and light-trap collections (with clupeiforms removed from the total catch) at the three platforms (Table 7). At GC 18, these groups of fish comprised 18% and 32% of the plankton net and light-trap collections, respectively. Dominant groups included gobiids, scombrids, and carangids. At GI 94, reef-dependent and reef-associated fishes comprised 10% of the plankton net catch and 17% of the light-trap catch. Blenniids were prominent in both plankton net and light-trap collections, as well as gobiids (plankton nets) and scombrids (light-traps). At ST54, these fishes comprised less than 1% of the plankton net collections and only 8% of the light-trap collections. Carangids (particularly *Chloroscombrus chrysurus*), gobiids, and scombrids dominated plankton net collections, while scombrids and blenniids dominated light-trap collections. At Belle Pass, reef-dependent and reef-associated fishes comprised approximately 15% and 2% of pushnet and light-trap collections. Samples by

47

Table 5. Total plankton net density (fish/100 m^3) and light-trap CPUE (fish/10 min) for fish collected at South Timbalier 54 with standard error (SE), rank, percent of total catch (%), and months collected for each taxa. (N) indicates taxa collected only with plankton nets. (L) indicates taxa collected only with light-traps. For ranks, tied values received the mean of the corresponding ranks. ‡ indicates a value <1.00%.

Taxa	Months Collected	Surface Net Density (SE) Rank (%)	Bottom Net Density (SE) Rank (%)	Bottom Light-trap CPUE (SE) Rank (%)	Surface Light-trap CPUE (SE) Rank (%)	Off-platform Light-trap CPUE (SE) Rank (%)
Osteichthyes Unidentified	Apr, May	3.93 (3.66) 12 ‡	0 (0)	0 (0)	0.50 (0.50) 6 (1.20)	0 (0)
Albuliformes Albulidae *Albula vulpes* (L) (bonefish)	Apr	0 (0)	0 (0)	0 (0)	0.01 (0.01) 42 ‡	0 (0)
Anguilliformes Unidentified (eel)	Jun	0 (0)	0 (0)	0 (0)	0 (0)	0.02 (0.02) 50 ‡
Muraenidae Unidentified (L) (moray eel)	Jun	0.43 (0.41) 40 ‡	0 (0)	0 (0)	0 (0)	0.02 (0.02) 50 ‡
Ophichthidae Unidentified (snake eel)	Apr, May, Jun	0.20 (0.18) 52 ‡	0 (0)	0 (0)	<0.01 (0.01) 50 ‡	0.02 (0.02) 50 ‡
Clupeiformes Unidentified (N) (herring/anchovy)	May	1.92 (1.92) 17 ‡	0 (0)	0 (0)	0 (0)	0 (0)
Clupeidae *Brevoortia patronus* (L) (gulf menhaden)	Apr	0 (0)	0 (0)	0 (0)	0 (0)	0.02 (0.02) 50 ‡
Etrumeus teres (N) (round herring)	Apr	0.04 (0.03) 68 ‡	0 (0)	0 (0)	0 (0)	0 (0)
Harengula jaguana (scaled sardine)	Apr, May, Jun, Jul	1.27 (0.50) 24 ‡	0 (0)	0 (0)	0.56 (0.17) 5 (1.29)	0.55 (0.22) 8 (1.43)
Opisthonema oglinum (Atlantic thread herring)	Apr, May, Jun, Jul	3689.84 (1964.23) 1 (96.56)	0 (0)	0.35 (0.14) 3 (7.05)	23.26 (9.41) 1 (54.60)	25.53 (7.93) 1 (66.71)
Sardinella aurita (Spanish sardine)	Apr	0.03 (0.03) 74 ‡	0 (0)	0 (0)	0 (0)	0.02 (0.02) 50 ‡
Engraulidae Unidentified (anchovy)	Apr, May, Jun, Jul	146.75 (39.54) 2 (1.49)	10.73 (7.58) 2 (46.38)	0.13 (0.06) 5 (2.90)	1.13 (0.53) 4 (2.71)	0.90 (0.20) 4 (2.36)
Anchoa spp. (anchovy spp.)	May	0.61 (0.61) 31 ‡	0 (0)	0 (0)	0 (0)	0 (0)

Table 5. (continued)

Taxa	Months Collected	Surface Net Density (SE) Rank (%)	Bottom Net Density (SE) Rank (%)	Bottom Light-trap CPUE (SE) Rank (%)	Surface Light-trap CPUE (SE) Rank (%)	Off-platform Light-trap CPUE (SE) Rank (%)
Anchoa hepsetus (L) (striped anchovy)	Jun	0 (0)	0 (0)	0 (0)	0.01 (0.01) 42 ‡	0 (0)
Anchoa mitchilli (bay anchovy)	Apr, May, Jun, Jul	4.23 (1.61) 11 ‡	0 (0)	0.04 (0.03) 13 ‡	0.38 (0.13) 9 ‡	0.31 (0.17) 11 ‡
Anchoa nasuta (L) (longnose anchovy)	May, Jun	0 (0)	0 (0)	0 (0)	0.06 (0.04) 21 ‡	0.02 (0.03) 33 ‡
Anchoa nasuta/hepsetus (longnose/striped anchovy)	Apr, May, Jun, Jul	2.27 (0.77) 16 ‡	0 (0)	0.57 (0.20) 2 (11.62)	9.89 (3.63) 2 (23.74)	3.66 (1.49) 2 (9.57)
Anchoviella perfasciata (N) (flat anchovy)	Apr	0.02 (0.02) 77.5 ‡	0 (0)	0 (0)	0 (0)	0 (0)
Engraulis eurystole (silver anchovy)	Apr, May, Jun, Jul	0.22 (0.15) 49 ‡	0 (0)	0 (0)	0.26 (0.07) 11 ‡	0.03 (0.02) 33 ‡
Stomiiformes						
Gonostomatidae						
Cyclothone braueri (N)	Apr	0.10 (0.06) 60 ‡	0 (0)	0 (0)	0 (0)	0 (0)
Aulopiformes						
Synodontidae						
Unidentified (L) (lizardfish)	Apr, May	0 (0)	0 (0)	0 (0)	0.01 (0.01) 42 ‡	0.02 (0.02) 50 ‡
Saurida brasiliensis (L) (largescale lizardfish)	May, Jun	0 (0)	0 (0)	0.04 (0.03) 9.5 (1.24)	0.06 (0.03) 21 ‡	0.08 (0.03) 26.5 ‡
Saurida suspicio (L)	May	0 (0)	0 (0)	0 (0)	0 (0)	0.02 (0.02) 50 ‡
Synodus foetens (inshore lizardfish)	Apr, May, Jun	0.21 (0.14) 50 ‡	0.26 (0.26) 11 (1.45)	2.88 (1.55) 1 (58.51)	3.16 (1.25) 3 (7.60)	0.27 (0.10) 12 ‡
Synodus poeyi (offshore lizardfish)	Apr, May	0.23 (0.19) 48 ‡	0 (0)	0 (0)	0 (0)	0.02 (0.02) 50 ‡
Myctophiformes						
Myctophidae						
Unidentified (lanternfish)	Apr, Jul	0.24 (0.13) 47 ‡	4.09 (3.52) 4 (4.35)	0 (0)	0 (0)	0.03 (0.2) 33 ‡
Gadiformes						
Bregmacerotidae						
Bregmaceros cantori (codlet)	Apr, May	1.85 (0.66) 20 ‡	0.26 (0.26) 11 (1.45)	0.06 (0.03) 9.5 (1.24)	0.01 (0.01) 42 ‡	0.10 (0.05) 24 ‡

Table 5. (continued)

Taxa	Months Collected	Surface Net Density (SE) Rank (%)	Bottom Net Density (SE) Rank (%)	Bottom Light-trap CPUE (SE) Rank (%)	Surface Light-trap CPUE (SE) Rank (%)	Off-platform Light-trap CPUE (SE) Rank (%)
Ophidiidae						
Lepophidium spp. (cusk-eel spp.)	Apr, May	0.41 (0.41) 42.5 ‡	0 (0)	0 (0)	0 (0)	0.02 (0.02) 50 ‡
Lepophidium staurophor (L)	Apr	0 (0)	0 (0)	0 (0)	0 (0)	0.02 (0.02) 50 ‡
Ophidion spp. (N) (cusk-eel spp.)	Apr	0.03 (0.03) 72 ‡	0 (0)	0 (0)	0 (0)	0 (0)
Ophidion nocomis/selenops (cusk-eel spp.)	May	3.09 (1.77) 13 ‡	0 (0)	0.02 (0.02) 18.5 ‡	0 (0)	0 (0)
Ophidion robinsi (L) (cusk-eel spp.)	May	0 (0)	0 (0)	0.02 (0.02) 18.5 ‡	0 (0)	0 (0)
Ophidion selenops (L) (mooneye cusk-eel)	May	0 (0)	0 (0)	0.02 (0.02) 18.5 ‡	0.01 (0.01) 42 ‡	0 (0)
Bythitidae						
Unidentified (N) (brotula)	May	0.41 (0.41) 42.5 ‡	0 (0)	0 (0)	0 (0)	0 (0)
Gobiesociformes						
Gobiesocidae						
Gobiesox strumosus (skilletfish)	Apr, May	0.03 (0.03) 69.5 ‡	0 (0)	0 (0)	0.06 (0.04) 21 ‡	0.03 (0.02) 36 ‡
Atheriniformes						
Exocoetidae						
Unidentified (N) (flyingfish)	Apr	0.03 (0.03) 71 ‡	0 (0)	0 (0)	0 (0)	0 (0)
Cypselurus spp. (N) (flyingfish spp.)	Apr	0.03 (0.03) 69.5 ‡	0 (0)	0 (0)	0 (0)	0 (0)
Cypselurus cyanopterus (L) (margined flyingfish)	Jun	0 (0)	0 (0)	0 (0)	0 (0)	0.02 (0.02) 50 ‡
Cypselurus furcatus (L) (spotfin flyingfish)	May	0 (0)	0 (0)	0 (0)	0 (0)	0.02 (0.02) 50 ‡
Atherinidae						
Unidentified (N) (silverside)	Apr	0.29 (0.20) 45 ‡	0 (0)	0 (0)	0 (0)	0 (0)
Membras martinica (L) (rough silverside)	Jun	0 (0)	0 (0)	0 (0)	0.02 (0.02) 32 ‡	0 (0)
Gasterosteiformes						

Table 5. (continued)

Taxa	Months Collected	Surface Net Density (SE) Rank (%)	Bottom Net Density (SE) Rank (%)	Bottom Light-trap CPUE (SE) Rank (%)	Surface Light-trap CPUE (SE) Rank (%)	Off-platform Light-trap CPUE (SE) Rank (%)
Syngnathidae						
Syngnathus spp. (N) (pipefish spp.)	Apr	0.03 (0.03) 74 ‡	0 (0)	0 (0)	0 (0)	0 (0)
Syngnathus louisiana (N) (chain pipefish)	Apr	0.02 (0.02) 80.5 ‡	0 (0)	0 (0)	0 (0)	0 (0)
Scorpaeniformes						
Scorpaenidae						
Scorpaena spp. (scorpionfish spp.)	Apr, Jun	0 (0)	0.26 (0.26) 11 (1.45)	0 (0)	0.02 (0.02) 32 ‡	0.02 (0.02) 50 ‡
Triglidae						
Prionotus spp. (searobin spp.)	Apr	0.58 (0.26) 36 ‡	0 (0)	0 (0)	0.01 (0.01) 42 ‡	0.02 (0.02) 50 ‡
Perciformes						
Unidentified	Apr, May, Jun, Jul	10.47 (3.57) 6 ‡	14.29 (14.29) 1 (10.14)	0 (0)	0.02 (0.02) 32 ‡	0.16 (0.07) 17.5 ‡
Serranidae						
Unidentified (N) (seabass/grouper)	Apr	0.06 (0.06) 65 ‡	0 (0)	0 (0)	0 (0)	0 (0)
Epinephelinae (N) (grouper)	Apr	0.03 (0.03) 74 ‡	0 (0)	0 (0)	0 (0)	0 (0)
Serraninae (seabass)	Apr, May	0.34 (0.24) 44 ‡	0 (0)	0 (0)	0.01 (0.01) 42 ‡	0 (0)
Priacanthidae						
Priacanthus spp. (L) (bigeye spp.)	May	0 (0)	0 (0)	0 (0)	0 (0)	0.02 (0.02) 50 ‡
Carangidae						
Unidentified (N) (jack)	Apr, Jun	0.43 (0.28) 41 ‡	0 (0)	0 (0)	0 (0)	0 (0)
Caranx crysos (L) (blue runner)	May, Jun, Jul	0 (0)	0 (0)	0.02 (0.02) 23.5 ‡	0.05 (0.03) 19 ‡	0.24 (0.08) 14 ‡
Caranx hippos/latus (crevalle/horse-eye jack)	May, Jun, Jul	2.70 (2.44) 14 ‡	0 (0)	0 (0)	0.04 (0.02) 26.5 ‡	0.61 (0.25) 6 (1.60)
Chloroscombrus chrysurus (Atlantic bumper)	May, Jun, Jul	30.00 (11.03) 4 ‡	0 (0)	0.02 (0.02) 18.5 ‡	0.09 (0.04) 17 ‡	0.11 (0.06) 22 ‡
Decapterus punctatus (round scad)	Apr, May, Jun	0.02 (0.02) 77.5 ‡	0 (0)	0 (0)	0.02 (0.02) 32 ‡	0.02 (0.02) 50 ‡

51

Table 5. (continued)

Taxa	Months Collected	Surface Net Density (SE) Rank (%)	Bottom Net Density (SE) Rank (%)	Bottom Light-trap CPUE (SE) Rank (%)	Surface Light-trap CPUE (SE) Rank (%)	Off-platform Light-trap CPUE (SE) Rank (%)
Oligoplites saurus (N) (leatherjack)	Jun	0.48 (0.37) 37 ‡	0 (0)	0 (0)	0 (0)	0 (0)
Selar crumenopthalmus (L) (bigeye scad)	May	0 (0)	0 (0)	0 (0)	0 (0)	0.02 (0.02) 50 ‡
Selene spp. (N) (moonfish/lookdown spp.)	May	0.61 (0.61) 31 ‡	0 (0)	0 (0)	0 (0)	0 (0)
Seriola spp. (L) (jack spp.)	Apr	0 (0)	0 (0)	0 (0)	0.01 (0.01) 49 ‡	0 (0)
Trachinotus carolinus (L) (Florida pompano)	May	0 (0)	0 (0)	0 (0)	0 (0)	0.03 (0.03) 33 ‡
Trachurus lathami (rough scad)	Apr, May	0.02 (0.02) 80.5 ‡	0 (0)	0 (0)	0.06 (0.05) 18 ‡	0.02 (0.02) 50 ‡
Lutjanidae Unidentified (N) (snapper)	Jul	0.17 (0.17) 54.5 ‡	0 (0)	0 (0)	0 (0)	0 (0)
Lutjanus spp. (N) (snapper spp.)	May, Jul	0.61 (0.45) 31 ‡	0 (0)	0 (0)	0 (0)	0 (0)
Lutjanus campechanus (red snapper)	May, Jun	0.61 (0.61) 31 ‡	0 (0)	0 (0)	0 (0)	0.02 (0.02) 50 ‡
Rhomboplites aurorubens (L) (vermilion snapper)	May, Jun	0 (0)	0 (0)	0.12 (0.07) 6 (2.49)	0 (0)	0 (0)
Gerreidae Unidentified (L) (jenny/mojarra)	May	0 (0)	0 (0)	0 (0)	0 (0)	0.02 (0.02) 50 ‡
Haemulidae Unidentified (N) (grunt)	May	0.61 (0.61) 31 ‡	0 (0)	0 (0)	0 (0)	0 (0)
Sparidae Unidentified (N) (porgy)	Apr	0.14 (0.14) 58 ‡	0 (0)	0 (0)	0 (0)	0 (0)
Calamus spp. (N) (porgy spp.)	Apr	0.10 (0.10) 61 ‡	0 (0)	0 (0)	0 (0)	0 (0)
Sciaenidae Unidentified (drum)	Apr, May, Jun	0.15 (0.15) 57 ‡	0 (0)	0 (0)	0.02 (0.02) 32 ‡	0.02 (0.02) 50 ‡
Bairdiella chrysoura (silver perch)	Jun	0.12 (0.12) 59 ‡	0 (0)	0 (0)	0 (0)	0.02 (0.02) 50 ‡

Table 5. (continued)

Taxa	Months Collected	Surface Net Density (SE) Rank (%)	Bottom Net Density (SE) Rank (%)	Bottom Light-trap CPUE (SE) Rank (%)	Surface Light-trap CPUE (SE) Rank (%)	Off-platform Light-trap CPUE (SE) Rank (%)
Cynoscion arenarius (sand seatrout)	Apr, May, Jun, Jul	42.16 (8.56) 3‡	7.99 (3.21) 3 (21.74)	0.10 (0.04) 7 (2.07)	0.42 (0.11) 8 (1.03)	0.56 (0.13) 7 (1.47)
Larimus fasciatus (N) (banded drum)	Apr	0.05 (0.04) 66‡	0 (0)	0 (0)	0 (0)	0 (0)
Menticirrhus spp. (kingfish spp.)	Apr, May, Jun, Jul	1.45 (0.36) 22‡	0 (0)	0 (0)	0 (0)	0.03 (0.02) 33‡
Stellifer lanceolatus (N) (star drum)	Apr	0.44 (0.25) 39‡	0 (0)	0 (0)	0 (0)	0 (0)
Mullidae *Upeneus parvus* (L) (dwarf goatfish)	Apr	0 (0)	0 (0)	0 (0)	0 (0)	0.02 (0.02) 50‡
Ephippidae *Chaetodipterus faber* (N) (Atlantic spadefish)	May, Jul	0.86 (0.39) 25‡	0 (0)	0 (0)	0 (0)	0 (0)
Pomacentridae *Abudefduf saxatilis* (L) (sergeant major)	May	0 (0)	0 (0)	0 (0)	0 (0)	0.10 (0.07) 24‡
Pomacentrus spp. (L) (damselfish spp.)	May	0 (0)	0 (0)	0 (0)	0 (0)	0.02 (0.02) 50‡
Mugilidae *Mugil cephalus* (L) (striped mullet)	Apr	0 (0)	0 (0)	0 (0)	0 (0)	0.02 (0.02) 50‡
Mugil curema (L) (white mullet)	May	0 (0)	0 (0)	0 (0)	0.01 (0.01) 42‡	0.05 (0.04) 29.5‡
Sphyraenidae *Sphyraena borealis* (L) (northern sennet)	May	0 (0)	0 (0)	0 (0)	0.01 (0.01) 42‡	0 (0)
Labridae Unidentified (L) (wrasse)	Jun	0 (0)	0 (0)	0.02 (0.02) 18.5‡	0 (0)	0 (0)
Scaridae Unidentified (N) (parrotfish)	Apr	0.02 (0.02) 77.5‡	0 (0)	0 (0)	0 (0)	0 (0)
Blenniidae Unidentified (blenny)	Apr, May, Jun, Jul	2.47 (0.90) 15‡	1.10 (1.10) 6 (1.45)	0.02 (0.02) 18.5‡	0.09 (0.03) 16‡	0.08 (0.05) 26.5‡

Table 5. (continued)

Taxa	Months Collected	Surface Net Density (SE) Rank (%)	Bottom Net Density (SE) Rank (%)	Bottom Light-trap CPUE (SE) Rank (%)	Surface Light-trap CPUE (SE) Rank (%)	Off-platform Light-trap CPUE (SE) Rank (%)
Hypsoblennius hentz/ionthas (feather/freckled blenny)	Apr, May, Jun	0.17 (0.17) 54.5 ‡	0 (0)	0 (0)	0.21 (0.08) 12 ‡	0.48 (0.22) 9.5 (1.26)
Hypsoblennius invemar (tessellated blenny)	Apr, May, Jun	0.61 (0.61) 31 ‡	0 (0)	0 (0)	0.11 (0.05) 15 ‡	0.48 (0.19) 9.5 (1.26)
Parablennius marmoreus (seaweed blenny)	May, Jul	0.20 (0.20) 53 ‡	0 (0)	0 (0)	0 (0)	0.02 (0.02) 50 ‡
Scartella/Hypleurochilus (blenny spp.)	Apr, May, Jun, Jul	1.89 (1.29) 19 ‡	0 (0)	0.06 (0.03) 9.5 (1.24)	0.49 (0.26) 7 (1.17)	0.16 (0.08) 17.5 ‡
Eleotridae						
Dormitator maculatus (N) (fat sleeper)	Apr	0.02 (0.02) 77.5 ‡	0 (0)	0 (0)	0 (0)	0 (0)
Gobiidae						
Unidentified (goby)	Apr, May, Jun, Jul	29.96 (12.71) 5 ‡	1.41 (0.96) 5 (4.35)	0.06 (0.03) 9.5 (1.24)	0.03 (0.02) 28 ‡	0.23 (0.08) 15 ‡
Microdesmidae						
Microdesmus spp. (wormfish spp.)	Apr, Jul	0.58 (0.43) 35 ‡	0 (0)	0 (0)	0.01 (0.01) 42 ‡	0 (0)
Microdesmus lanceolatus (N) (lancetail wormfish)	Jun, Jul	1.28 (0.86) 23 ‡	0 (0)	0 (0)	0 (0)	0 (0)
Trichiuridae						
Trichiurus lepturus (Atlantic cutlassfish)	Apr, May, Jun	0 (0)	0.52 (0.52) 8.5 (2.90)	0.18 (0.07) 4 (3.73)	0.01 (0.01) 42 ‡	0 (0)
Scombridae						
Unidentified (N) (mackerel)	Apr, Jul	0.25 (0.18) 46 ‡	0 (0)	0 (0)	0 (0)	0 (0)
Auxis spp. (mackerel spp.)	May, Jun, Jul	0 (0)	0 (0)	0 (0)	0.02 (0.02) 32 ‡	0.26 (0.17) 13 ‡
Euthynnus alletteratus (little tunny)	May, Jun, Jul	0.47 (0.27) 38 ‡	0 (0)	0.02 (0.02) 23.5 ‡	0.37 (0.23) 10 ‡	1.08 (0.47) 3 (2.82)
Scomberomorus cavalla (king mackerel)	Apr, May, Jun, Jul	5.39 (3.15) 10 ‡	0 (0)	0.04 (0.03) 13 ‡	0.05 (0.04) 24 ‡	0.10 (0.05) 24 ‡
Scomberomorus maculatus (Spanish mackerel)	Apr, May, Jun, Jul	6.56 (2.09) 9 ‡	0 (0)	0 (0)	0.18 (0.06) 13 ‡	0.81 (0.18) 5 (2.11)
Stromateidae						
Ariomma spp. (N) (driftfish spp.)	Apr	0.05 (0.04) 67 ‡	0.52 (0.52) 8.5 (2.90)	0 (0)	0 (0)	0 (0)

Table 5. (continued)

Taxa	Months Collected	Surface Net Density (SE) Rank (%)	Bottom Net Density (SE) Rank (%)	Bottom Light-trap CPUE (SE) Rank (%)	Surface Light-trap CPUE (SE) Rank (%)	Off-platform Light-trap CPUE (SE) Rank (%)
Peprilus burti (gulf butterfish)	Apr, May	1.65 (1.23) 21‡	0 (0)	0.02 (0.02) 18.5‡	0.14 (0.05) 14‡	0.13 (0.05) 20.5‡
Peprilus alepidotus (harvestfish)	Apr, May, Jul	1.92 (0.77) 18‡	0 (0)	0.04 (0.03) 13‡	0.04 (0.02) 26.5‡	0.15 (0.06) 19‡
Pleuronectiformes						
Bothidae						
Unidentified (N) (lefteye flounder)	May	0.81 (0.81) 26‡	0 (0)	0 (0)	0 (0)	0 (0)
Citharichthys spilopterus (bay whiff)	Apr, May, Jun	0.21 (0.13) 51‡	0 (0)	0 (0)	0 (0)	0.05 (0.04) 29.5‡
Cyclopsetta fimbriata (L) (spotfin flounder)	May	0 (0)	0 (0)	0 (0)	0 (0)	0.02 (0.02) 50‡
Etropus crossotus (fringed flounder)	Apr, May, Jun	7.59 (2.94) 8‡	0.89 (0.89) 7 (1.45)	0 (0)	0.05 (0.02) 24‡	0.13 (0.06) 20.5‡
Syacium spp. (L) (flounder spp.)	May	0.61 (0.61) 31‡	0 (0)	0 (0)	0 (0)	0 (0)
Soleidae						
Unidentified (sole)	Jun, Jul	0.06 (0.06) 63.5‡	0 (0)	0.02 (0.02) 18.5‡	0 (0)	0 (0)
Achirus lineatus (lined sole)	Apr, May, Jul	0.16 (0.10) 56‡	0 (0)	0 (0)	0.02 (0.02) 32‡	0 (0)
Gymnachirus spp. (N) (sole spp.)	May	0.09 (0.09) 62‡	0 (0)	0 (0)	0 (0)	0 (0)
Trinectes maculatus (N) (hogchoker)	Apr, May	0.70 (0.42) 27‡	0 (0)	0 (0)	0 (0)	0 (0)
Symphurus spp. (tonguefish spp.)	Apr, May, Jun, Jul	8.84 (3.84) 7‡	0 (0)	0 (0)	0.01 (0.01) 42‡	0.06 (0.04) 28‡
Tetraodontiformes						
Tetraodontidae						
Sphoeroides spp. (puffer spp.)	Apr, May, Jun	0.06 (0.06) 63.5‡	0 (0)	0 (0)	0.05 (0.03) 24‡	0.21 (0.12) 16‡
Sphoeroides parvus (L) (least puffer)	Apr	0 (0)	0 (0)	0 (0)	0.01 (0.01) 42‡	0 (0)

55

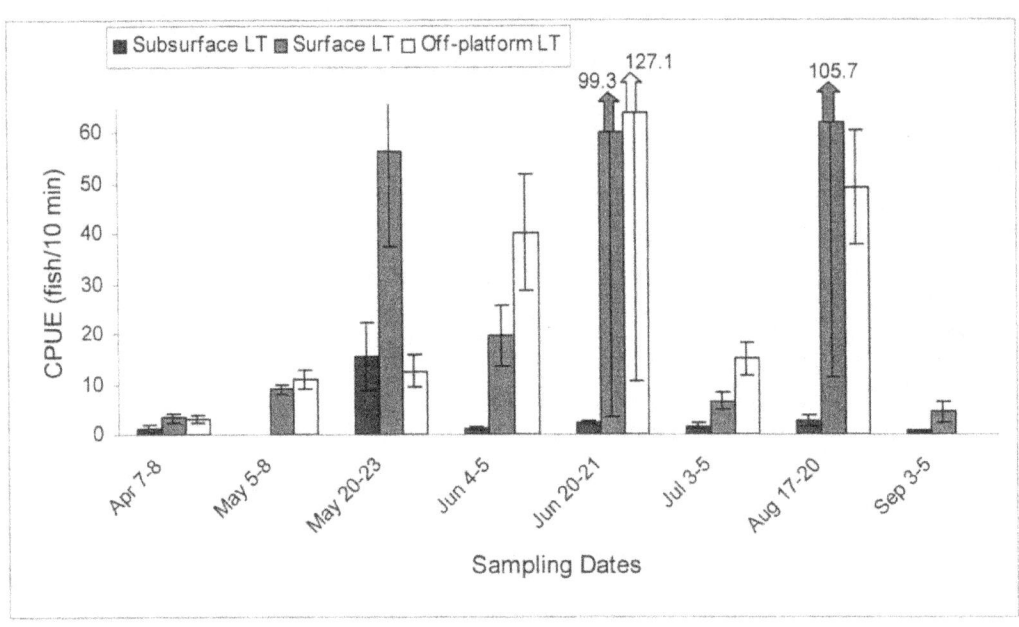

With clupeiform fishes

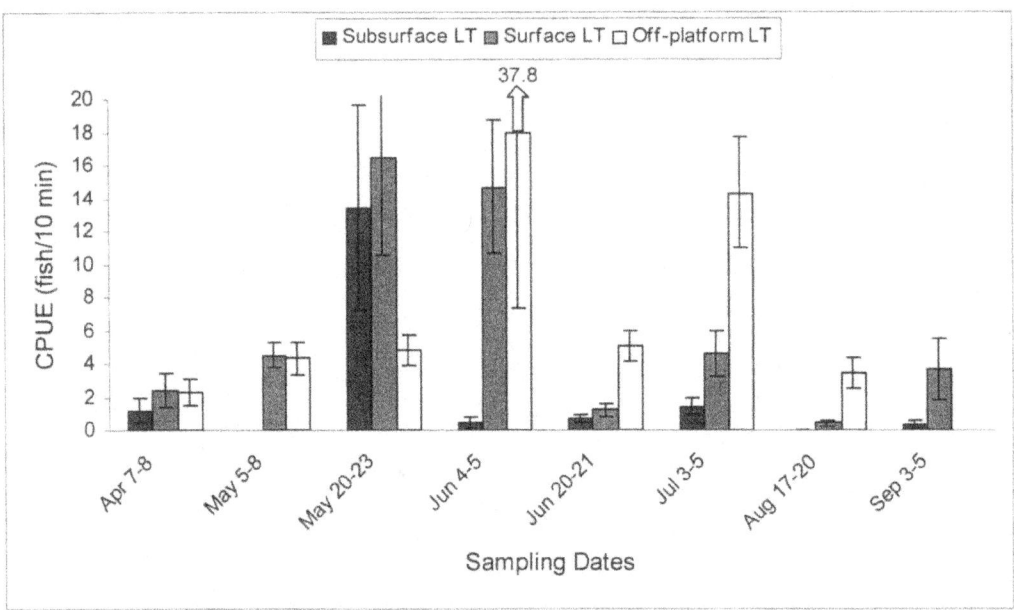

Without clupeiform fishes

Figure 11. Mean light-trap CPUEs and standard errors for data with and without clupeiform fishes included for each sampling trip at South Timbalier 54 (1997). Arrows above bars point toward the mean for that gear. No subsurface light-trap samples were taken during May 5-8. No off-platform light-trap samples were taken during September 3-5. No non-clupeiform fish were present in subsurface light-trap samples (n=4) during August 17-20.

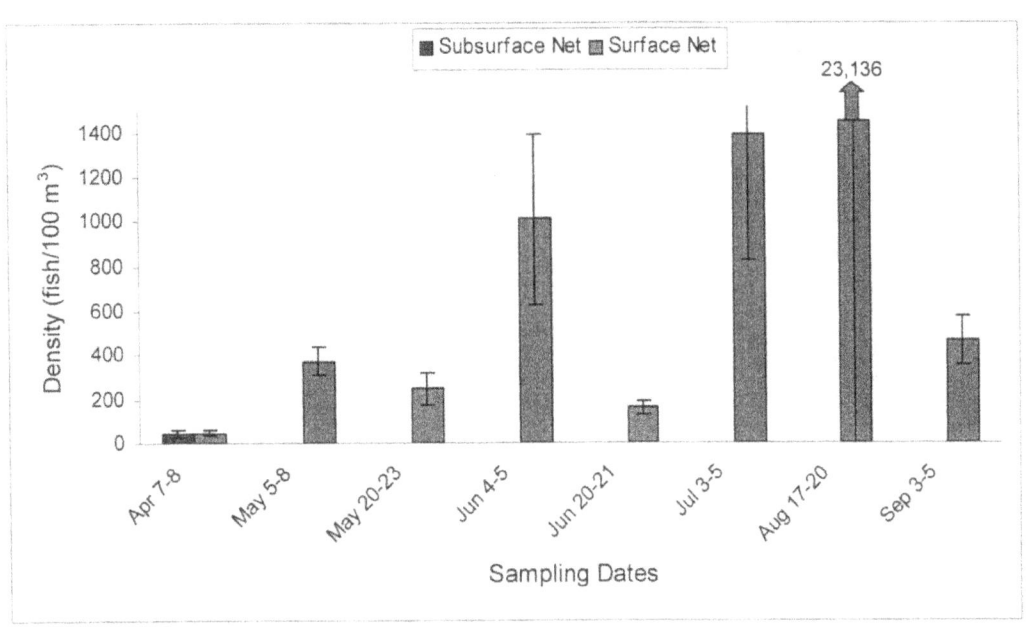

With clupeiform fishes

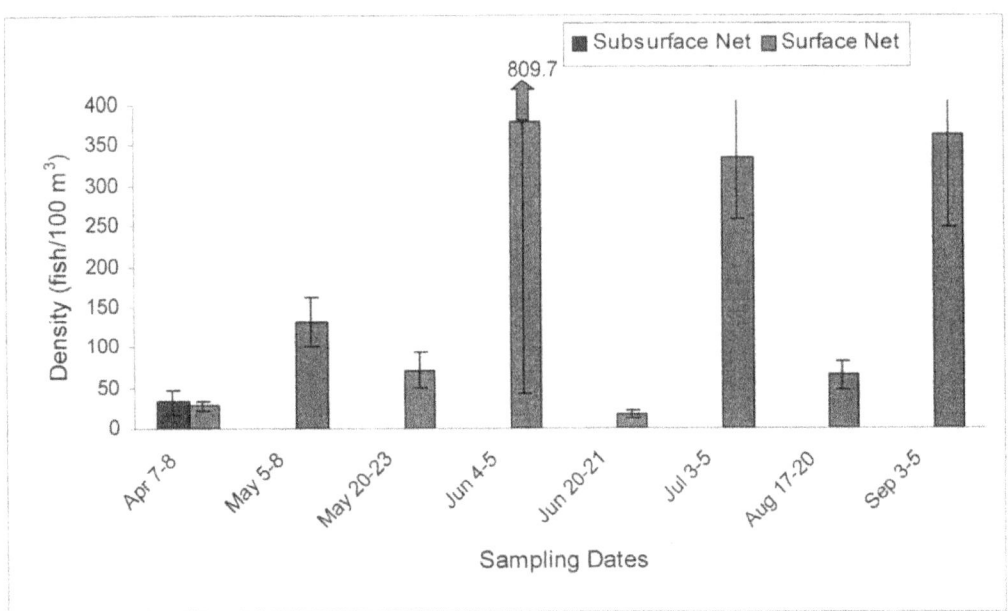

Without clupeiform fishes

Figure 12. Mean plankton net densities and standard errors for data with and without clupeiform fishes included for each sampling trip at South Timbalier 54 (1997). Subsurface net samples were only taken during April 7-8.

Table 6. Total mean light-trap CPUE (fish/10 min) and pushnet density (fish/100 m³) for fish collected at Belle Pass with standard error (SE), rank, percent of total catch (%), and months collected for each taxa. For ranks, tied values received the mean of the corresponding ranks. ‡ indicates a value <1.00%.

Taxa	Months Collected	Light-trap CPUE (SE) Rank (%)	Pushnet Density (SE) Rank (%)
Osteichthyes			
Unidentified	Apr, May, Jun, Jul, Aug	0.14 (0.06) 17 ‡	1.23 (0.65) 20 ‡
Elopiformes			
Elopidae			
Elops saurus (ladyfish)	Apr, May, Jun, Jul, Aug	<0.01 (<0.01) 48 ‡	0.22 (0.06) 36 ‡
Megalops atlanticus (tarpon)	Aug	0 (0)	0.03 (0.01) 60 ‡
Anguilliformes			
Unidentified (eel)	Apr, May, Jun, Jul, Aug	<0.01(<0.01) 48‡	0.17(0.08) 41‡
Ophichthidae			
Unidentified (snake eel)	Apr, May, Jun	0.03(0.02) 31‡	0.03(0.03) 57‡
Bascanichthys spp. (sooty/whip eel spp.)	Jun, Jul, Aug	0 (0)	0.13(0.03) 44‡
Myrophis punctatus (speckled worm eel)	Apr, May, Jun, Jul	0.04(0.02) 28‡	0.64(0.31) 27‡
Ophichthus gomesi (shrimp eel)	Jul	0 (0)	0.15(0.07) 42‡
Ophichthus melanoporus (blackpored eel)	Aug	0 (0)	<0.01(<0.01) 82‡
Congridae			
Paraconger caudilimbatus (margintail conger)	Jun	0 (0)	<0.01(<0.01) 82‡
Clupeiformes			
Unidentified (herring/anchovy)	May, Jun, Jul, Aug	0.01(<0.01) 41‡	10.85(3.88) 5(2.05)
Clupeidae			
Unidentified (herring)	Apr, May, Aug	0.07(0.04) 22‡	2.48(1.42) 13‡
Brevoortia spp. (menhaden spp.)	Apr, Aug	0.15(0.08) 16‡	2.77(2.09) 11‡
Brevoortia patronus (gulf menhaden)	Apr, May, Jun, Jul, Aug	0.04(0.03) 27‡	0.60(0.37) 29‡
Harengula jaguana (scaled sardine)	May, Jun, July, Aug	1.12(0.36) 4‡	0.53(0.10) 30‡
Opisthonema oglinum (Atlantic thread herring)	May, Jun, July, Aug	0.28(0.12) 11‡	0.40(0.10) 32‡
Engraulidae			
Unidentified (anchovy)	Apr, May, Jun, Jul, Aug	16.33(7.07) 2(13.47)	138.43(21.12) 2(27.74)
Anchoa hepsetus (striped anchovy)	Apr, May, Jun, Jul, Aug	0.73(0.24) 6‡	1.30(0.50) 18‡
Anchoa mitchilli (bay anchovy)	Apr, May, Jun, Jul, Aug	95.80(37.97) 1(79.01)	153.25(33.48) 1(38.23)
Anchoa nasuta (longnose anchovy)	May, Jun, Jul, Aug	0.24(0.08) 13‡	0.18(0.06) 38‡
Anchoa nasuta/hepsetus (longnose/striped anchovy)	Apr, May, Jun, Jul, Aug	0.64(0.22) 7‡	1.90(0.45) 15‡
Siluriformes			
Ariidae			
Arius felis (hardhead catfish)	May, Jul	0 (0)	0.09(0.06) 48‡
Bagre marinus (gafftopsail catfish)	Jul, Aug	0 (0)	0.10(0.08) 46‡
Aulopiformes			
Synodontidae			
Unidentified (lizardfish)	May	0 (0)	<0.01(<0.01) 88‡

Table 6. (continued)

Taxa	Months Collected	Light-trap CPUE (SE) Rank (%)	Pushnet Density (SE) Rank (%)
Synodus spp. (lizardfish spp.)	Apr, May	0 (0)	0.02(0.02) 61‡
Synodus foetens (inshore lizardfish)	Apr, May, Jun, Jul, Aug	0.15(0.04) 15‡	0.93(0.14) 23‡
Paralepidae			
Paralepis atlantica (duckbill barracudina)	Apr	0 (0)	<0.01(<0.01) 90‡
Gadiformes			
Ophidiidae			
Unidentified (cuskeel)	Apr	0 (0)	<0.01(<0.01) 89‡
Lepophidium spp. (cusk-eel spp.)	Jun	0 (0)	<0.01(<0.01) 108‡
Gobiesociformes			
Gobiesocidae			
Gobiesox strumosus (skilletfish)	Apr, May, Jun, Jul, Aug	0.47(0.13) 10‡	1.55(0.25) 16‡
Atheriniformes			
Exocoetidae			
Unidentified (flyingfish)	May, Jun	0 (0)	0.01(<0.01) 80‡
Cypselurus spp. (flying fish spp.)	Jun	<0.01(<0.01) 48‡	0 (0)
Hyporhamphus unifasciatus (silverstriped halfbeak)	May, Jun, Jul, Aug	<0.01(<0.01) 48‡	0.04(0.01) 55‡
Atherinidae			
Unidentified (silverside)	Apr, May, Jun, Jul, Aug	0 (0)	0.18(0.08) 40‡
Membras martinica (rough silverside)	Apr, May, Jun, Jul, Aug	1.30(0.56) 3(1.09)	0.98(0.22) 21‡
Menidia beryllina (inland silverside)	May	0 (0)	0.02(0.02) 66‡
Gasterosteiformes			
Syngnathidae			
Hippocampus erectus (lined seahorse)	Jun	0 (0)	<0.01(<0.01) 99‡
Syngnathus spp. (pipefish spp.)	Apr, May, Jun, Jul, Aug	<0.01(<0.01) 48‡	0.09(0.03) 49‡
Syngnathus louisiana (chain pipefish)	Jul	0 (0)	<0.01(<0.01) 111‡
Scorpaeniformes			
Triglidae			
Prionotus spp. (searobin spp.)	Jun	0 (0)	<0.01(<0.01) 110‡
Prionotus roseus (bluespotted searobin)	Jul	0 (0)	<0.01(<0.01) 101‡
Prionotus tribulus (bighead searobin)	Jul	0 (0)	<0.01(<0.01) 94‡
Perciformes			
Serranidae			
Epinephelinae (grouper spp.)	Apr	0 (0)	<0.01(<0.01) 97‡
Rachycentridae			
Rachycentron canadum (cobia)	May	0 (0)	<0.01(<0.01) 86‡
Carangidae			
Unidentified (jack)		0 (0)	0.02(0.02) 62‡
Caranx spp. (jack spp.)	Aug	0 (0)	0.64(0.26) 28‡
Caranx hippos/latus (crevalle/horse-eye jack)	Jun, Jul, Aug	<0.01(<0.01) 48‡	0.09(0.04) 47‡

Table 6. (continued)

Taxa	Months Collected	Light-trap CPUE (SE) Rank (%)	Pushnet Density (SE) Rank (%)
Chloroscombrus chrysurus (Atlantic bumper)	Jun, Jul, Aug	0.05(0.02) 23‡	0.28(0.15) 35‡
Oligoplites saurus (leatherjack)	Aug	<0.01(<0.01) 48‡	0.02(<0.01) 71‡
Selene vomer (lookdown)	Jul	0 (0)	<0.01(<0.01) 98‡
Selene setapinnis (Atlantic moonfish)	Jul	0 (0)	<0.01(<0.01) 104‡
Lutjanidae			
Lutjanus griseus (gray snapper)	Jun, Jul, Aug	0 (0)	0.03(0.01) 59‡
Lutjanus synagris (lane snapper)	Jul, Aug	0.01(<0.01) 38‡	0.07(0.02) 51‡
Lutjanus spp. (snapper spp.)	Aug	<0.01(<0.01) 48‡	0 (0)
Gerreidae			
Unidentified (jenny/mojarra)	May, Jun, Aug	0.02(0.01) 34‡	0.19(0.07) 37‡
Eucinostomus spp. (mojarra/jenny spp.)	Jun, Aug	<0.01(<0.01) 48‡	0.02(0.01) 70‡
Haemulidae			
Unidentified (grunt)	Jul	0 (0)	<0.01(<0.01) 102‡
Sparidae	Apr, May		
Unidentified (porgy)		0 (0)	0.02(0.01) 63‡
Sparidae Type B (porgy spp.)	May	0 (0)	0.02(<0.01) 68‡
Sciaenidae			
Unidentified (drum)	May, Jun, Jul, Aug	0.02(0.01) 34‡	2.54(0.96) 12‡
Bairdiella chrysoura (silver perch)	Apr, May, Jun, Jul, Aug	0.12(0.08) 19‡	3.07(0.73) 10‡
Cynoscion arenarius (sand seatrout)	Apr, May, Jun, Jul, Aug	0.59(0.28) 9‡	40.74(8.02) 4(7.85)
Cynoscion nebulosus (spotted seatrout)	Apr, May, Jun, Aug	0.01(<0.01) 38‡	0.85(0.21) 24‡
Cynoscion nebulosus/arenarius (spotted/sand seatrout)	Jul	0 (0)	0.01(0.01) 74‡
Menticirrhus spp. (kingfish spp.)	Apr, May, Jul, Aug	0.03(0.01) 29‡	0.51(0.09) 31‡
Menticirrhus americanus/littoralis (gulf/northern kingfish)	Jun, Aug	0 (0)	0.02(0.01) 64‡
Micropogonias undulatus (Atlantic croaker)	Apr, Jul	0 (0)	0.04(0.02) 56‡
Pogonias cromis (black drum)	May	0.01(<0.01) 38‡	0.74(0.21) 26‡
Sciaenops ocellatus (red drum)	Aug	<0.01(<0.01) 48‡	1.29(0.59) 19‡
Stellifer lanceolatus (star drum)	Apr, Jun, Jul	0 (0)	0.05(0.02) 54‡
Mullidae			
Unidentified (goatfish)	May	0 (0)	<0.01(<0.01) 87‡
Ephippidae			
Chaetodipterus faber (Atlantic spadefish)	Jun, Aug	0 (0)	0.05(0.02) 52‡
Mugilidae			
Mugil cephalus (striped mullet)	Apr	0 (0)	<0.01(<0.01) 97‡
Mugil curema (white mullet)	Apr, May, Jun	0 (0)	0.02(<0.01) 69‡

60

Table 6. (continued)

Taxa	Months Collected	Light-trap CPUE (SE) Rank (%)	Pushnet Density (SE) Rank (%)
Polynemidae			
Polydactylus octonemus	Aug	0 (0)	<0.01(<0.01)
(Atlantic threadfin)			93‡
Labridae			
Unidentified	Apr	0 (0)	0.01(<0.01)
(wrasse)			77‡
Scaridae			
Sparisoma spp.	Apr	0 (0)	0.01(<0.01)
(parrotfish spp.)			72‡
Uranoscopidae			
Unidentified	Jun	0 (0)	<0.01(<0.01)
(stargazer)			92‡
Blenniidae			
Unidentified	May, Jun, Jul, Aug	0.02(0.01)	0.03(0.02)
(blenny)		35‡	58‡
Chasmodes spp.	Apr	0 (0)	<0.01(<0.01)
(striped/Florida blenny)			100‡
Hypleurochilus bermudensis	Aug	0 (0)	<0.01(<0.01)
(barred blenny)			95‡
Hypsoblennius spp.	Jul	0 (0)	<0.01(<0.01)
(blenny spp.)			104(<.1.00)
Hypsoblennius hentz/ionthas	Apr, May, Jun, Jul, Aug	1.04(0.27)	1.95((0.45)
(feather/tessellated blenny)		5‡	14‡
Scartella cristata	Apr, May, Jun, Jul, Aug	0.03(0.02)	0.34(0.08)
(molly miller)		31‡	33‡
Eleotridae			
Unidentified	Jun, Jul, Aug	0.01(<0.01)	0.02(0.01)
(sleeper)		38‡	67‡
Eleotridae Type A	Jun, Aug	<0.01(<0.01)	0.18(0.06)
(sleeper spp.)		48‡	39‡
Dormitator maculatus	Apr, May, Jun, Jul, Aug	0.12(0.06)	0.96(0.34)
(fat sleeper)		18‡	22‡
Gobiidae			
Unidentified	Apr, May, Jun, Jul, Aug	0.03(0.01)	0.81(0.23)
(goby)		31‡	25‡
Bathygobius soporator	Jun, Jul	0 (0)	0.01(<0.01)
(frillfin goby)			76‡
Evorthodus lyricus/Gobionellus boleosoma	Jun, Jul, Aug	0 (0)	0.01(<0.01)
(lyre goby/darter goby)			78‡
Gobionellus oceanicus	Apr, May, Jun, Jul, Aug	0.11(0.06)	8.82(2.13)
(highfin goby)		20‡	6(1.97)
Gobiosoma spp.	Apr, May, Jun, Jul, Aug	0.26(0.18)	1.48(0.43)
(goby spp.)		12‡	17‡
Gobiosoma bosc	Apr, May, Jun, Jul, Aug	0.59(0.16)	46.88(7.88)
(naked goby)		8‡	3(10.64)
Microgobius spp.	May, Jun, Jul, Aug	0.04(0.03)	4.17(1.30)
(goby spp.)		26‡	9(1.05)
Microdesmidae			
Microdesmus longipinnis	Jun, Jul, Aug	0.05(0.02)	0.14(0.04)
(pink wormfish)		24‡	43‡
Trichiuridae			
Unidentified	May	0 (0)	<0.01(<0.01)
(snake mackerel)			91‡
Trichiurus lepturus	Apr, Jul	0 (0)	0.01(<0.01)
(Atlantic cutlassfish)			79‡
Scombridae			
Unidentified	May, Jun	0 (0)	0.01(<0.01)
(mackerel)			73‡
Scomberomorus spp.	Aug	<0.01(<0.01)	0 (0)
(mackeral spp.)		48‡	
Scomberomorus maculatus	May, Aug	0 (0)	<0.01(<0.01)
(Spanish mackeral)			83‡

Table 6. (continued)

Taxa	Months Collected	Light-trap CPUE (SE) Rank (%)	Pushnet Density (SE) Rank (%)
Stromateidae			
Peprilus alepidotus (harvestfish)	Jun, Jul, Aug	0 (0)	0.01(<0.01) 75‡
Peprilus burti (gulf butterfish)	Apr	0 (0)	<0.01(<0.01) 85‡
Pleuronectiformes			
Bothidae			
Unidentified (lefteye flounder)	Apr, Jun	0 (0)	0.02(0.01) 65‡
Citharichthys spp. (whiff/sanddab spp.)	Apr, May, Jun, Jul, Aug	0.08(0.03) 21‡	6.53(1.02) 7(1.49)
Citharichthys spilopterus (bay whiff)	Jul	0 (0)	<0.01(<0.01) 81‡
Etropus crossotus (fringed flounder)	Jul	0 (0)	<0.01(<0.01) 104‡
Soleidae			
Achirus lineatus (lined sole)	Jun	0 (0)	<0.01(<0.01) 84‡
Trinectes maculatus (hogchoker)	May, Jun, Jul, Aug	0 (0)	0.07(0.02) 50‡
Cynoglossidae			
Symphurus spp. (tonguefish spp.)	Apr, May, Jun, Jul, Aug	0.05(0.02) 25‡	5.66(0.89) 8(1.27)
Symphurus plagiusa (blackcheek tonguefish)	Jul	0 (0)	<0.01(<0.01) 106‡
Tetraodontiformes			
Balistidae			
Monacanthus hispidus (planehead filefish)	Jun	0 (0)	<0.01(<0.01) 110‡
Tetraodontidae			
Unidentified (puffer)	May, Jun	0 (0)	0.05(0.02) 53‡
Sphoeroides spp. (puffer spp.)	Apr, May, Jun, Aug	0.01(<0.01) 38‡	0.12(0.04) 45‡
Sphoeroides parvus (least puffer)	Apr, May, Jun, Jul, Aug	0.17(0.06) 14‡	0.34(0.08) 34‡

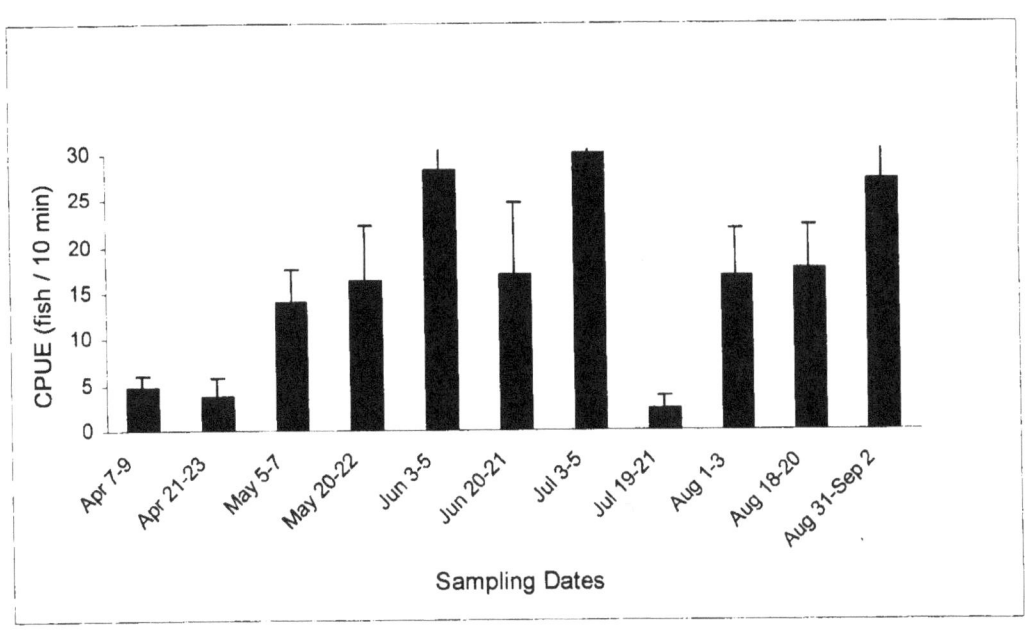

With clupeiform fishes

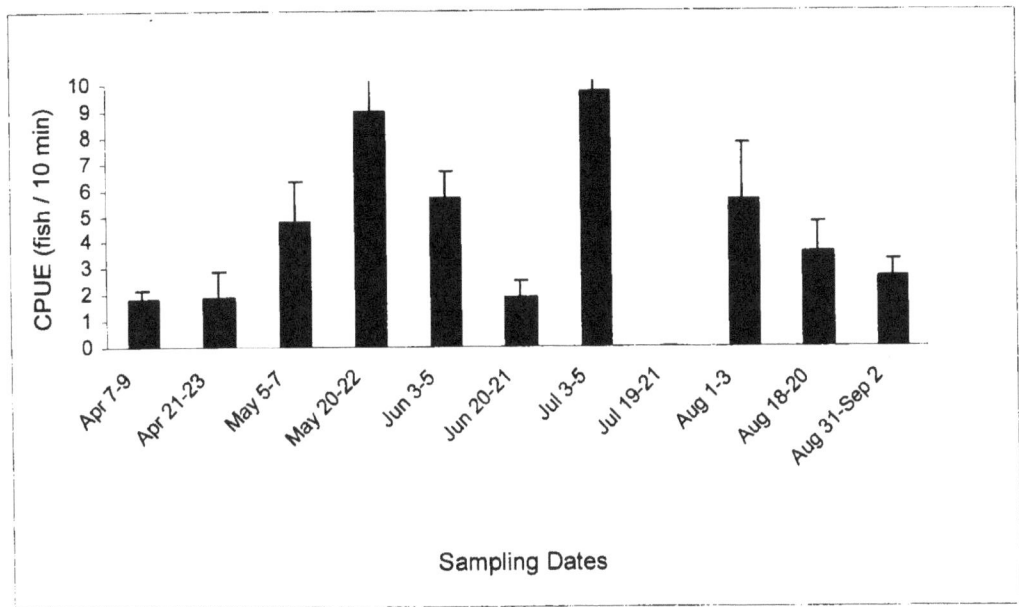

Without clupeiform fishes

Figure 13. Mean light-trap CPUEs and standard errors for data with and without clupeiform fishes included for each sampling trip at Belle Pass (1997). No non-clupeiform were collected during July 19-21.

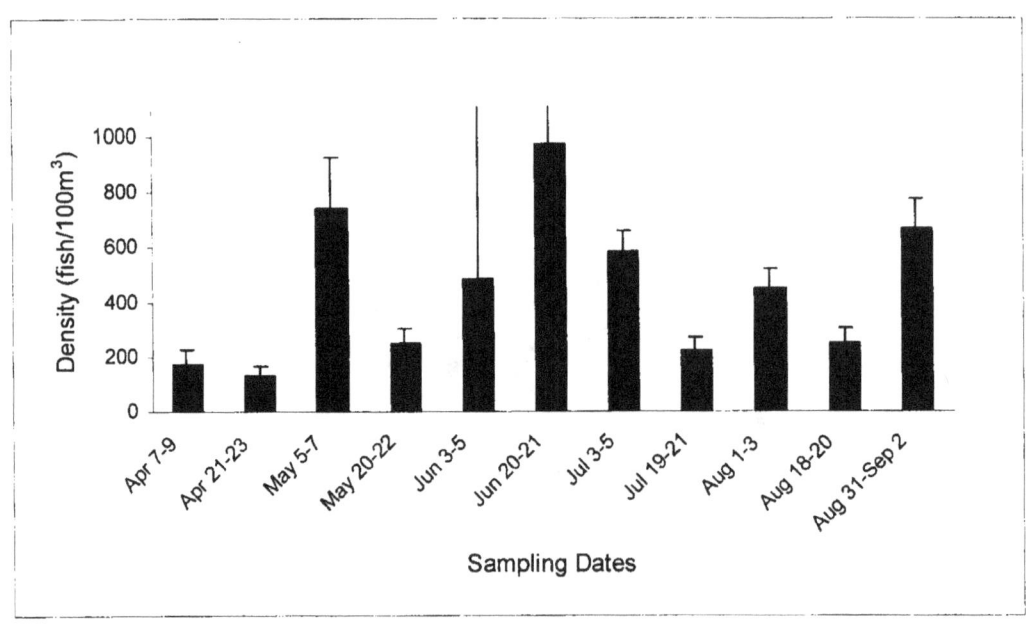

With clupeiform fishes

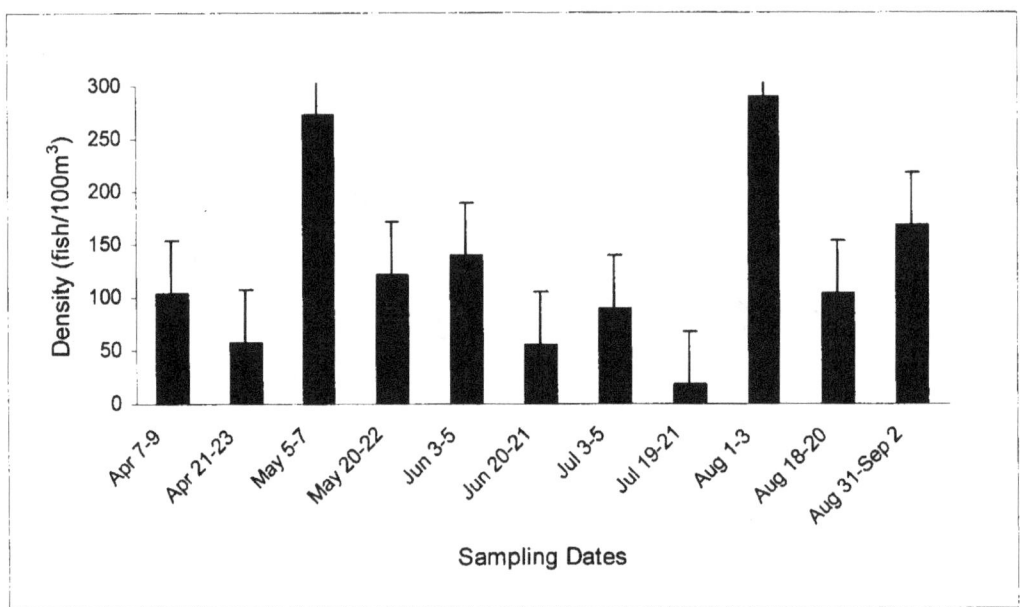

Without clupeiform fishes

Figure 14. Mean pushnet densities and standard errors for data with and without clupeiform fishes included for each sampling trip at Belle Pass (1997).

Table 7. Total plankton net density (fish/100m³), pushnet density (fish/100m³), and light-trap CPUE (fish/10 min) for reef-dependent (RD) and reef-associated (RA) families of fish collected at each site with standard error (SE). Densities calculated for the platforms include surface, subsurface, and offplatform samples. CPUEs calculated for the platforms include both surface and subsurface samples. † indicates a value <0.01.

Taxa	Ecology	Green Canyon Plankton net density (SE)	Green Canyon Light-trap CPUE (SE)	Grand Isle Plankton net density (SE)	Grand Isle Light-trap CPUE (SE)	South Timbalier Plankton net density (SE)	South Timbalier Light-trap CPUE (SE)	Belle Pass Pushnet density (SE)	Belle Pass Light-trap CPUE (SE)
Anguilliformes									
Muraenidae									
Unidentified (moray eel)	RA	0.01	0.02	0.25	†	0.40	0.01		
		0.01	0.01	0.12	†	0.38	0.01		
Beryciformes									
Holocentridae	RA								
Holocentrus spp. (squirrelfish spp.)		0.12	0.06	0.09	0.01				
		0.07	0.02	0.04	†				
Perciformes									
Serranidae	RA								
Unidentified (seabass/grouper)		0.75		0.12		0.05			
		0.43		0.07		0.05			
Anthiinae (sea perch)		0.43	0.01	0.25	†				
		0.15	0.01	0.12	†				
Epinephelinae (grouper)		0.35	†	0.03	0.01	0.03		†	
		0.16	†	0.02	†	0.03		†	
Grammistinae		0.05		0.03					
		0.03		0.02					
Serraninae (sea bass)	RA			0.65	0.03	0.31	0.01		
				0.18	0.01	0.22	0.01		
Priacanthidae	RA								
Unidentified (bigeye)		0.09	†						
		0.06	†						
Priacanthus spp. (bigeye/glasseye spp.)				0.02			0.01		
				0.02			0.01		
Apogonidae	RA								
Unidentified (cardinalfish)		0.01							
		0.01							
Apogon spp. (cardinalfish spp.)		0.01							
		0.01							
Rachycentridae	RA								
Rachycentron canadum (cobia)				0.08				†	
				0.04				†	
Carangidae	RA								
Unidentified (jack)		0.35		0.10	†	0.40		0.02	
		0.19		0.06	†	0.26		0.02	
Caranx spp. (jack spp.)		0.02	†	0.08				0.64	
		0.02	†	0.05				0.26	

Table 7. (continued)

Taxa	Ecology	Green Canyon Plankton net density (SE)	Green Canyon Light-trap CPUE (SE)	Grand Isle Plankton net density (SE)	Grand Isle Light-trap CPUE (SE)	South Timbalier Plankton net density (SE)	South Timbalier Light-trap CPUE (SE)	Belle Pass Pushnet density (SE)	Belle Pass Light-trap CPUE (SE)
Caranx crysos (blue runner)		2.03 (0.89)	0.17 (0.04)	0.89 (0.30)	0.07 (0.02)		0.11 (0.03)		
Caranx hippos/latus (crevalle/horse-eye jack)		2.72 (0.69)	0.09 (0.02)	0.26 (0.16)	0.07 (0.02)	2.49 (2.25)	0.21 (0.08)	0.09 (0.04)	† (†)
Chloroscombrus chrysurus (Atlantic bumper)		0.38 (0.16)	0.01 (0.01)	0.65 (0.20)	0.01 (0.01)	27.64 (10.19)	0.08 (0.03)	0.28 (0.15)	0.05 (0.02)
Decapterus punctatus (round scad)		0.02 (0.02)	0.01 (0.01)		0.02 (0.01)	0.02 (0.02)	0.02 (0.01)		
Elagatis bipinnulata (rainbow runner)		0.13 (0.08)	† (†)						
Oligoplites saurus (leatherjack)			† (†)	0.08 (0.06)		0.45 (0.34)		0.02 (†)	† (†)
Selar crumenophthalmus (bigeye scad)		0.07 (0.06)		0.23 (0.10)			0.01 (0.01)		
Selene spp. (moonfish/lookdown spp.)						0.56 (0.56)		†	
Selene vomer (lookdown)		0.16 (0.16)		0.03 (0.02)				†	
Selene setapinnis (Atlantic moonfish)								†	
Seriola spp. (jack spp.)		0.22 (0.12)	† (†)	0.02 (0.02)			† (†)		
Seriola dumerili/rivoliana (greater amberjack/almaco jack)					0.01 (†)				
Seriola fasciata (lesser amberjack)					† (†)				
Trachinotus carolinus (Florida pompano)					† (†)		0.01 (0.01)		
Trachinotus falcatus/goodei (permit/palometa)					0.01 (0.01)				
Trachurus lathami (rough scad)		0.14 (0.08)		0.09 (0.05)	0.03 (0.01)	0.02 (0.02)	0.04 (0.02)		
Lutjanidae	RA								
Unidentified (snapper)		0.03 (0.03)	0.01 (0.01)	0.08 (0.04)	† (†)	0.16 (0.16)			
Lutjanus spp. (snapper spp.)		0.15 (0.09)	† (†)	0.35 (0.12)	0.01 (0.01)	0.56 (0.42)			
Lutjanus griseus (gray snapper)								0.03 (0.01)	† (†)

66

Table 7. (continued)

Taxa	Ecology	Green Canyon Plankton net density (SE)	Green Canyon Light-trap CPUE (SE)	Grand Isle Plankton net density (SE)	Grand Isle Light-trap CPUE (SE)	South Timbalier Plankton net density (SE)	South Timbalier Light-trap CPUE (SE)	Belle Pass Pushnet density (SE)	Belle Pass Light-trap CPUE (SE)
Lutjanus synagris (lane snapper)								0.07 (0.02)	0.01 (†)
Lutjanus apodus/vivanus (schoolmaster/silk snapper)			0.01 (†)						
Lutjanus campechanus (red snapper)			0.01 (0.01)	0.01 (0.01)	0.01 (0.01)	0.56 (0.56)	0.01 (0.01)		
Pristipomoides aquilonaris (wenchman)		1.25 (0.56)							
Rhomboplites aurorubens (vermilion snapper)		0.03 (0.03)		0.39 (0.17)	0.09 (0.02)		0.03 (0.02)		
Haemulidae Unidentified (grunt)	RA					0.56 (0.56)		† (†)	
Sparidae Unidentified (porgy)	RA	0.02 (0.02)		0.02 (0.02)	0.01 (†)	0.13 (0.13)		0.02 (0.01)	
Sparidae Type B (porgy sp.)								0.02 (0.01)	
Calamus spp. (porgy spp.)					† (†)	0.09 (0.09)			
Lagodon rhomboides (pinfish)		0.24 (0.16)							
Mullidae Unidentified (goatfish)	RA		† (†)	0.13 (0.07)	0.02 (0.01)			† (†)	
Mullus auratus (red goatfish)			† (†)		0.02 (0.01)				
Pseudupeneus maculatus (spotted goatfish)					0.02 (0.01)				
Upeneus parvus (dwarf goatfish)					0.13 (0.03)		0.01 (0.01)		
Ephippidae *Chaetodipterus faber* (Atlantic spadefish)	RA	0.03 (0.02)				0.79 (0.36)		0.05 (0.02)	
Chaetodontidae Unidentified (butterflyfish)	RD	0.02 (0.02)		0.01 (0.01)					
Pomacentridae Unidentified (damselfish)	RD				0.01 (0.01)				

67

Table 7. (continued)

Taxa	Ecology	Green Canyon		Grand Isle		South Timbalier		Belle Pass	
		Plankton net density (SE)	Light-trap CPUE (SE)	Plankton net density (SE)	Light-trap CPUE (SE)	Plankton net density (SE)	Light-trap CPUE (SE)	Pushnet density (SE)	Light-trap CPUE (SE)
Abudefduf saxatilis (sergeant major)	RA				0.01		0.03		
					0.01		0.02		
Abudefduf taurus (night sergeant)					†				
Chromis spp. (chromis spp.)				0.15	0.15				
				0.15	0.04				
Pomacentrus spp. (damselfish spp.)			0.07	0.06	0.17		0.01		
			0.03	0.03	0.05		0.01		
Sphyraenidae	RA								
Sphyraena borealis (northern sennet)					†		0.01		
					†		0.01		
Sphyraena guachancho (guaguanche)	RD	0.32	0.01	0.94	0.01				
		0.27	0.01	0.31					
Labridae	RD								
Unidentified (wrasse)	RD			0.10	†	0.02	0.01	0.01	
				0.08	†	0.02	0.01	†	
Scaridae									
Unidentified (parrotfish)	RD	7.33	0.03						
		2.11	0.01						
Sparisoma spp. (parrotfish spp.)								0.01	
								†	
Opisthognathidae	RA								
Unidentified (jawfish)				0.47	0.23				
				0.17	0.07				
Opisthognathus spp. (jawfish spp.)				0.03					
				0.03					
Opisthognathus aurifrons (yellowhead jawfish)				0.03	0.01				
				0.03	0.01				
Opisthognathus lonchurus (moustache jawfish)				0.05					
				0.05					
Blenniidae	RA								
Unidentified (blenny)		0.55	0.08	3.02	0.26	2.36	0.07	0.03	0.02
		0.34	0.05	2.05	0.07	0.83	0.02	0.02	0.01
Chasmodes spp. (striped/Florida blenny)								†	
Hypleurochilus bermudensis (barred blenny)								†	
Hypsoblennius spp. (blenny spp.)								†	

68

Table 7. (continued)

Taxa	Ecology	Green Canyon Plankton net density (SE)	Green Canyon Light-trap CPUE (SE)	Grand Isle Plankton net density (SE)	Grand Isle Light-trap CPUE (SE)	South Timbalier Plankton net density (SE)	South Timbalier Light-trap CPUE (SE)	Belle Pass Pushnet density (SE)	Belle Pass Light-trap CPUE (SE)
Hypsoblennius hentz/ionthas (feather/freckled blenny)					0.61 / 0.19	0.16 / 0.16	0.25 / 0.08	1.95 / 0.45	1.04 / 0.27
Hypsoblennius invemar (tessellated blenny)		0.03 / 0.03	†	0.02 / 0.02	3.35 / 0.64	0.56 / 0.56	0.20 / 0.07		
Ophioblennius atlanticus (redlip blenny)		0.44 / 0.32	0.01 / †	0.22 / 0.22					
Parablennius marmoreus (seaweed blenny)				0.01 / 0.01	3.01 / 0.40	0.19 / 0.19	0.01 / 0.01		
Scartella cristata (molly miller)								0.34 / 0.08	0.03 / 0.02
Scarella/Hypleurochilus (blenny spp.)				0.14 / 0.08	0.42 / 0.08	1.74 / 1.18	0.28 / 0.12		
Gobiidae	RA								
Unidentified (goby)		6.73 / 1.75	0.20 / 0.14	8.18 / 0.96	0.09 / 0.02	27.7 / 11.7	0.10 / 0.03	0.81 / 0.23	0.03 / 0.01
Bathygobius soporator (frillfin goby)								0.01 / †	
Evorthodus lyricus/Gobionellus boleosoma (lyre goby/darter goby)					†			0.01 / †	
Bollmannia communis (ragged goby)					†				
Gobionellus oceanicus (highfin goby)				0.01 / 0.01	†				
Gobiosoma spp. (goby spp.)					†			1.48 / 0.43	0.26 / 0.18
Gobiosoma bosc (naked goby)								46.88 / 7.88	0.59 / 0.16
Microgobius spp. (goby spp.)								4.17 / 1.30	0.04 / 0.03
Scombridae	RA								
Unidentified (mackerel)		1.42 / 0.72	0.01 / 0.01	0.26 / 0.15	0.05 / 0.03	0.23 / 0.17		0.01 / †	
Acanthocybium solandri (wahoo)		0.03 / 0.03							
Auxis spp. (mackerel spp.)		1.26 / 0.33	0.19 / 0.05	4.00 / 1.25	0.34 / 0.07		0.09 / 0.05		
Euthynnus alletteratus (little tunny)		0.47 / 0.17	0.07 / 0.02	4.33 / 0.74	1.29 / 0.23	0.43 / 0.25	0.51 / 0.18		

Table 7. (continued)

Taxa	Ecology	Green Canyon		Grand Isle		South Timbalier		Belle Pass	
		Plankton net density (SE)	Light-trap CPUE (SE)	Plankton net density (SE)	Light-trap CPUE (SE)	Plankton net density (SE)	Light-trap CPUE (SE)	Pushnet density (SE)	Light-trap CPUE (SE)
Katsuwonus pelamis				0.03	0.03				
(skipjack tuna)									
Scomber japonicus				0.02	0.01				
(chub mackerel)									
Scomberomorus spp.					0.01			0.01	
(mackerel spp.)					0.01			†	
Scomberomorus cavalla		0.06	0.02	0.10	0.13	4.97	0.06	†	
(king mackerel)		0.05	0.01	0.04	0.04	2.91	0.02		
Scomberomorus maculatus		0.51	0.01	0.28	0.07	6.05	0.33	†	
(Spanish mackerel)		0.28	†	0.12	0.02	1.94	0.07		
Thunnus spp.		0.07	0.01		†				
(tuna spp.)		0.07	0.01		†				
Thunnus thynnus		0.11			†				
(bluefin tuna)		0.07							
Tetraodontiformes									
Balistidae	RA								
Unidentified				0.01	†			†	
(leatherjacket)				0.01	†			†	
Monacanthus hispidus									
(planehead filefish)									

70

both gears were dominated by gobiids and blenniids, particularly *Gobiosoma bosc* and *Hypsoblennius hentz/ionthas*.

In general, trends in seasonality were consistent for taxa collected at the different sites across the shelf (Tables 3-6; Ditty et al. 1988). Many groups (e.g., clupeiforms, carangids, and scombrids) were present throughout the sampling periods for GI 94, ST 54, and the Belle Pass jetty, and throughout the spring-summer at GC 18. At GC 18, the only site that included fall and winter sampling, only a few taxa were represented solely during these months, and included *Etremeus teres* (January-February), *Diplophos taenia* (November) and *Mugil cephalus* (October-November and January-February), among others.

Between and Within Site Comparisons of Sampling Gears

In general within the light-trap collections, surface light-traps had the highest mean total CPUEs at all three platforms (Figure 15a). At GC 18 values ranged from 2.3-5.0 fish/10 min and both surface light-trap and off-platform light-trap CPUEs were significantly higher than the subsurface light-trap CPUEs (Tukey's Studentized Range Test, α=0.05). Overall light-trap CPUEs at GI 94 were the highest and ranged from 25.1-148.2 fish/10 min with significant differences detected between all gear depths/locations. Although graphically it appears that the subsurface light-trap and off-platform light-trap mean CPUEs are similar, the statistical results are based on the ranks, which accounts for the apparent discrepancy. The trend observed at ST 54 was the same as that at GC 18, but the CPUEs were much higher, ranging from 4.9-42.2 fish/10 min. When clupeiform fishes were excluded from these analyses, CPUEs were considerably lower but the same trends were detected with the exception of ST 54 (Figure 15b). Significant differences were detected at ST 54 between all three gear depths/locations, a result of large reductions in the CPUEs of the off-platform light-trap and surface light-trap once clupeiforms were removed. Light-trap CPUEs (without clupeiforms) ranged from 0.7-3.2 fish/10 min at GC 18, 6.5-58.2 fish/10 min at GI 94, and 3.8-7.2 fish/10 min at ST 54.

No significant difference was detected in mean total plankton net densities between the two depths at GC 18 (Tukey's Studentized Range Test, α=0.05; Figure 16a), whereas surface nets had significantly higher mean total densities than subsurface nets at ST 54 and GI 94. The mean total density for surface nets at ST 54 was very high (4,024 fish/100 m^3) due in large part to the very high densities of *Opisthonema oglinum*. In contrast, no *O. oglinum* were collected in the subsurface collections. Likewise, high densities of *O. oglinum* contributed to the high surface net total density at GI 94 (388.2 fish/100 m^3). When clupeiform fishes were removed from the analyses, mean densities were reduced considerably, but the vertical trends were the same with the exception of GI 94 where mean densities in subsurface nets were larger, but not significantly (Figure 16b). In both analyses (with and without clupeiforms) mean densities at GC 18 for the subsurface net were somewhat higher than the surface nets but not significantly so.

Significant trends were also observed within dominant species in mean CPUEs and densities between the different sampling depths and locations within sites. At GC 18, *Caranx crysos* and *Auxis* spp. appeared to behave similarly, since they were collected in significantly higher CPUEs from surface waters (both within the platform structure and off-platform) than from subsurface waters (Tukey's Studentized Range tests, α=0.05; Figure 17). While with *C.*

71

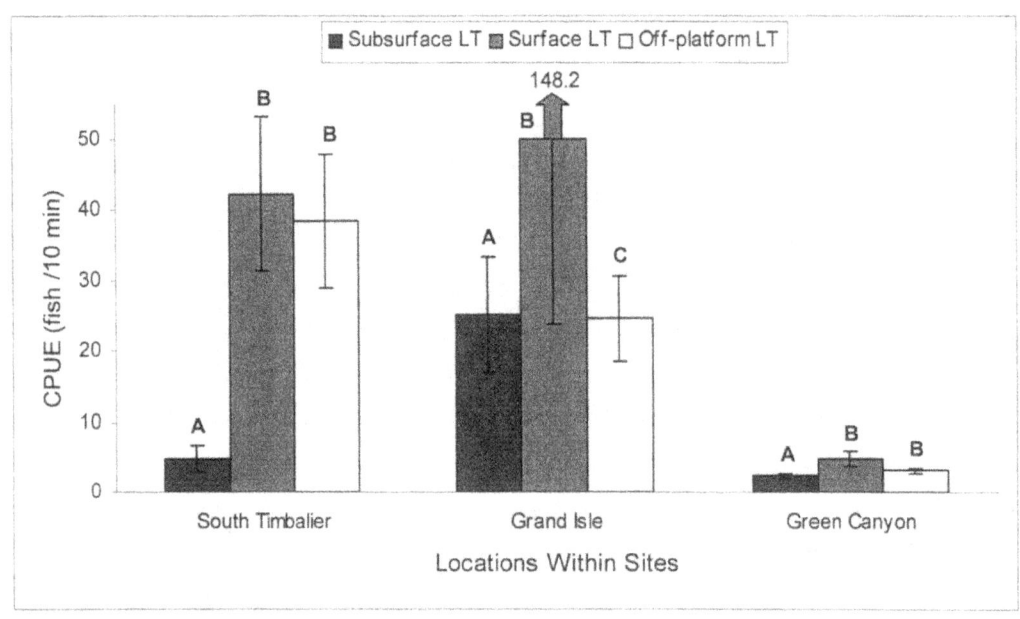

With clupeiform fishes

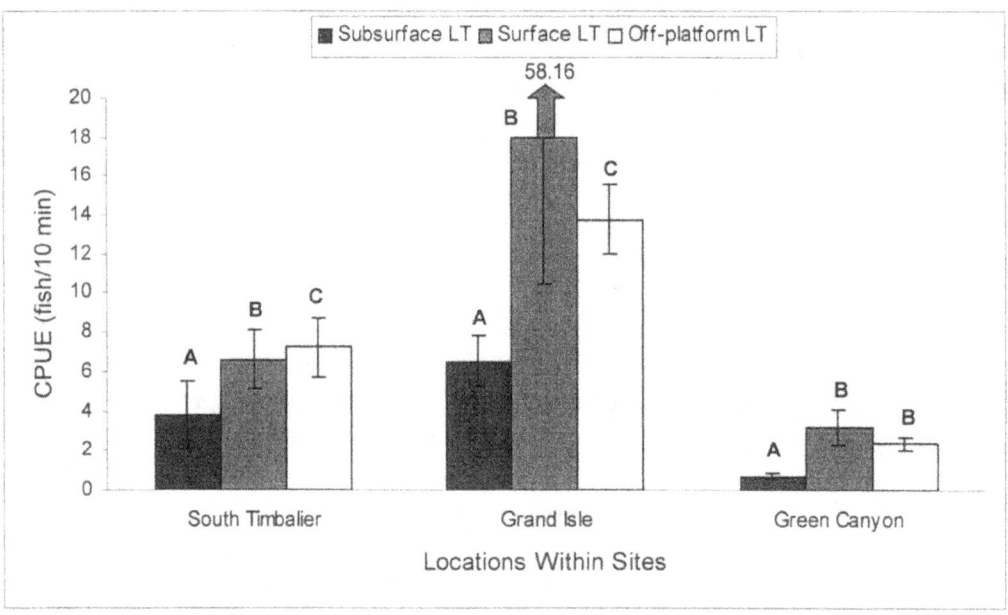

Without clupeiform fishes

Figure 15. Mean light-trap CPUEs (with standard error bars) for data with and without clupeiform fishes included for depths/locations within each platform site. Arrows above bars point toward the mean for that gear. Within each location, the same letter above each bar indicates no significant difference between the gear types based on Tukey's Studentized Range test on ranked data (α=0.05). Different letters designate significant differences.

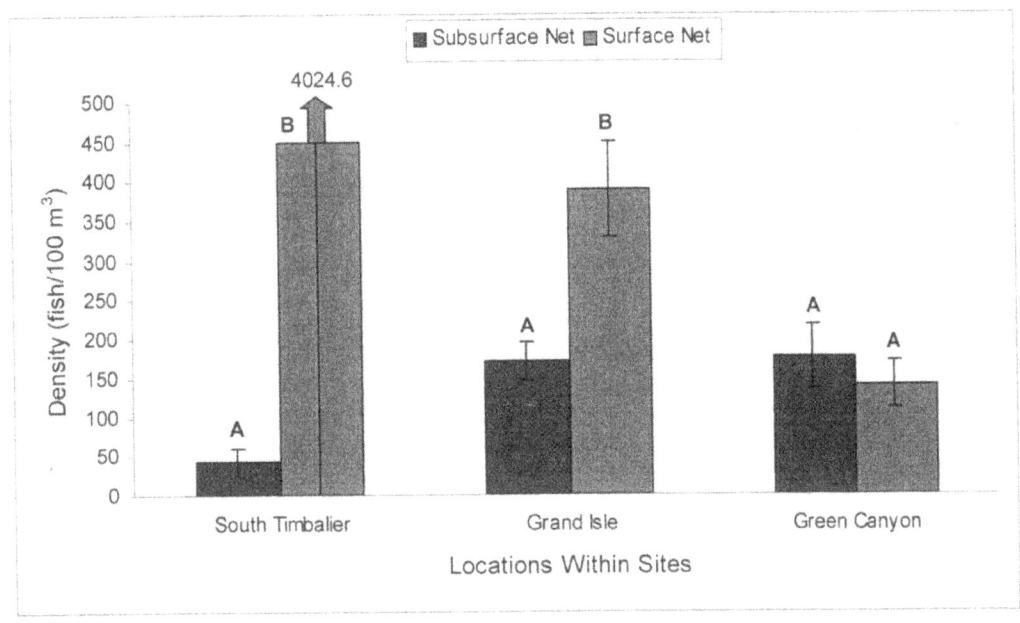

With clupeiform fishes

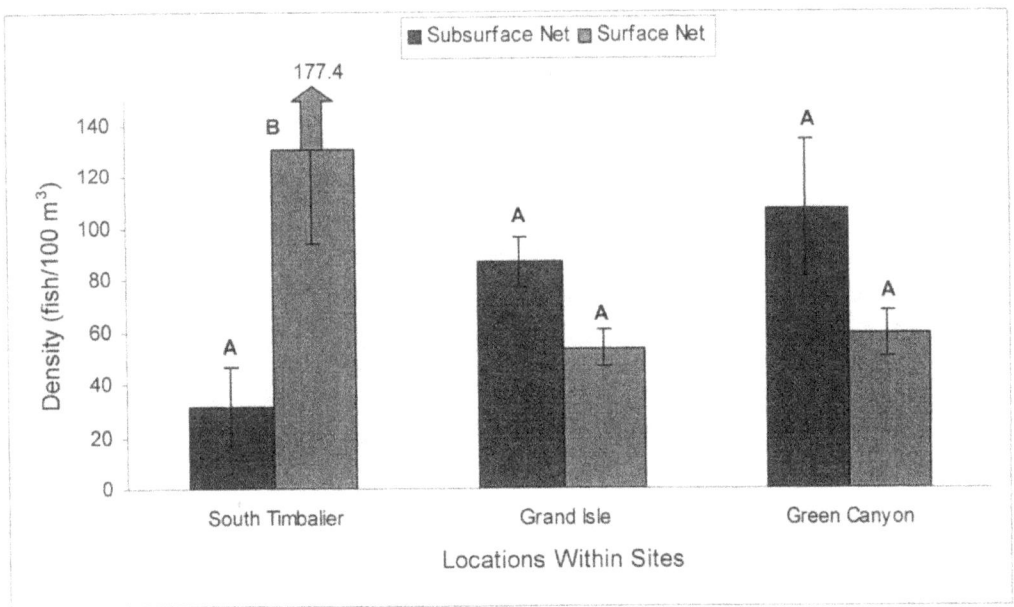

Without clupeiform fishes

Figure 16. Mean plankton net densities (with standard error bars) for data with and without clupeiform fishes included for depths within each platform site. Arrows above bars point toward the mean for that gear. Within each location, the same letter above each bar indicates no significant difference between gear types based on t-tests on log-transformed data ($\alpha=0.05$). Different letters designate significant differences.

hippos/latus, significantly higher CPUEs were taken in off-platform collections than with either depth within the platform. No significant differences were detected between the depths and locations for *Anchoa nasuta/hepsetus*. There was no clear pattern for *Opisthonema oglinum* where mean CPUEs were significantly different between surface and subsurface light-trap samples, but neither of these values differed from the off-platform CPUE.

In general, differences in mean plankton net densities at GC 18 were higher in subsurface collections than surface collections (Figure 18): *Citharichthys spilopterus* (Student's t-test, p=0.006); *Symphurus* spp. (p=0.046); *Mugil cephalus* (p=0.081); and *Caranx hippos/latus* (p=0.260). By contrast, mean surface plankton net density was greater for *Opisthonema oglinum* (p=0.001).

At GI 94, three of the dominant species collected with light-traps appeared to be surface oriented (Figure 19). Mean CPUEs for *Opisthonema oglinum*, *Hypsoblennius invemar*, and *Euthynnus alletteratus* were significantly higher in surface and off-platform light-trap samples than in subsurface light-trap samples (Tukey's Studentized Range tests, α=0.05). Significantly higher CPUEs were observed within the platform structure for *Engraulis eurystole* and *Anchoa nasuta/hepsetus* regardless of depth of capture. Mean CPUEs for *Synodus foetens* were significantly higher in the surface light-trap samples. No significant difference was observed between depths or locations for *Anchoa nasuta*. Mean surface plankton net densities (Figure 20) were significantly higher for the clupeiform fishes: *O. oglinum* (Student's t-test, p<0.0001) and *Anchoa* spp. (p<0.005). Mean plankton net densities were significantly higher in the subsurface samples for *Bregmaceros cantori*. No significant difference was observed between the two depths for *Symphurus* spp.

At ST 54, the patterns in mean CPUEs between the depths and locations within sites were not as clear (Figure 21). Significant differences were detected for all depths and locations for *Opisthonema oglinum* (Tukey's Studentized Range test, α=0.05). Surface collections were greater than subsurface, i.e. the highest mean CPUEs were for off-platform samples, followed by surface light-trap collections within the platform and then subsurface samples. For *Anchoa nasuta/hepsetus* surface oriented collections also appeared to be higher with mean surface light-trap CPUEs being significantly higher than that for the subsurface samples, but not for off-platform samples (α=0.05). Similarly for *Euthynnus alletteratus*, the mean off-platform light-trap CPUE was significantly higher than the subsurface light-trap CPUE but not significantly different from the mean surface light-trap CPUE (α=0.05). For *Synodus foetens*, the mean surface light-trap CPUE was significantly higher than that for off-platform samples, but not the subsurface samples and there was no significant differences between subsurface and off-platform mean CPUEs (α=0.05).

The mean surface density for *Opisthonema oglinum* was significantly higher than the subsurface density (Student's t-test, p<0.0007; Figure 22). Mean surface net densities were higher for *Cynoscion arenarius*, *Chloroscombrus chrysurus*, and *Etropus crossotus*, although no significant differences were detected. Conversely, the mean subsurface net density was significantly higher than the surface net density for *Ariomma* spp. (p<0.030).

74

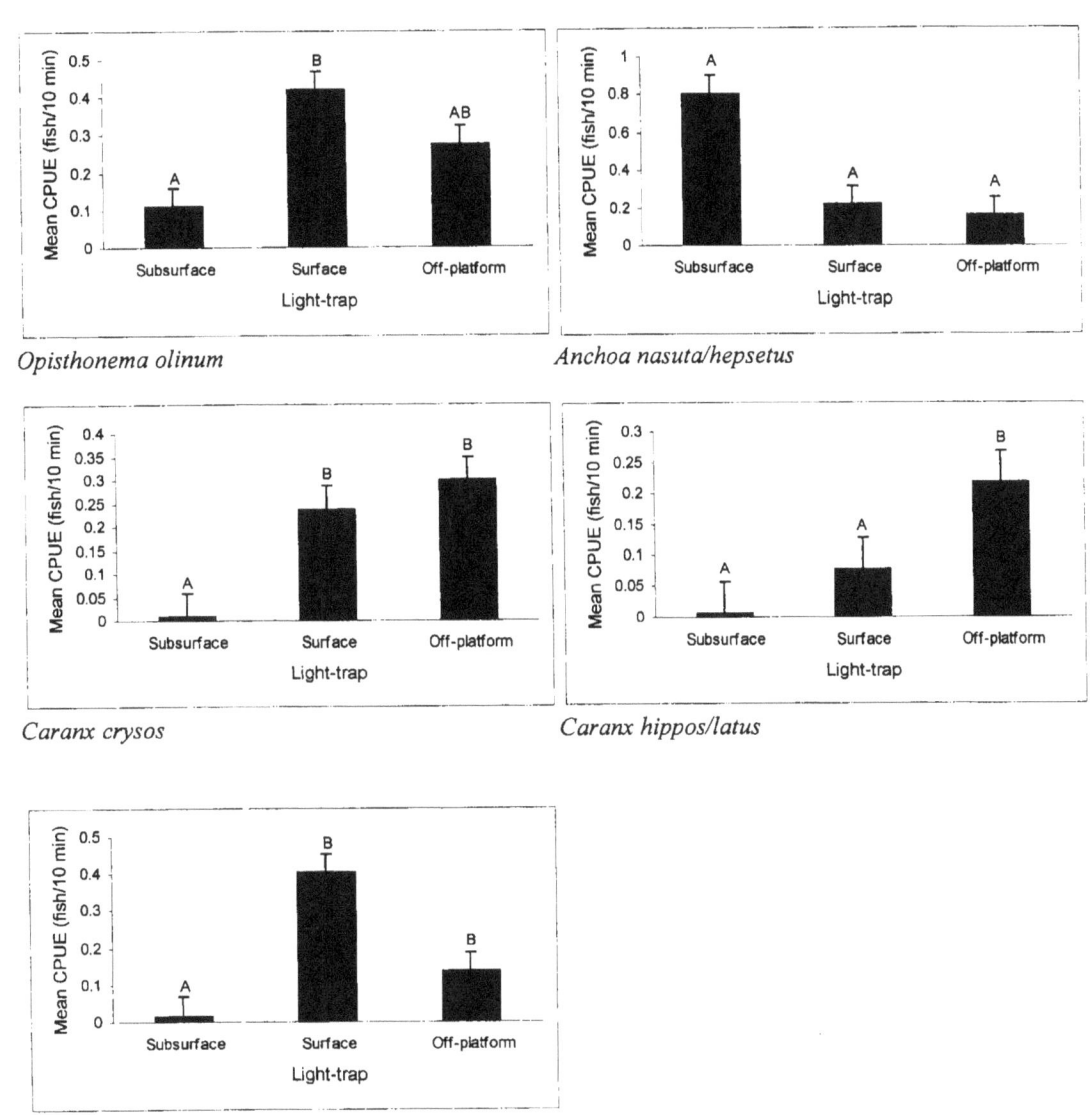

Opisthonema olinum

Anchoa nasuta/hepsetus

Caranx crysos

Caranx hippos/latus

Auxis spp.

Figure 17. Mean total CPUEs (with standard error bars) for dominant species collected with light-traps at Green Canyon 18 (1995-1996). The same letter above each bar indicates no significant difference between the gear locations based on Tukey's Studentized Range tests on ranked data ($\alpha=0.05$). Different letters indicate significant differences.

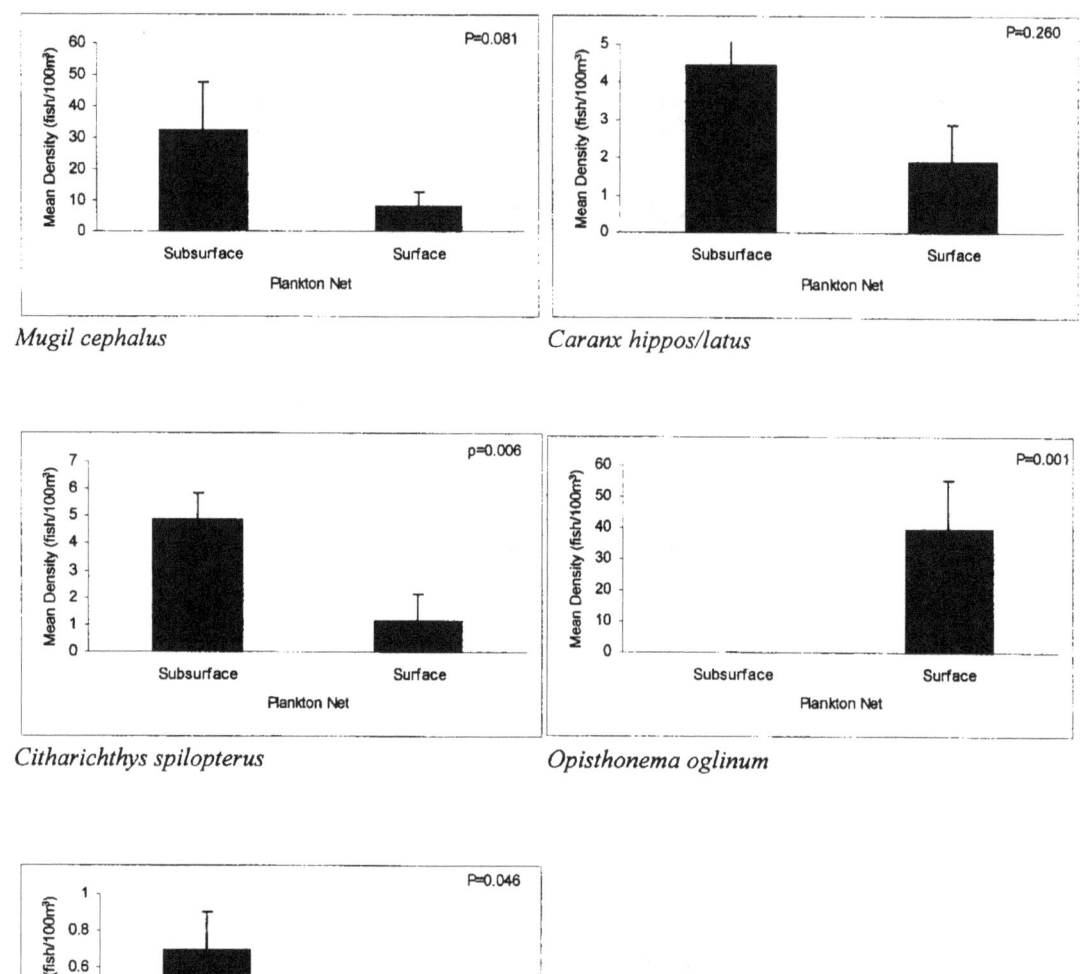

Mugil cephalus

Caranx hippos/latus

Citharichthys spilopterus

Opisthonema oglinum

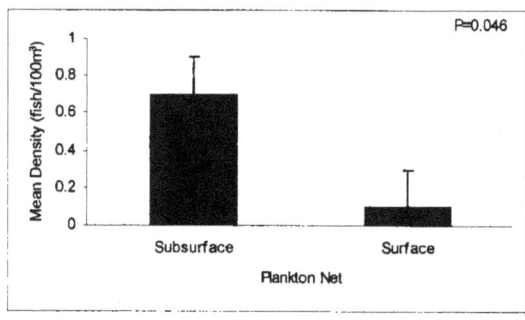

Symphurus spp.

Figure 18. Mean total densities (with standard error bars) for dominant species collected with plankton nets at Green Canyon 18 (1995-1996). The p-values indicate statistical significance from t-tests on log-transformed data.

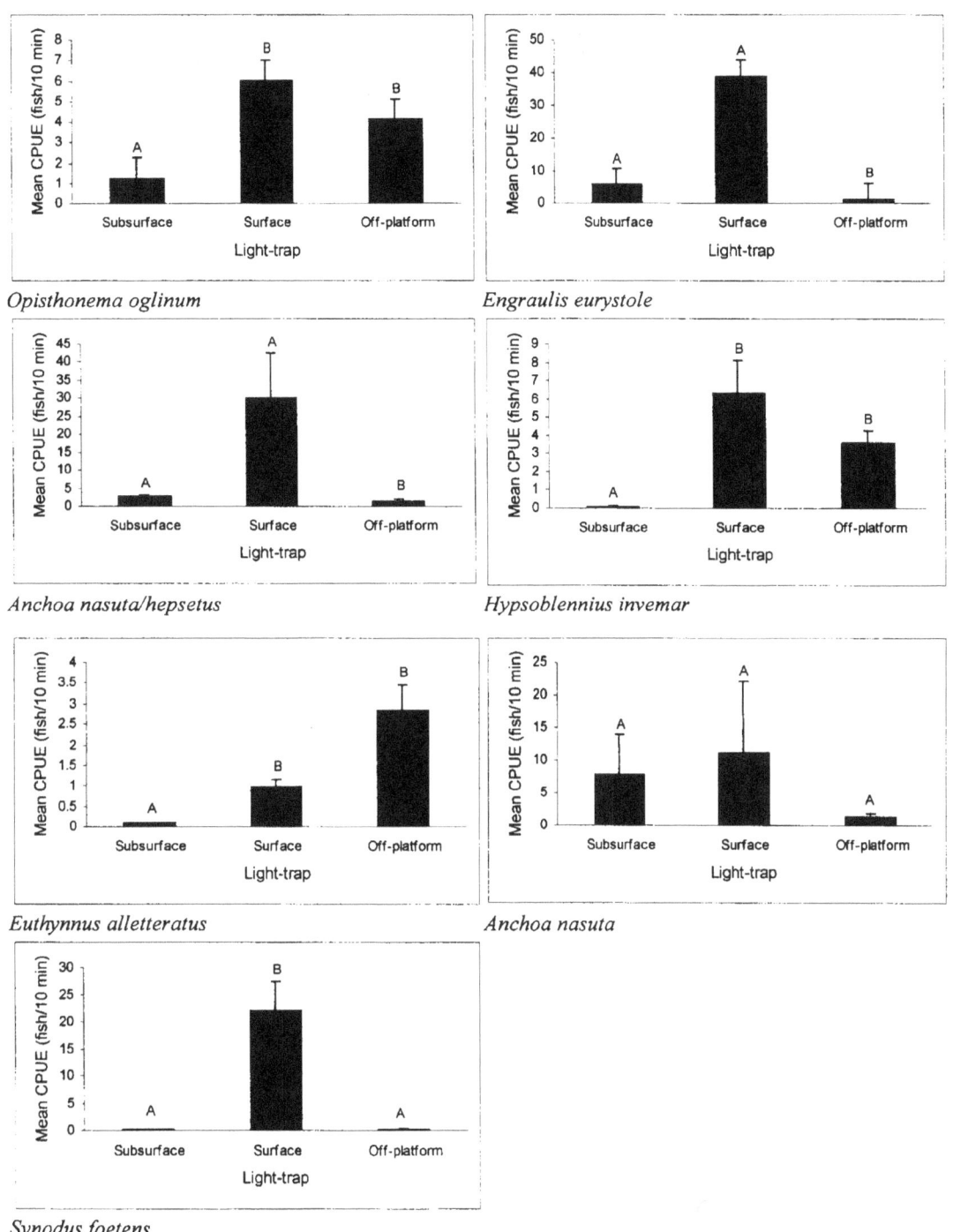

Opisthonema oglinum

Engraulis eurystole

Anchoa nasuta/hepsetus

Hypsoblennius invemar

Euthynnus alletteratus

Anchoa nasuta

Synodus foetens

Figure 19. Mean total CPUEs (with standard error bars) for dominant species collected with light-traps at Grand Isle 94 (1996). The same letter above each bar indicates no significant difference between the gear locations based on Tukey's Studentized Range tests on ranked data (α=0.05). Different letters indicate significant differences.

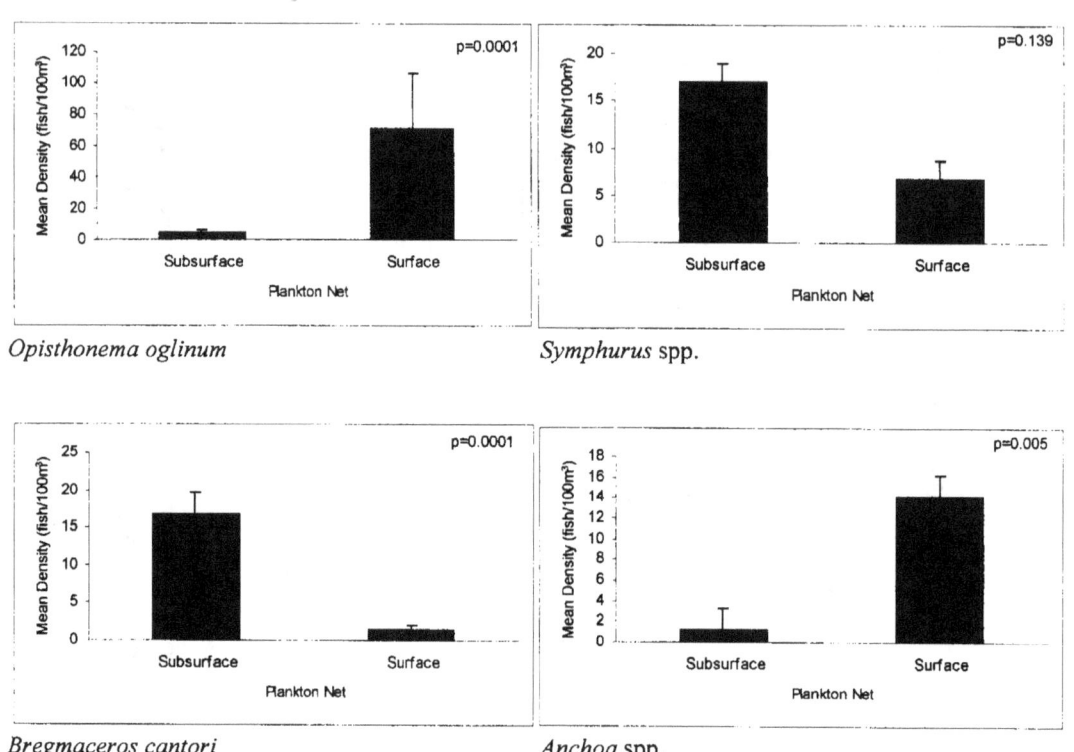

Opisthonema oglinum   *Symphurus* spp.

Bregmaceros cantori   *Anchoa* spp.

Figure 20. Mean total densities (with standard error bars) for dominant species collected with plankton nets at Grand Isle 94 (1996). The p-values indicate statistical significance from t-tests on log-transformed data.

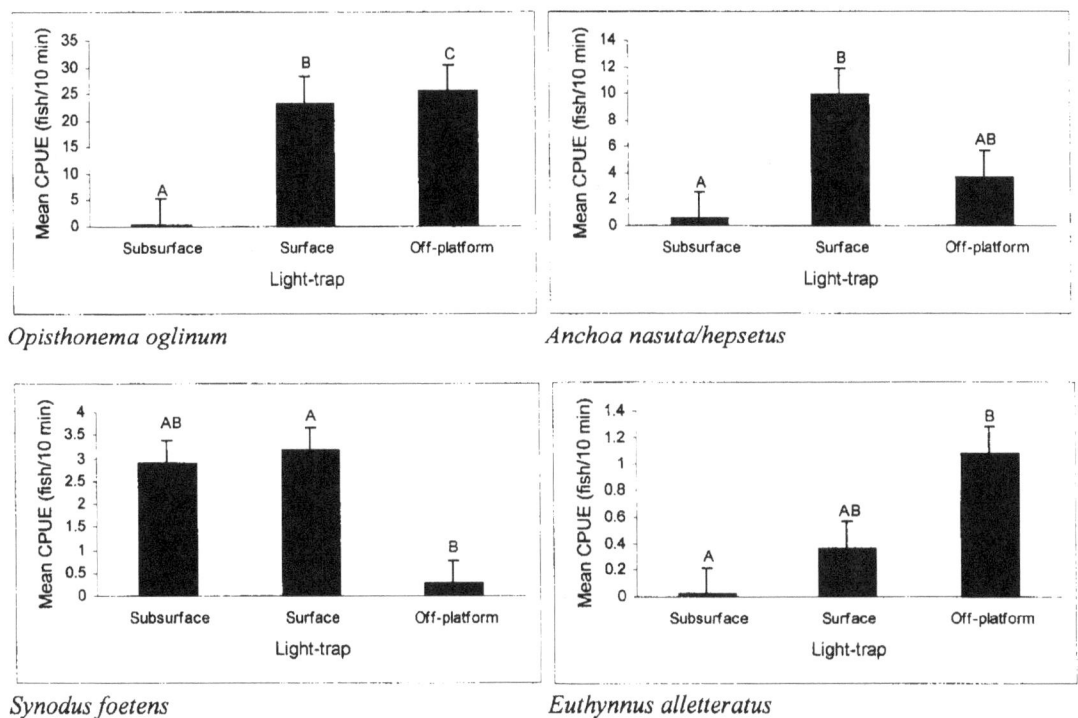

Opisthonema oglinum

Anchoa nasuta/hepsetus

Synodus foetens

Euthynnus alletteratus

Figure 21. Mean total CPUEs (with standard error bars) for dominant species collected with light-traps at South Timbalier 54 (1997). The same letter above each bar indicates no significant difference between the gear locations based on Tukey's Studentized Range tests on ranked data (α=0.05). Different letters indicate significant differences.

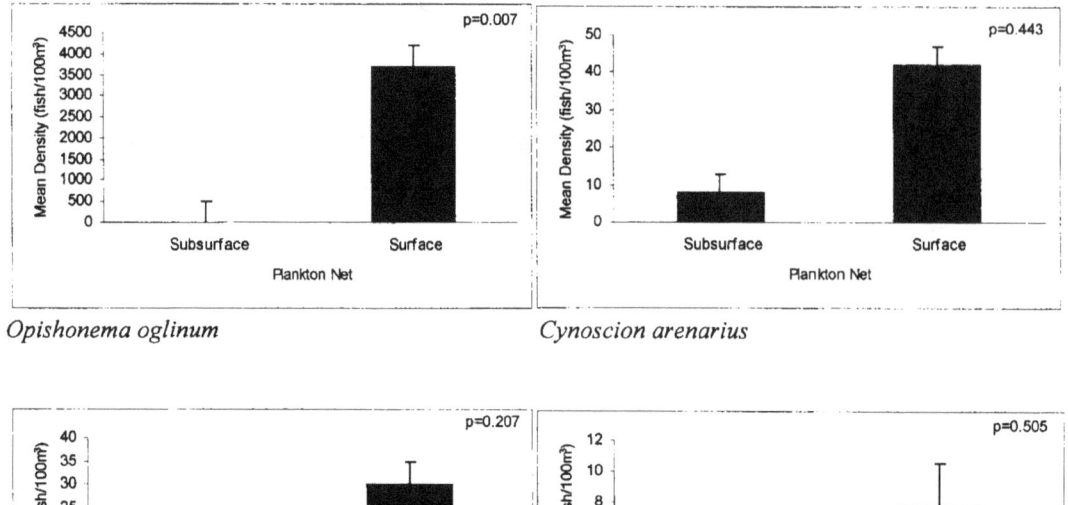

Opishonema oglinum   *Cynoscion arenarius*

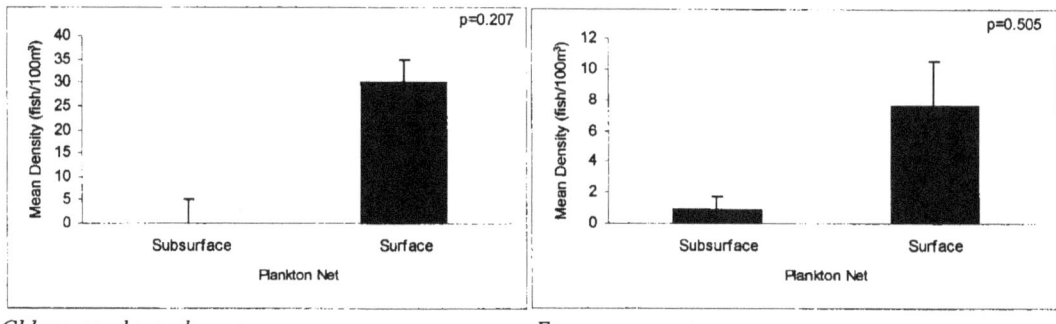

Chloroscombrus chrysurus   *Etropus crossotus*

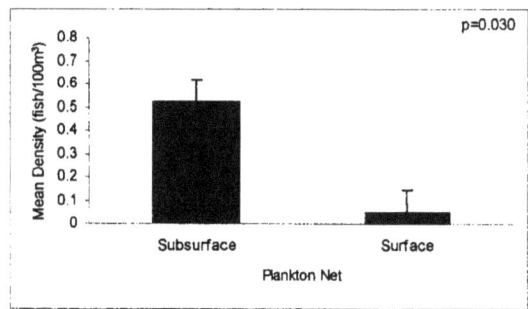

Ariomma spp.

Figure 22. Mean total densities (with standard error bars) for dominant species collected with plankton nets at South Timbalier 54 (1997). The p-values indicate statistical significance from t-tests on log-transformed data.

Length-Frequency Analyses

Eight taxa from GC 18 met the required criteria for K-S analyses (i.e., at least 10 specimens collected by each gear). In seven of the eight taxa, differences between size distributions for the two gear types were found to be statistically significant (K-S tests, p≤ 0.05; Figure 23). In general, there was some size overlap in all gear comparisons, although the degree of overlap and shapes of the size distributions differed. For *Auxis* spp., *Caranx crysos*, and *Mugil cephalus* the plankton net samples caught predominantly smaller individuals, while the light-trap samples generally encompassed these smaller sizes as well as larger larvae and juveniles. For *C. hippos/latus*, *Engraulis eurystole*, and *Euthynnus alletteratus* there was less overlap at the smaller sizes and modal size classes for the light-trap samples were generally larger. Only for *Symphurus* spp. was the modal length of light-trap samples smaller than that for net collections (p<0.05). The size distributions of *Opisthonema oglinum* were not significantly different.

At GI 94, 15 of the 16 taxa analyzed for differences between the two gear types' size distributions were highly significant (K-S tests, p<0.001; Figure 24). Size distributions for *Bregmaceros cantori*, *Synodus foetens*, *Scomberomorus cavalla,* and *Trichiurus lepturus* appeared to overlap substantially more at the smaller sizes, but in each instance the light-trap samples encompassed a significantly broader range of size classes. For *Anchoa mitchilli, A. nasuta/hepsetus, Auxis spp.*, *Caranx crysos*, *Engraulis eurystole*, *Harengula jaguana*, and *Synodus poeyi* there was some overlap in size distributions, with the plankton net capturing smaller larvae, but modal sizes for light-trap samples were always larger. With *Opisthonema oglinum*, the two gears overlapped somewhat at the smaller sizes but the light-trap collections displayed three (and possibly four) modal groups, whereas the net collections displayed only two or possibly three. Although significantly different, size distributions for *Rhomboplites aurorubens* exhibited a similar bimodal distribution for each gear type. For *Scomberomorus maculatus* there was no overlap at all in the sizes of larvae captured with the two gears. With only one taxon, *Sauridia brasiliensis*, were plankton nets not only able to better catch small sizes, but also larger size classes as well. Only one dominant taxa, *Symphurus* spp., did not exhibit significant differences in size distributions between gears (p=0.385).

At ST 54 differences between the two gear types' size distributions for 9 of the 11 taxa analyzed were highly significant (K-S tests, p<0.01; Figure 25). In general, light-trap size-frequency distributions for *Anchoa mitchilli, A. nasuta/hepsetus, Opisthonema oglinum, Peprilus burti, P. paru*, and *Scomberomorus maculatus* encompassed that of the plankton net distributions, but also included larger sizes. Little overlap in size distributions was observed for *Euthynnus alletteratus* and *Harengula jaguana*, with light-trap collections being much larger. Distributions for *Etropus crossotus* broadly overlapped but plankton nets collected a wider range of smaller size classes more frequently. Two species, *Bregmaceros cantori* and *Chloroscombrus chrysurus* did not exhibit a significant difference in size distributions between the two gear types (p=0.998 and p=0.133, respectively).

In contrast to the platform sites, size distributions at the Belle Pass jetty for pushnet vs. light-trap collections were significantly different (K-S tests, p<0.001) for only 7 of the 18 taxa analyzed (Figure 26). Size distributions for *Anchoa hepsetus* and *A. mitchilli* were similar for

81

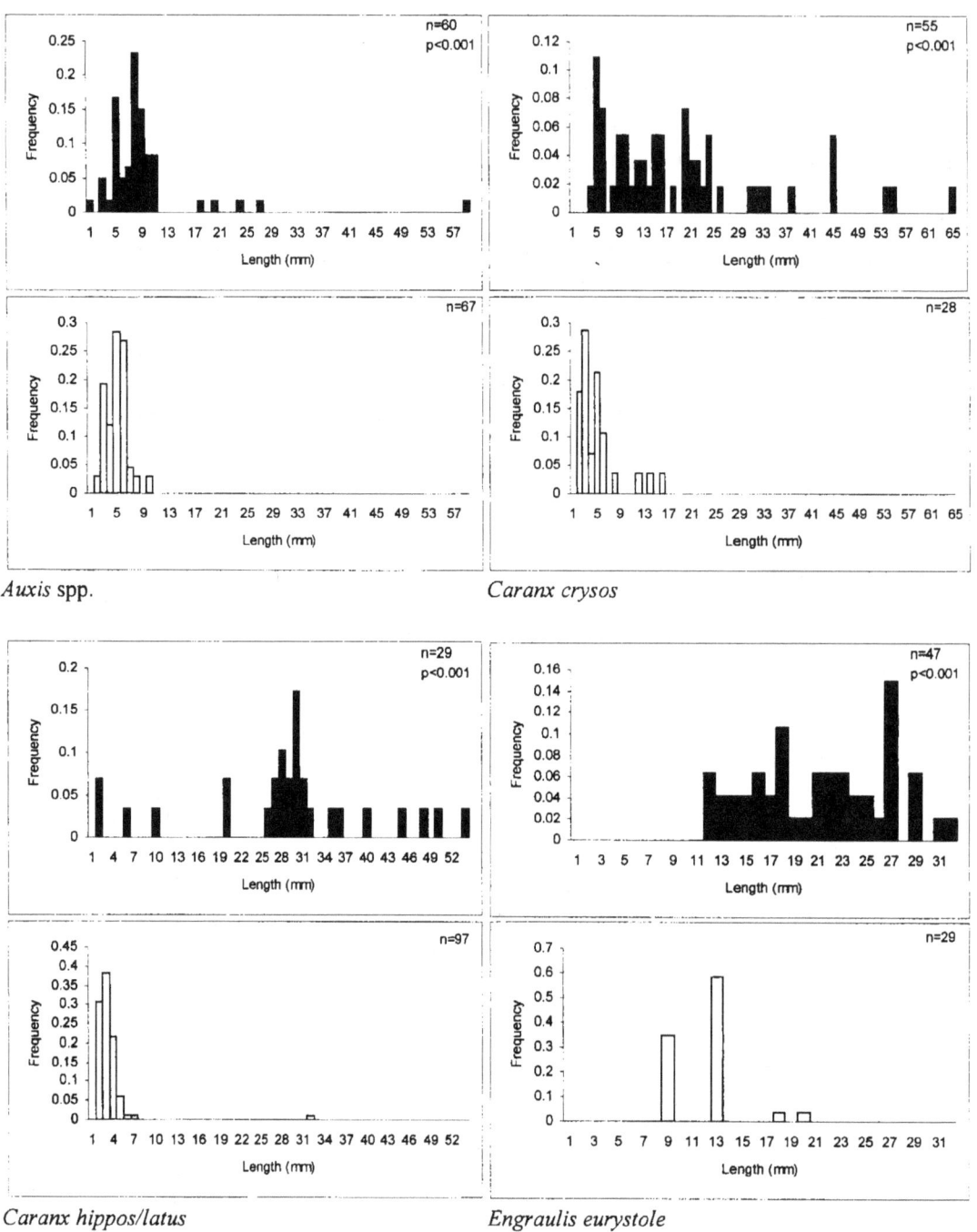

Figure 23. Size distributions of fish collected with light-traps (shaded bars) and plankton nets (open bars) at the Green Canyon site (1995-1996). Fish length-frequency distributions were analyzed with Kolmogorov-Smirnov tests (p-values are represented in the upper panel of each gear pairing along with each sample size). For analyses, at least 10 individuals were required for each gear type.

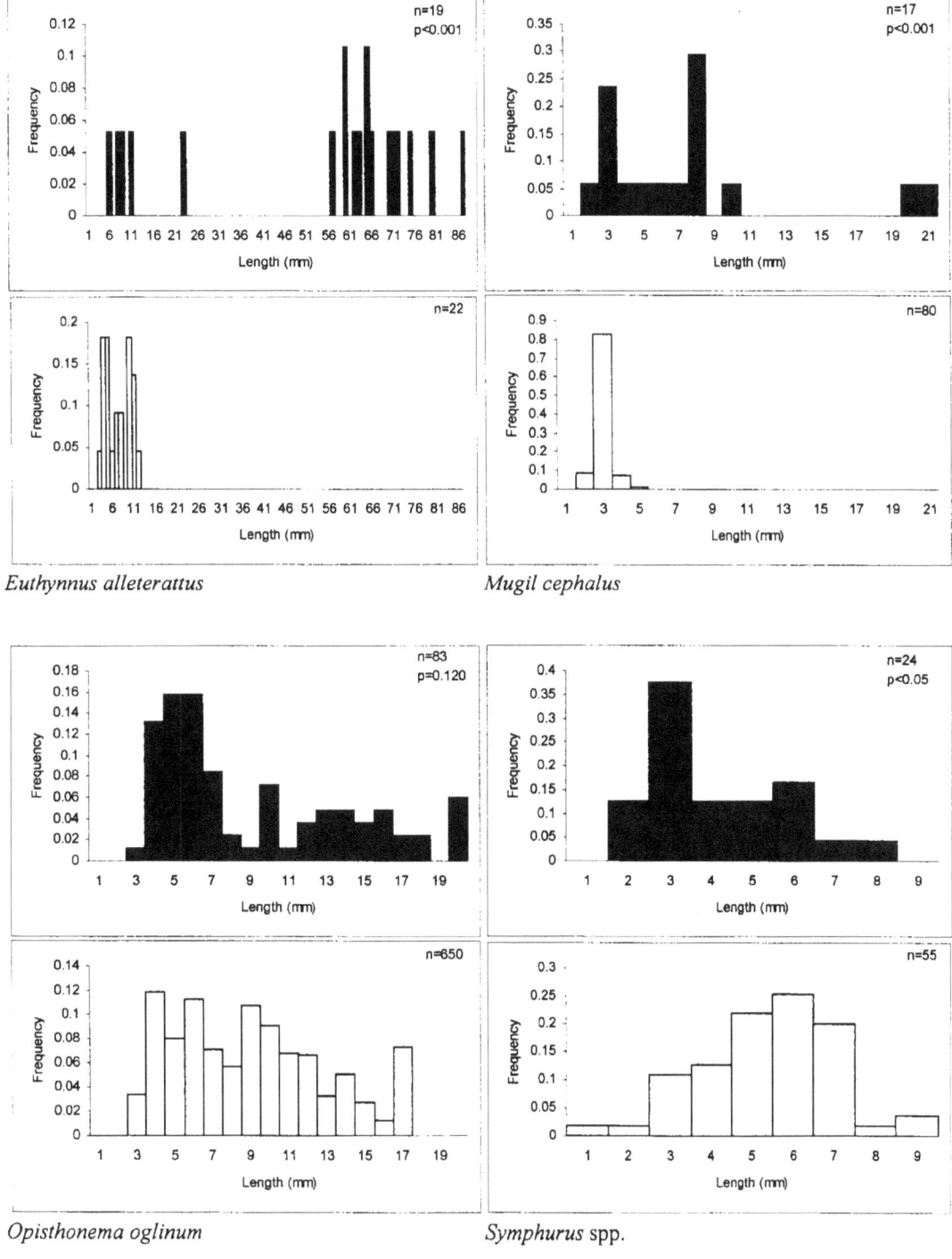

Euthynnus alleterattus

Mugil cephalus

Opisthonema oglinum

Symphurus spp.

Figure 23. (continued)

83

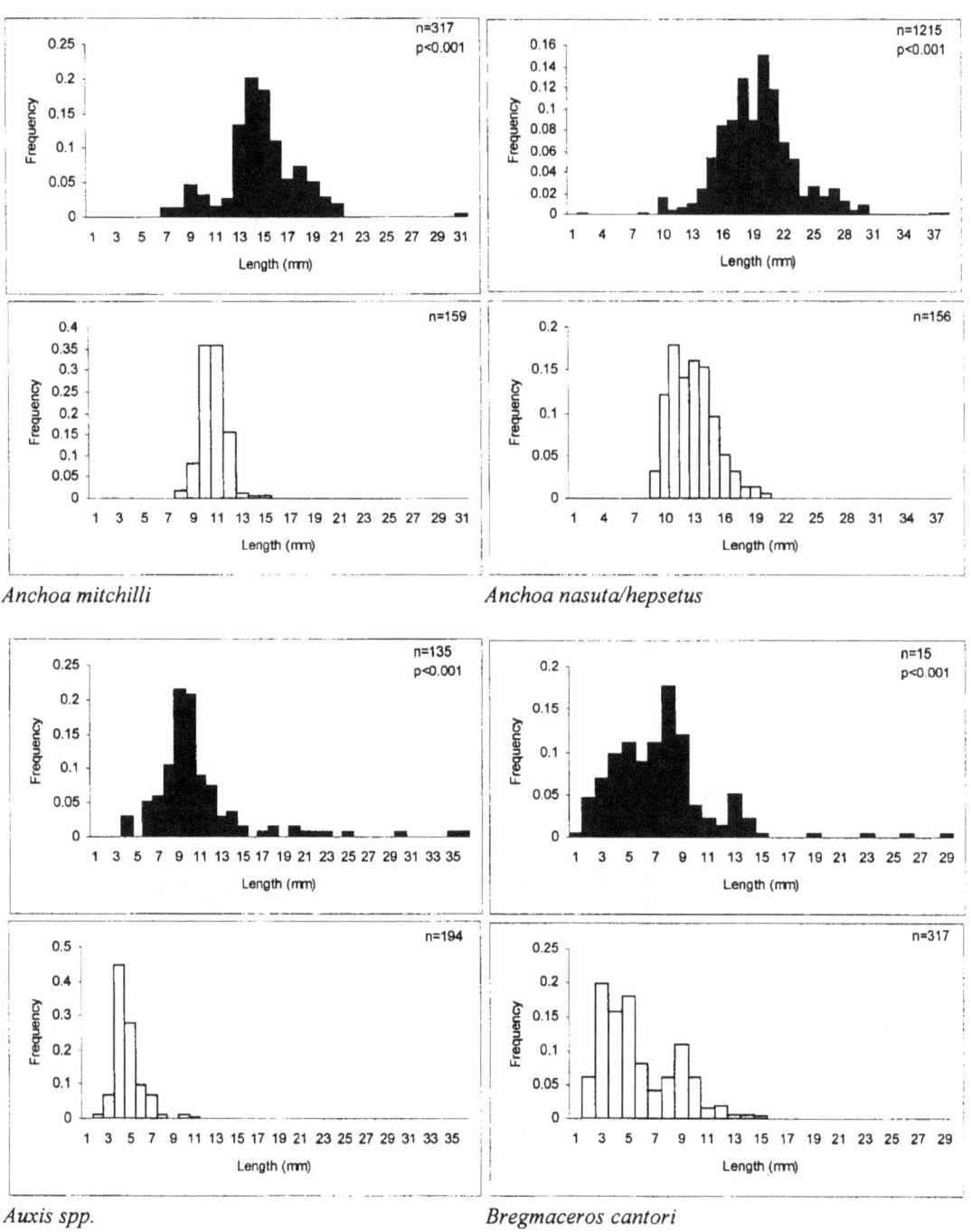

Figure 24. Size distributions of fish collected with light-traps (shaded bars) and plankton nets (open bars) at the Grand Isle site (1996). Fish length-frequency distributions were analyzed with Kolmogorov-Smirnov tests (p-values are represented in the upper panel of each gear pairing along with each sample size). For analyses, at least 10 individuals were required for each gear type.

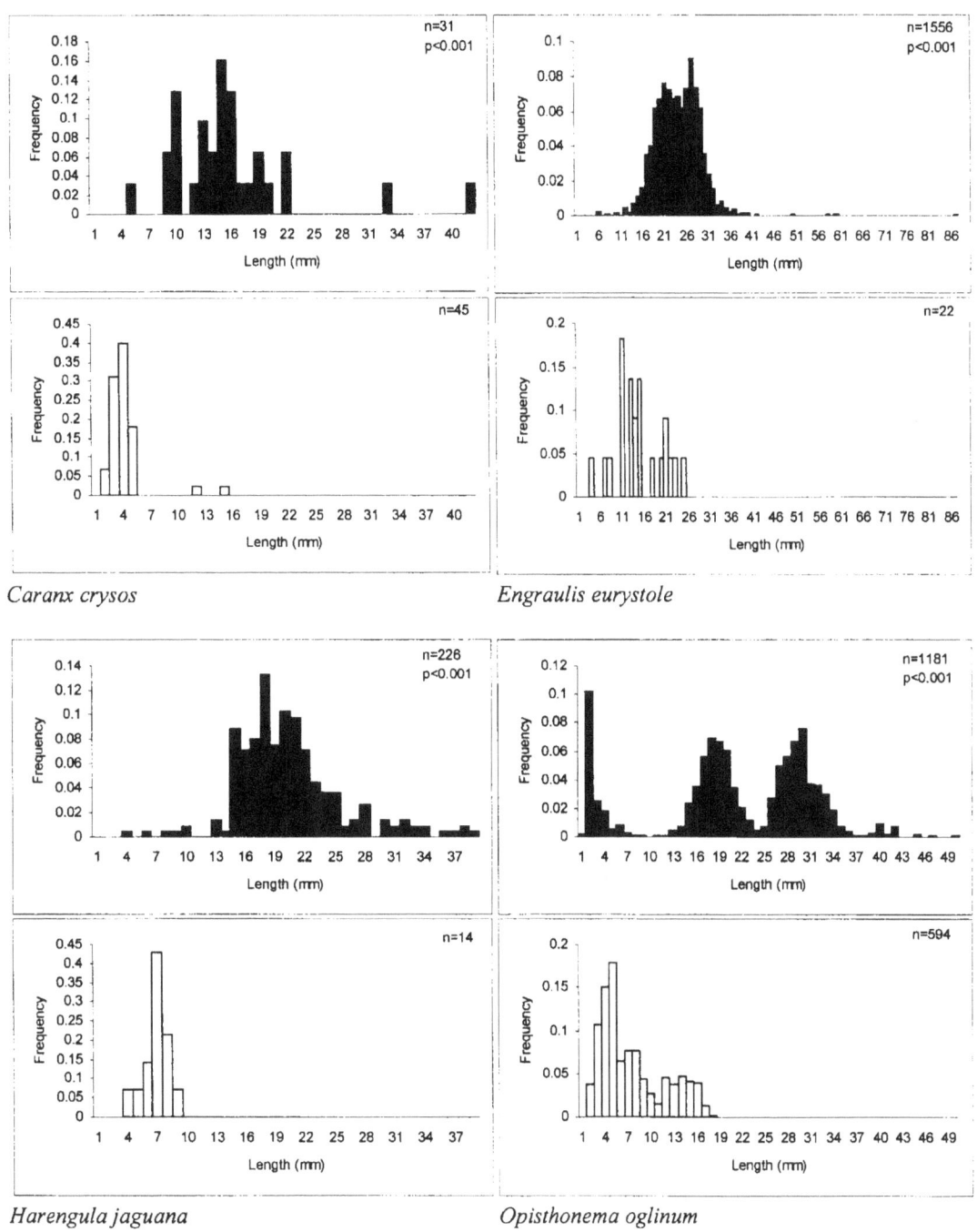

Caranx crysos

Engraulis eurystole

Harengula jaguana

Opisthonema oglinum

Figure 24. (continued)

85

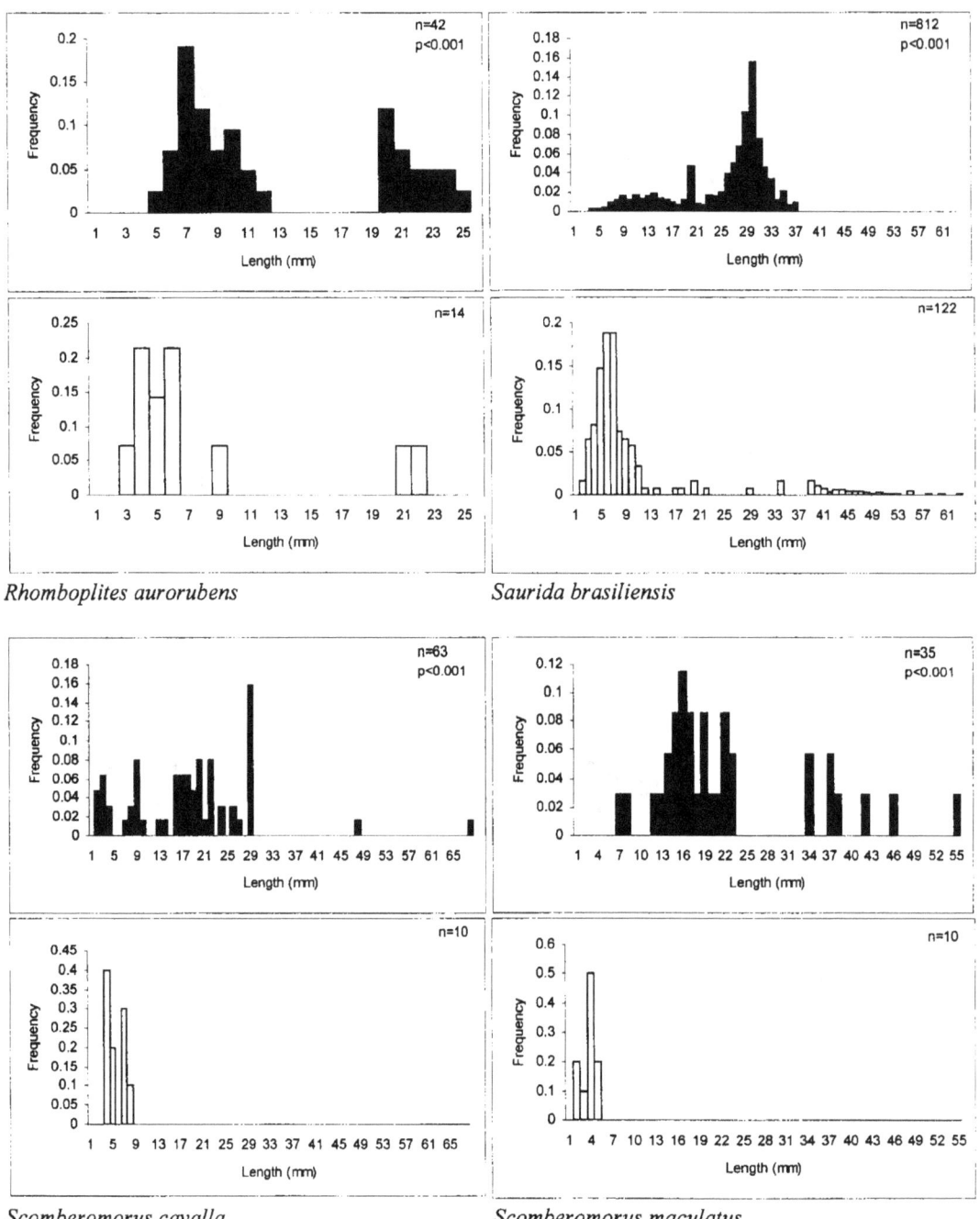

Rhomboplites aurorubens

Saurida brasiliensis

Scomberomorus cavalla

Scomberomorus maculatus

Figure 24. (continued)

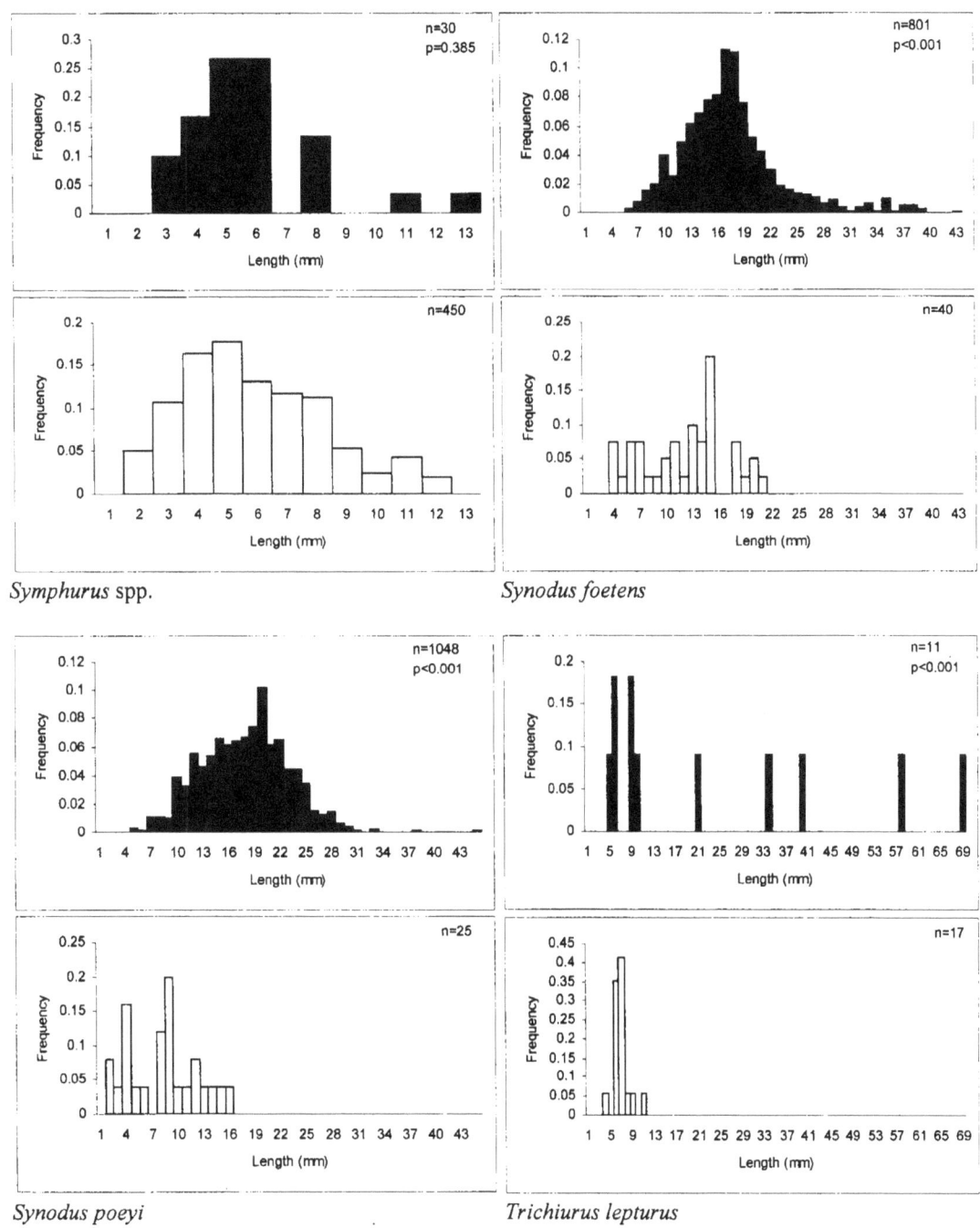

Symphurus spp.

Synodus foetens

Synodus poeyi

Trichiurus lepturus

Figure 24. (continued)

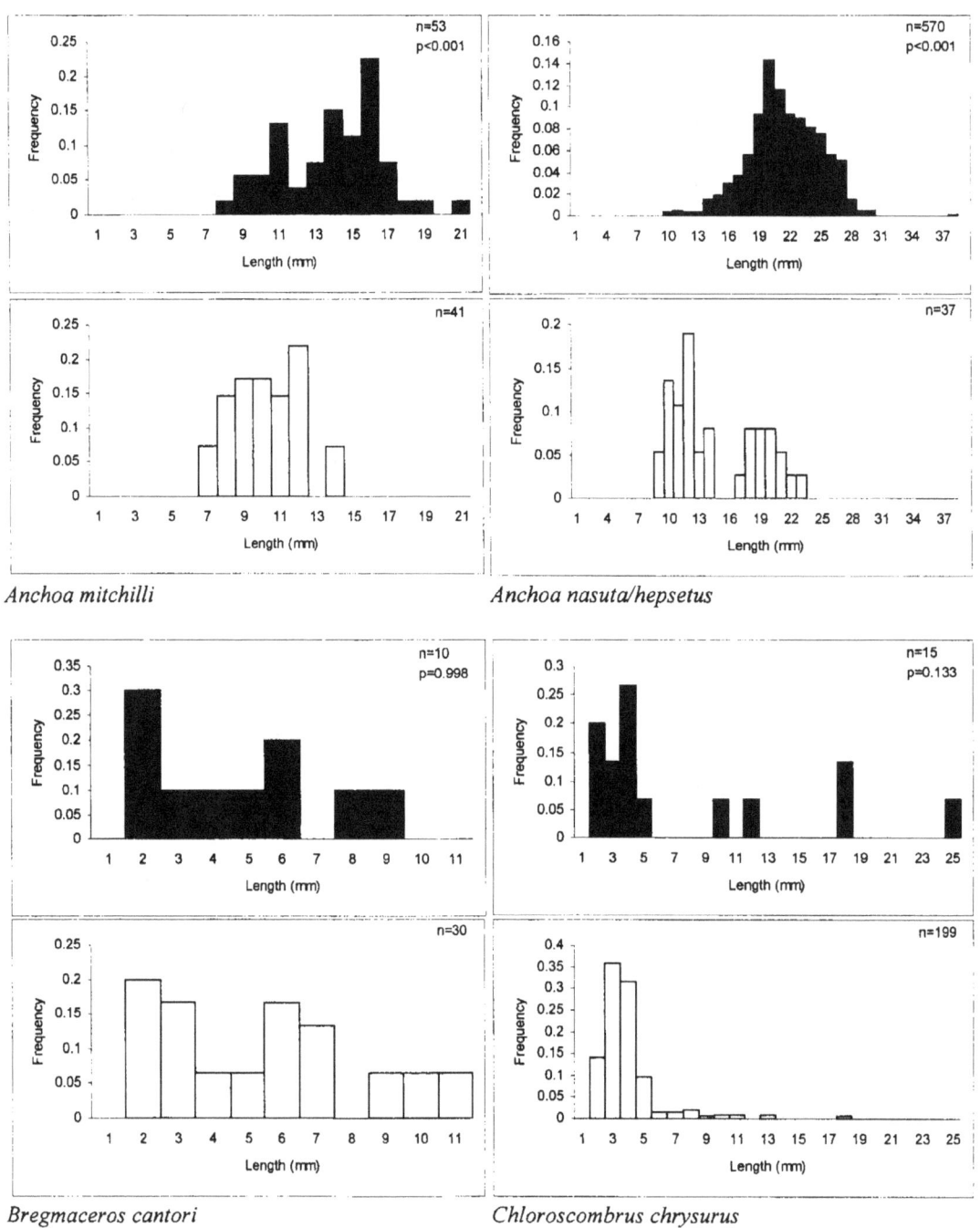

Figure 25. Size distributions of fish collected with light-traps (shaded bars) and plankton nets (open bars) at the South Timbalier site (1997). Fish length-frequency distributions were analyzed with Kolmogorov-Smirnov tests (p-values are represented in the upper panel of each gear pairing along with each sample size). For analyses, at least 10 individuals were required for each gear type.

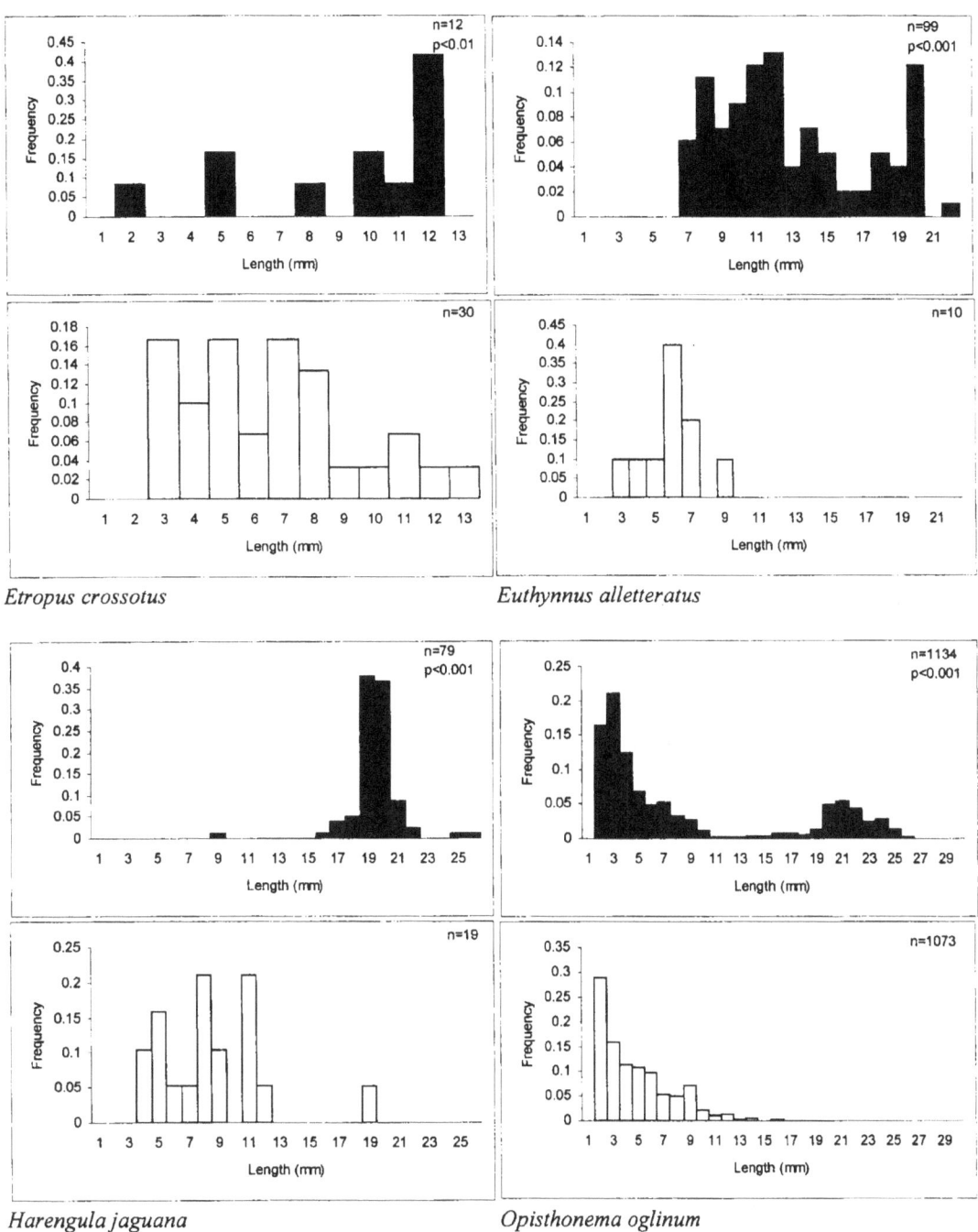

Etropus crossotus

Euthynnus alletteratus

Harengula jaguana

Opisthonema oglinum

Figure 25. (continued)

89

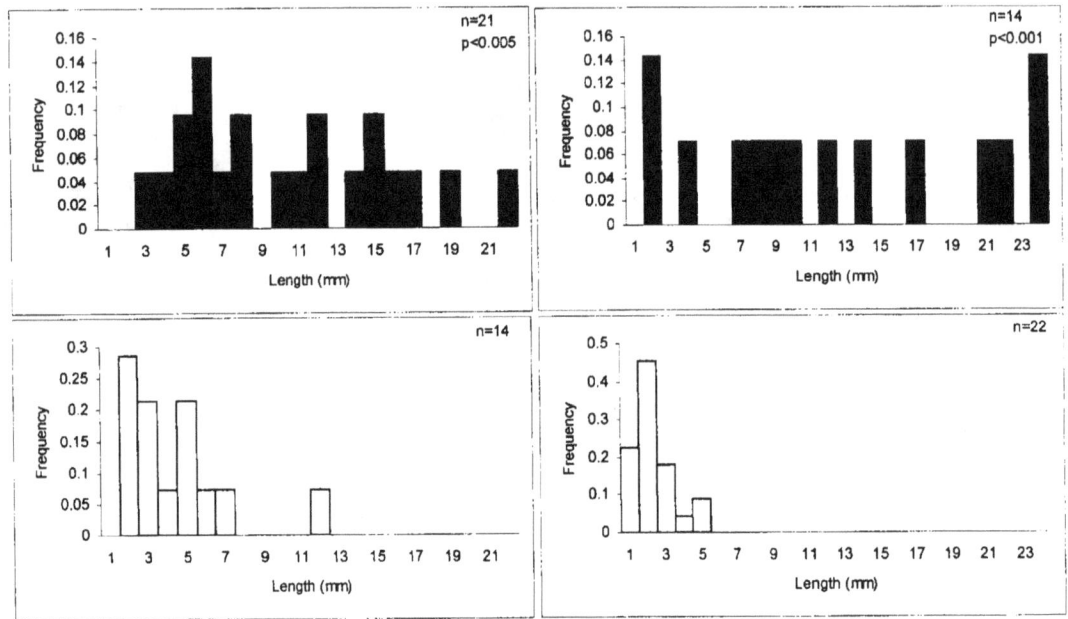

Peprilus burti   *Peprilus paru*

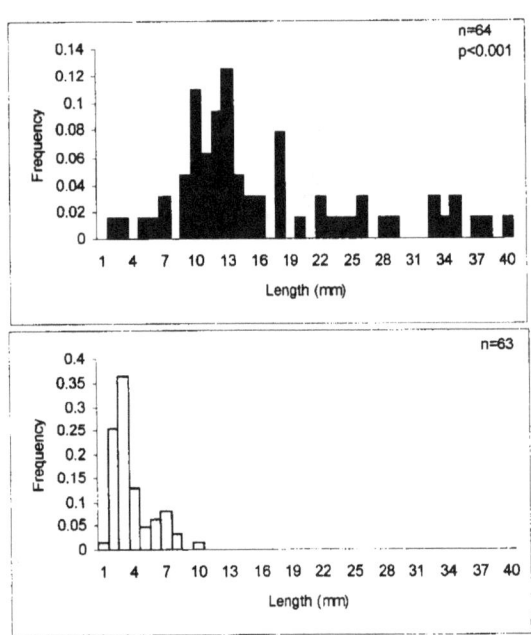

Scomberomorus maculatus

Figure 25. (continued)

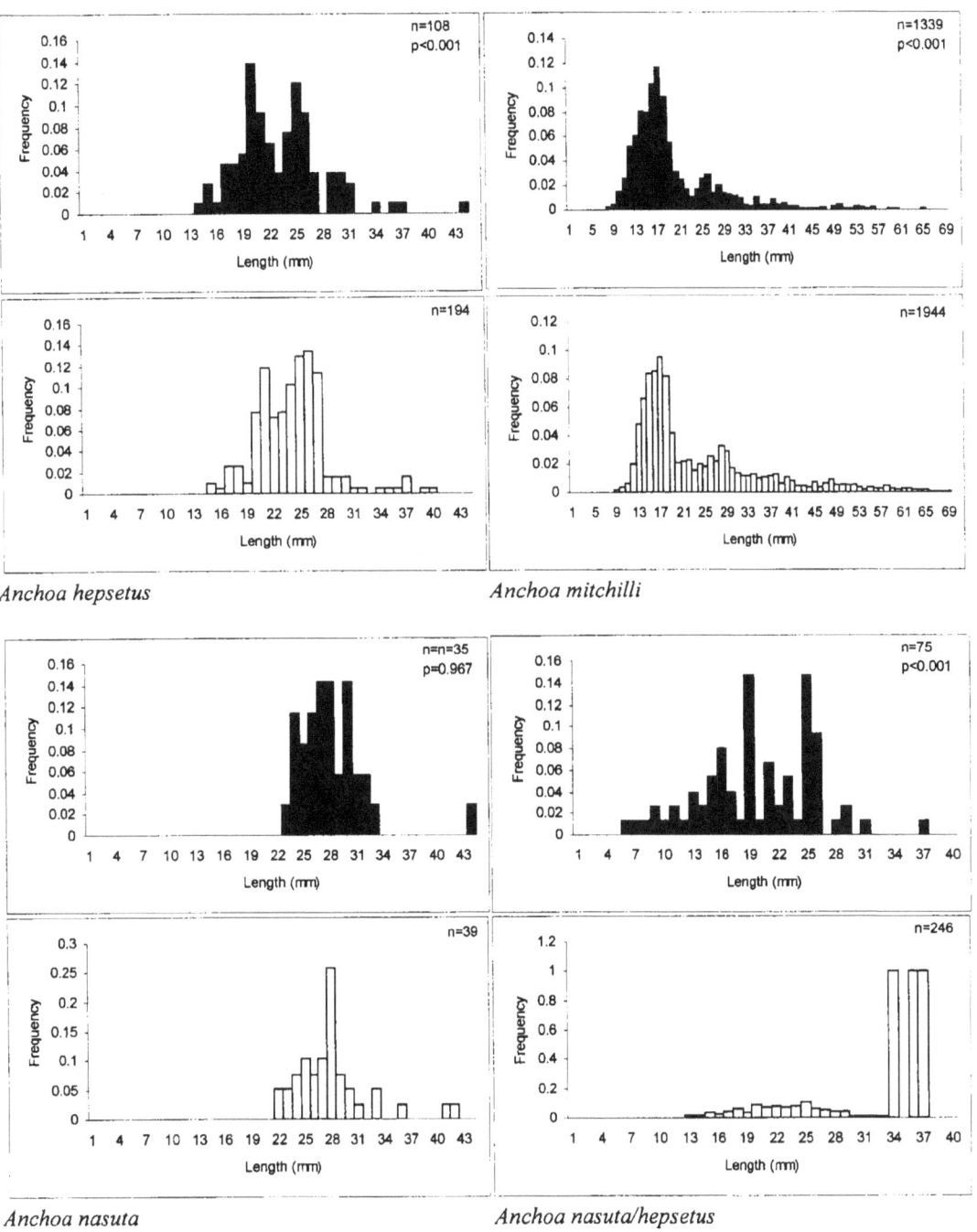

Figure 26. Size distributions of fish collected with light-traps (shaded bars) and a pushnet (open bars) at the Bell Pass site (1997). Fish length frequency distributions were analyzed with Kolmogorov-Smirnov tests (p-values are represented in the upper panel of each gear pairing along with each sample size). For analyses, at least 10 individuals were required for each gear type.

91

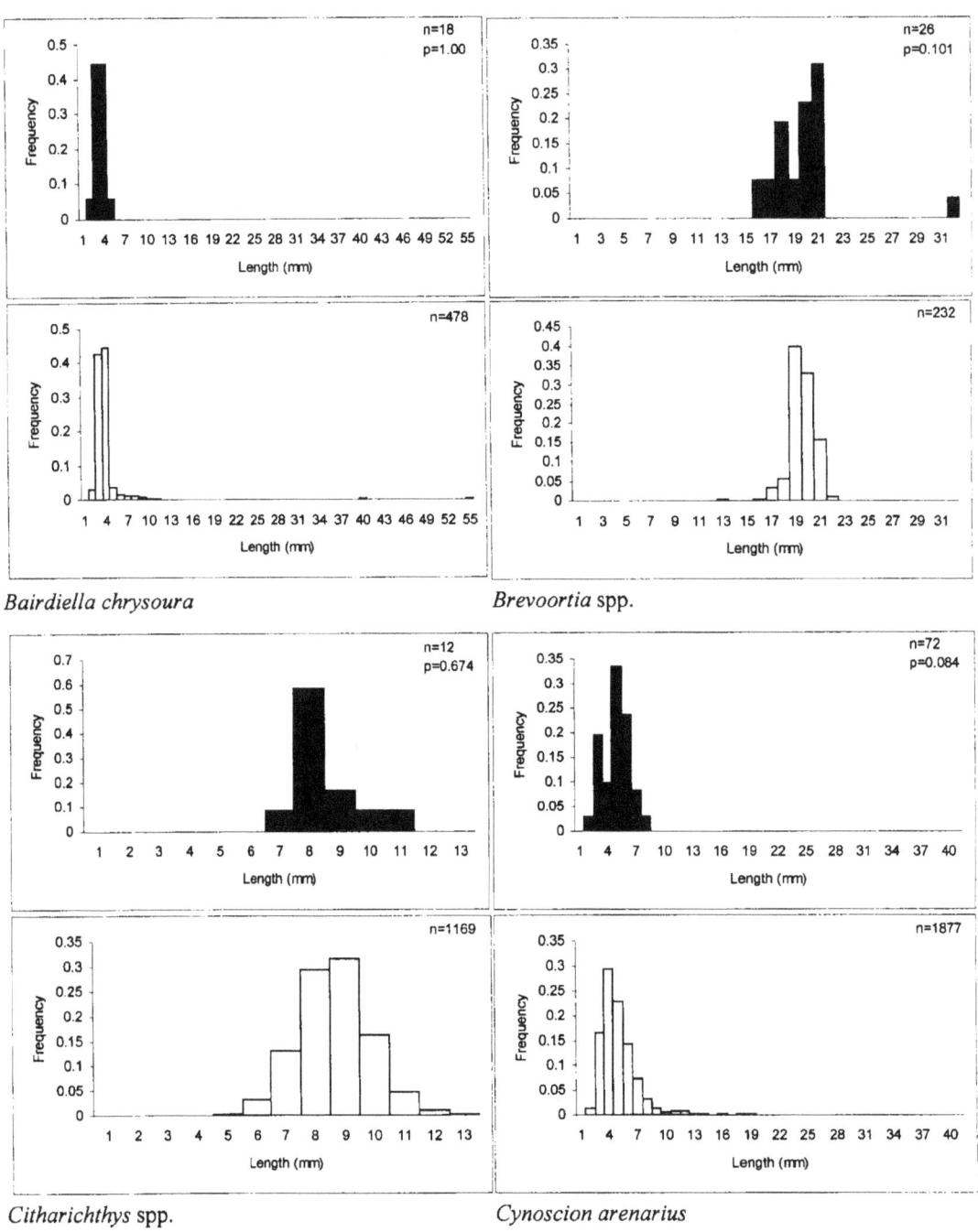

Bairdiella chrysoura

Brevoortia spp.

Citharichthys spp.

Cynoscion arenarius

Figure 26. (continued)

92

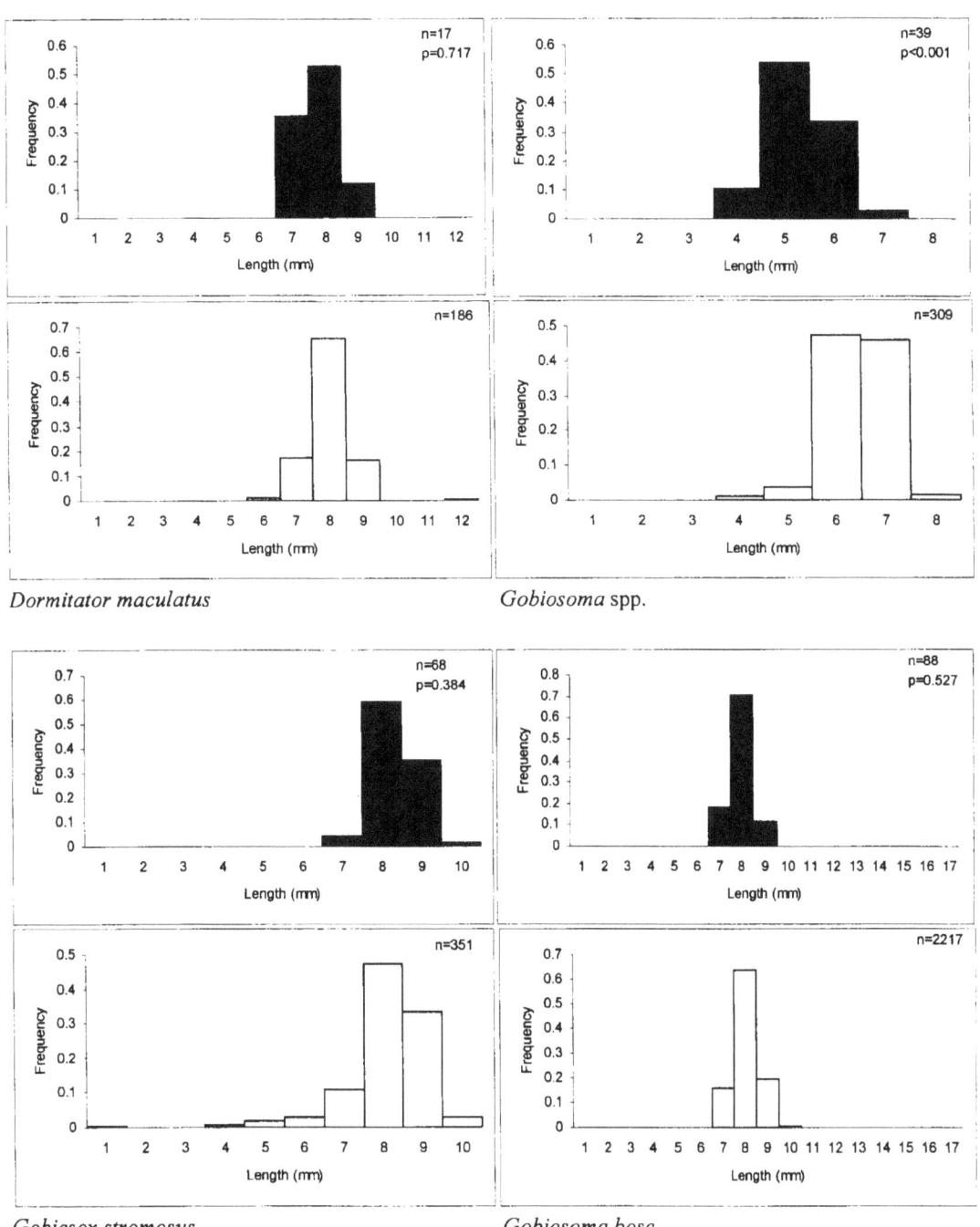

Dormitator maculatus

Gobiosoma spp.

Gobiesox stromosus

Gobiosoma bosc

Figure 26. (continued)

93

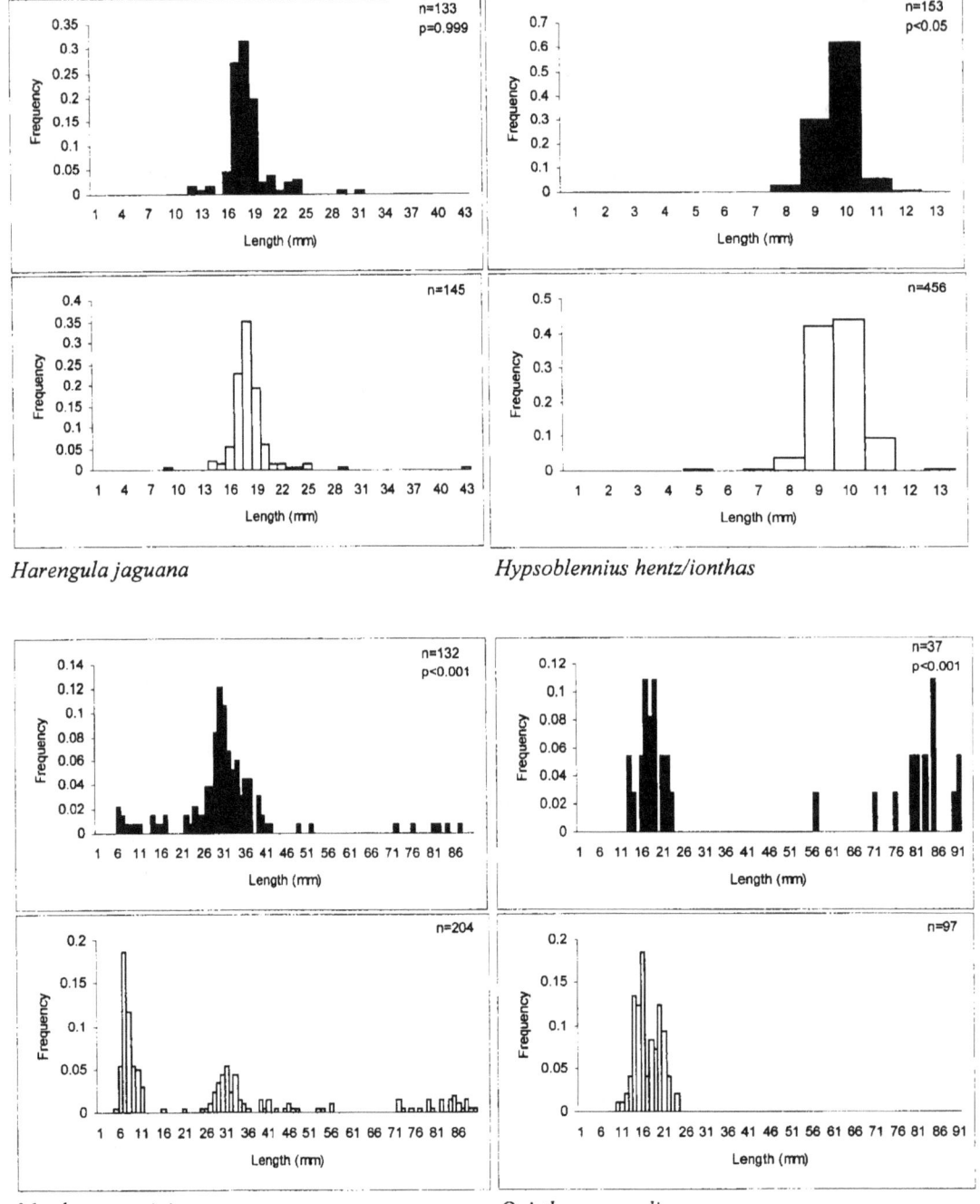

Harengula jaguana

Hypsoblennius hentz/ionthas

Membras martinica

Opisthonema oglinum

Figure 26. (continued)

94

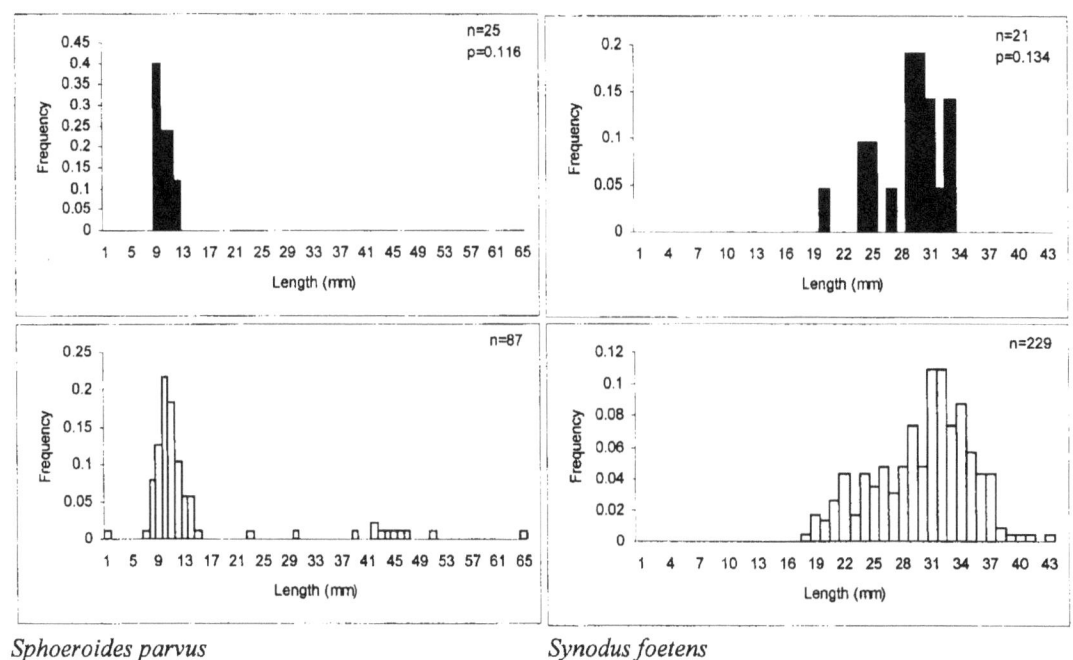

Sphoeroides parvus　　　　　　　　*Synodus foetens*

Figure 26. (continued)

both gear types, but the pushnet samples collected a more complete spectrum of larger individuals with greater frequency. There was also a good degree of overlap in the size distributions for *A. nasuta/hepsetus*, *Gobiosoma* spp., and *Hypsoblennius hentz/ionthas*, but in each instance the pushnet samples collected larger individuals with greater frequency, although with *Gobiosoma* spp. the light-trap collections had a smaller modal length. In contrast, light-trap size distributions for *Membras martinica* and *Opisthonema oglinum* had an intermediate dominant mode or an additional larger mode, respectively. All of the other taxa analyzed did not have significant differences in size distributions between the two gear types.

By using multiple gears and methodologies, we were able to confirm the presence of a number of taxa with a full range of life history stages, ranging from recently-spawned larvae to juveniles. For example, at GC 18 the plankton net collected *Euthynnus alletteratus* individuals within a smaller size range (3.0-12.0 mm) than the light-trap (6.2-87.0 mm). If our plankton net collections were not supplemented with light-trap catches, we would have not been able to confirm the presence of larger juveniles at this site.

Lunar Periodicity

At GI 94, mean total CPUE for light-traps during full moon phases was significantly higher than during new moon phases (Student's t-test, $p<0.0004$; Figure 27a). This trend was reversed when clupeiforms were removed from these analyses ($p<0.0001$; Figure 27b). No significant difference was detected in mean plankton densities between the two lunar phases ($p<0.1128$; Figure 27c), but when clupeiforms were removed full moon densities were significantly higher ($p<0.0055$; Figure 27d). In general, the GI 94 comparison (May 1996) involving the three lunar phases (first quarter, new, and third quarter moon phases) yielded no significant differences in mean light-trap CPUEs between the three periods with or without clupeiforms (Tukey's Studentized Range test, $\alpha=0.05$; Figure 28a and b), although mean CPUEs appeared to be higher during the first quarter moon period, but not significantly so. Mean plankton net density was also significantly higher during the first quarter moon period, but not so when clupeiform fishes were removed from the analyses (Figure 28c and d).

At ST 54, both mean light-trap CPUE and mean plankton net density were higher during full moon phases than during new moon phases (Student's t-test, $p<0.01$; Figures 29a and c). Once clupeiform fishes were removed, however, there were no significant differences in CPUEs between new and full moon phases ($p<0.5635$; Figure 29b), while the trend reversed for plankton net densities, i.e., mean total density during new moon phases was significantly higher than during full moons ($p<0.034$; Figure 29d).

At Belle Pass, mean CPUEs and pushnet densities were significantly higher during new moon periods, with or without clupeiforms (Student's t-tests, $p<0.005$ and $p<0.0003$, respectively for light-traps and $p<0.0001$ for nets; Figure 30).

Belle Pass Sampling Station Comparisons

At the Belle Pass jetty, there was no significant difference (Tukey's Studentized Range test, $\alpha=0.05$; Figure 31a) in mean light-trap CPUE between the four sampling stations, i.e., west

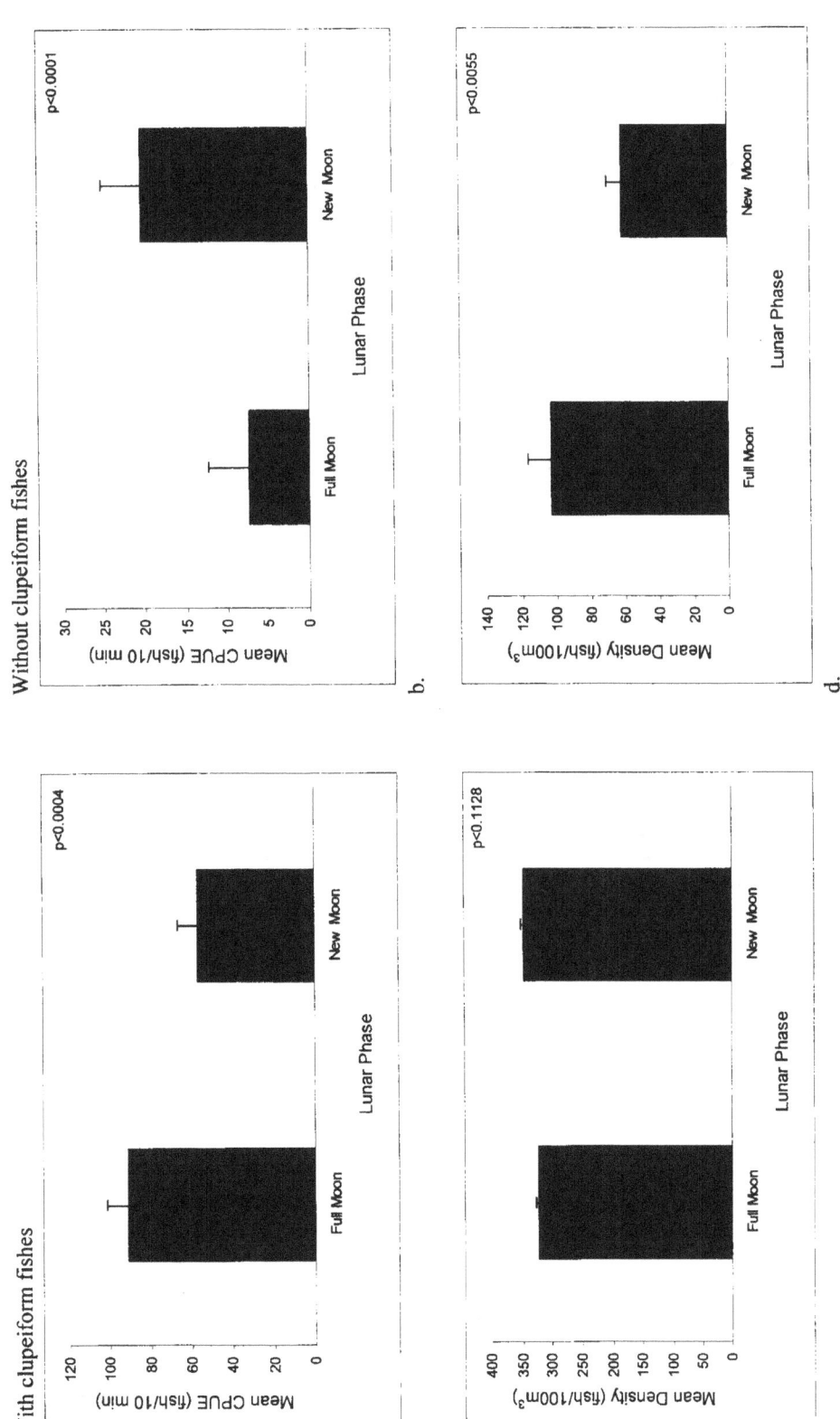

Figure 27. Mean light-trap CPUE and plankton net density (with standard error bars) for each lunar phase sampled at Grand Isle 94 (Apr.-Sept. 1996) for data with (a, c) and without clupeiform fishes (b, d) included. The p-values indicate statistical significance from t-tests.

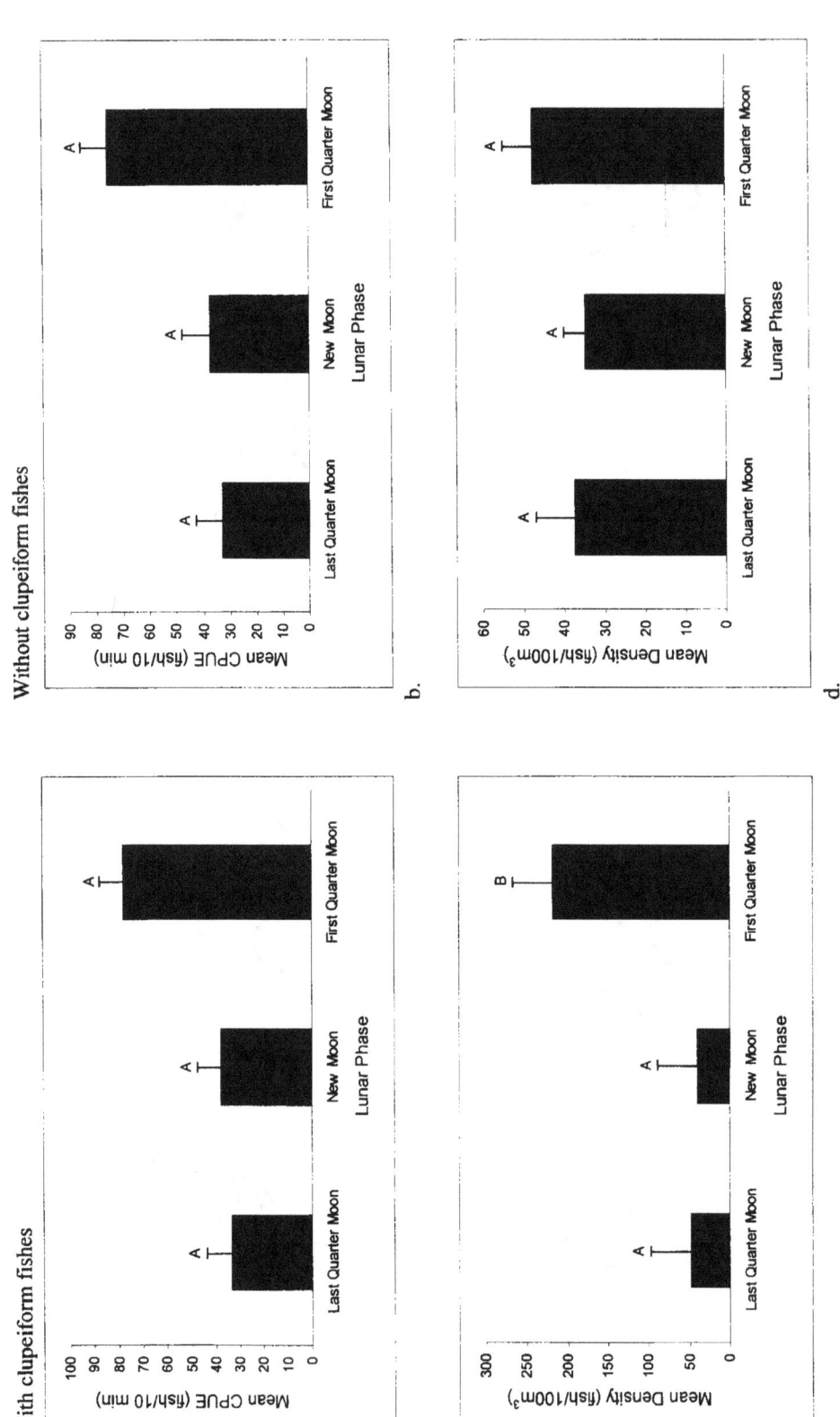

Figure 28. Mean light-trap CPUE and plankton net density (with standard error bars) for each lunar phase sampled in May 1996 at Grand Isle 94 for data with (a, c) and without clupeiform fishes (b, d) included. The same letter above each bar indicates no significant difference between the lunar phases based on Tukey's Studentized Range tests on ranked data (α=0.05). Different letters indicate significant differences.

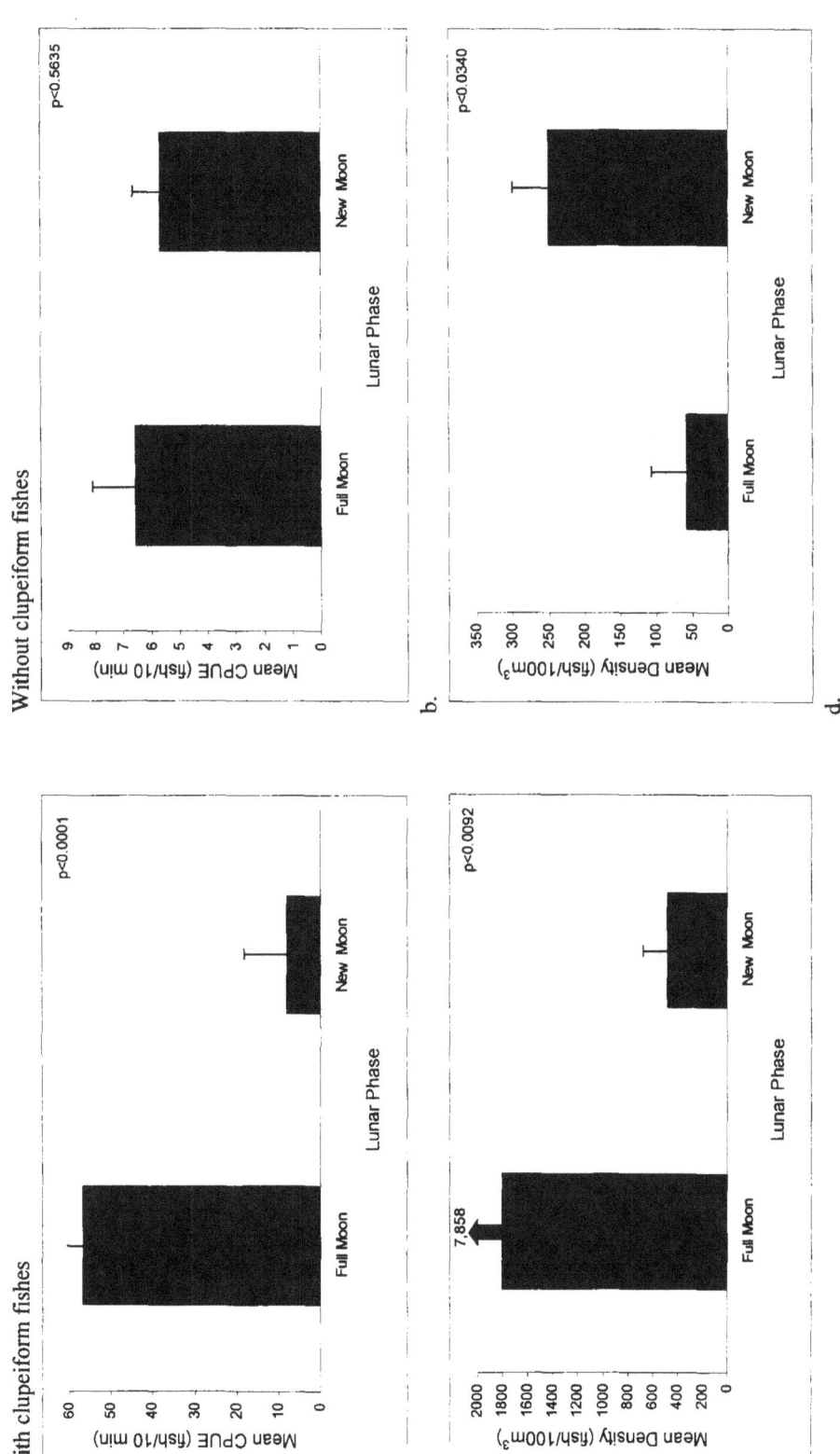

Figure 29. Mean light-trap CPUE and plankton net density (with standard error bars) for each lunar phase sampled at South Timbalier 54 (Apr.-Sept. 1997) for data with (a, c) without clupeiform fishes (b, d) included. The p-values represent statistical significance from t-tests.

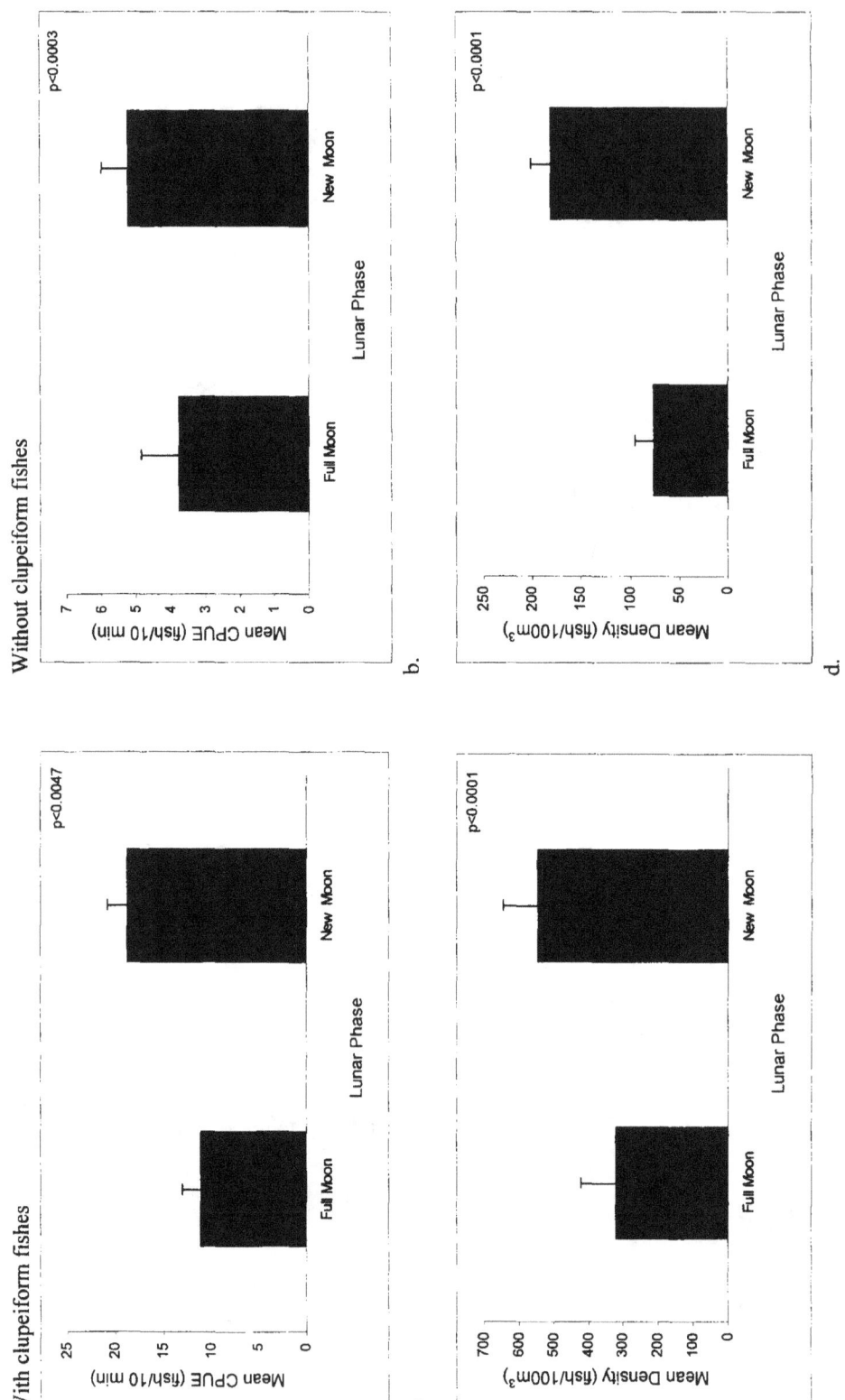

Figure 30. Mean light-trap CPUE and pushnet density (with standard error bars) for each lunar phase sampled at Belle Pass (Apr.-Sept. 1997) for data with (a, c) and without clupeiform fishes (b, d) included. The p-values represent statistical significance from t-tests.

100

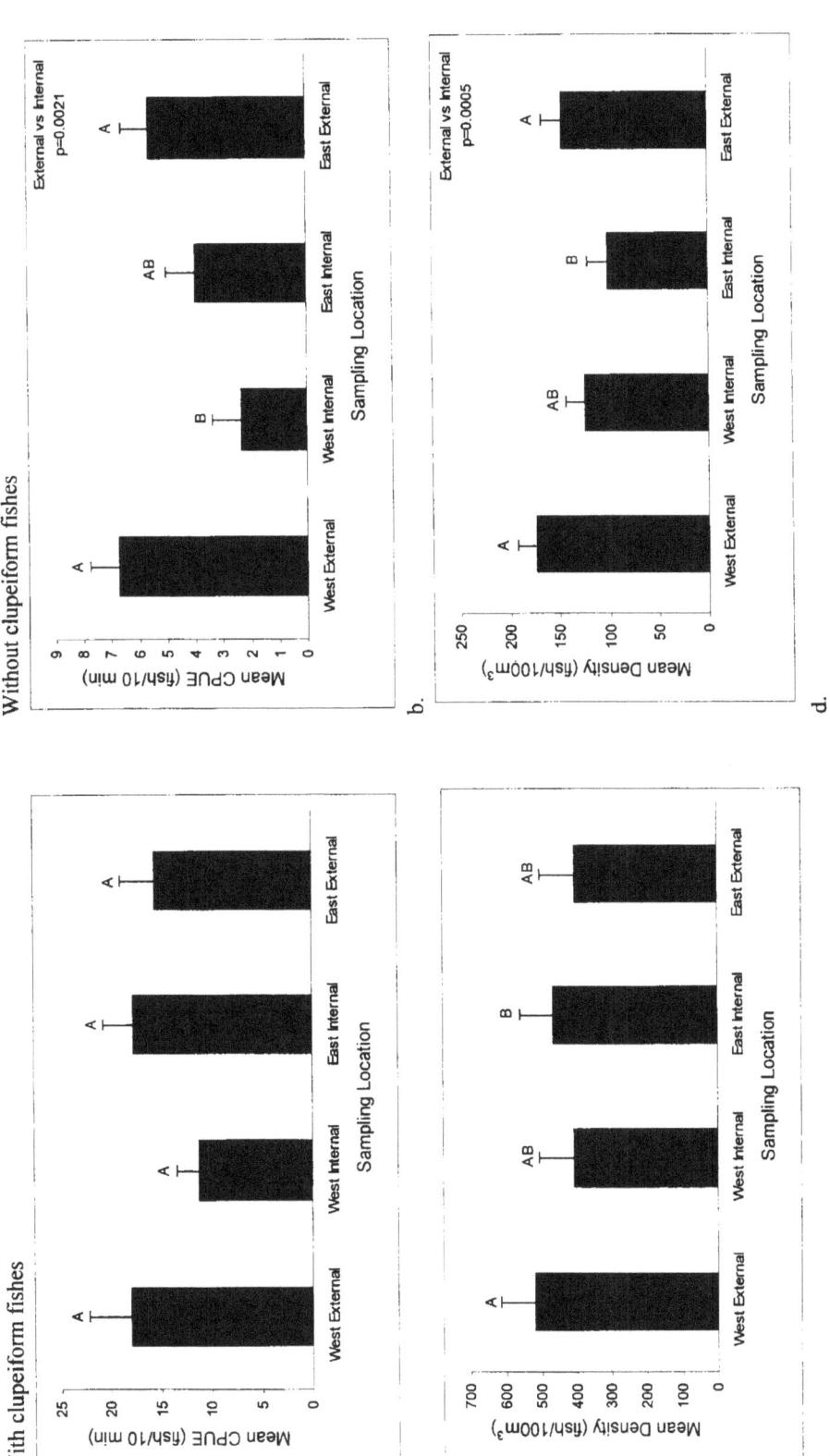

Figure 31. Mean light-trap CPUE and pushnet density (with standard error bars) for each station sampled at Belle Pass (1997) for data with (a, c) and without clupeiform fishes (b, d) included. The same letter above each bar indicates no significant difference between the stations based on Tukey's Studentized Range tests (α=0.05). Different letters indicate significant differences. Statistical contrast results (p-values) are presented for significant results only.

exterior (WE), west interior (WE), east interior (EI), or east exterior (EE). Once clupeiform fishes were removed from the analyses, however, mean CPUEs for the external stations (WE and EE) were significantly greater than that for the WI station, but not the EI station ($\alpha=0.05$; Figure 31b). Additionally, SAS statistical contrast results indicated an overall statistical difference between the external stations and internal (or estuarine) stations with higher mean CPUEs at the external stations. Mean pushnet density was significantly higher at the WE station than at the EI station, but no other differences were detected ($\alpha=0.05$; Figure 31c). Once clupeiform fishes were removed from the analyses, both external stations had significantly higher mean pushnet densities than the EI station, but not the WI station ($\alpha=0.05$; Figure 31d).

Similarity and Diversity of Larval and Juvenile Fish Assemblages Between Sites

Schoener's Index of Niche Overlap values range from 0 to 1 (no similarity to identical taxonomic compositions). Of the 14 comparisons between the six sites (i.e., the 3 platforms and jetty along the transect and the 2 pilot studies), Belle Pass, with values ranging from 0.01-0.07, and WC 352 (inner shelf), with values ranging from 0.01-0.16, differed the most from the other sites (Table 8). Inexplicably from the point of view of geography or water depth, the most similar sites (0.53) were GC 18 (shelf slope) and ST 54 (inner shelf) followed by GC 18 and WC 71D (western inner shelf/coastal) with a comparative value of 0.52. These relative similarities in taxonomic compositions changed when the single, most dominant taxon from each site was removed from the analyses. In many cases, the similarity indices were greater for adjacent sites: GI 94 (mid-shelf) and ST 54 (0.45); GI 94 and GC 18 (0.29); and ST 54 and Belle Pass (0.25). In other instances, although similarities were dramatically reduced, the values were still relatively high for sites that were distant from each other or represented large depth differences: ST 54 and GC 18 (0.35); WC 71D and GC 18 (0.31); and WC 71D and GI 94 (0.29).

The diversity data, however, were much more similar along the transect of the three platforms and the jetty. There was no significant difference in the diversity of the net samples (passive plankton net or pushnet) between the sites (platforms or Belle Pass; $\alpha=0.05$; Figure 32). The light-trap samples at GC 18 had significantly lower mean Shannon-Weiner diversity index values, while GI 94 had significantly higher mean diversity values than the other locations (Tukey's Studentized Range test, $\alpha=0.05$; Figure 32). The diversity of light-trap collections at the two more coastal sites, ST 54 and Belle Pass, were intermediate and not significantly different from one another.

Similarity and Diversity of Larval and Juvenile Fish Assemblages Within Sites

Within site comparisons of gears and surface sampling locations indicated that off-platform and surface light-trap collections were more similar to each other (0.45-0.76) than each was to surface plankton net collections (0.27-0.71), although the disparity between the index gear comparisons is smaller at ST 54 (0.59-0.71; Table 9). Overall, total light-trap collections were relatively different from total plankton net samples at GC 18 and GI 94 (0.38 and 0.32), but much more similar at ST 54 and Belle Pass (0.63 and 0.61), the two coastal sites, which were more strongly influenced by coastal herrings and anchovies.

Table 8. Schoener's similarity indices for all sampling sites. Values range from 0-1 (no similarity-identical) and include taxa (at least to the level of genus) from all gears used at each site. Values in parentheses represent indices calculated with the most dominant taxa from each site removed. (BP) Belle Pass, (ST) South Timbalier, (GI) Grand Isle, (GC) Green Canyon, (WC71D) West Cameron 71D, (WC352) West Cameron 352.

	GC 18	GI 94	ST 54	BP	WC 71D	WC 352
GC 18	1	.	.	.	.	.
GI 94	0.32 (0.29)[a]	1	.	.	.	.
ST 54	0.53 (0.35)[a]	0.15 (0.45)	1	.	.	.
BP	0.07 (0.15)[a]	0.07 (0.09)	0.02 (0.25)	1	.	.
WC 71D	0.52 (0.31)[b]	0.32 (0.29)[b]	0.17 (0.17)[b]	0.01 (0.06)[b]	1	.
WC 352	0.06 (0.13)[d]	0.16 (0.06)[c]	0.01 (0.12)[c]	0.03 (0.04)[c]	‡	1

[a] indices computed with April-August samples only
[b] indices calculated with July samples only
[c] indices calculated with April, May and August samples only
[d] index calculated with November, February, April, May and August samples only
‡ no seasonal overlap in sampling efforts between WC 352 and WC 71D

Table 9. Schoener's similarity indices for different surface gear and location comparisons. (OL) off-platform light-trap, (SL) surface light-trap, (SN) surface net, (TL) total light-traps, (TN) total nets.

	OL vs SL	OL vs SN	SL vs SN	TL vs TN
Green Canyon 18	0.53	0.32	0.31	0.38
Grand Isle 94	0.45	0.37	0.27	0.32
South Timbalier 54	0.76	0.71	0.59	0.63
Belle Pass			0.61	0.61‡

‡ calculation is the same as with SL vs. SN

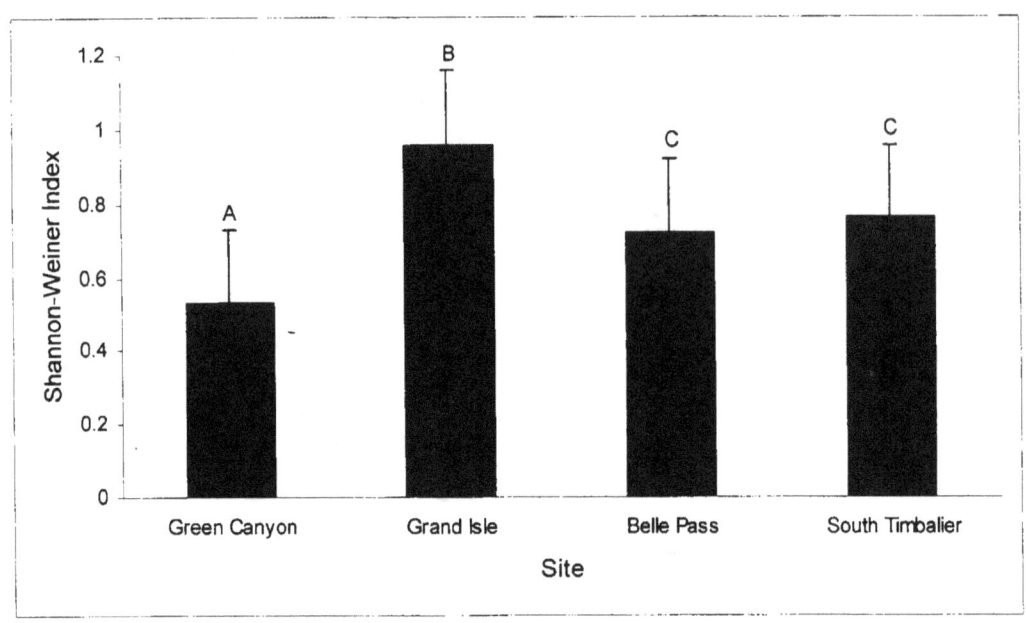

Light-traps

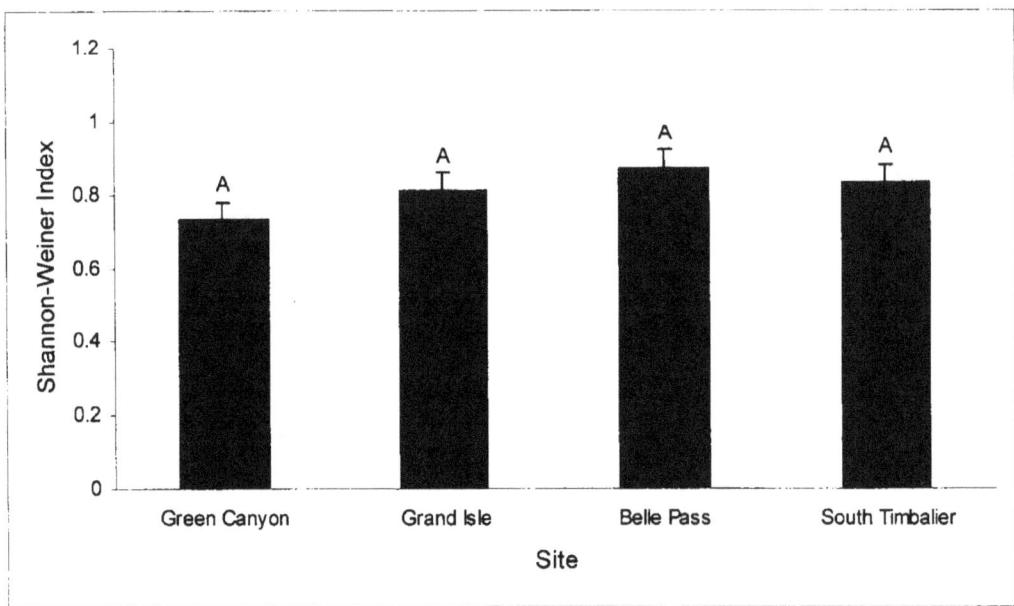

Plankton nets

Figure 32. Mean Shannon-Weiner diversity indices (with standard error bars) for light-trap collections and plankton net (GC 18, GI 94, and ST 54) or pushnet (Belle Pass) collections from each sampling site. The same letter above each bar indicates no significant difference between the sites based on Tukey's Studentized Range tests ($\alpha=0.05$). Different letters indicate significant differences.

104

There was little difference in the Shannon-Weiner diversity index values from gear and depth/location samples collected at GC 18 and ST 54 (Figure 33). In both instances, only subsurface light-trap samples had significantly lower diversity values than the other gear and depth/location combinations (α=0.05). No clear pattern in diversity was discernable at the GI 94 site other than surface net collections were significantly different from light-trap collections and that off platform light-trap collections were different from net collections regardless of depth. At the Belle Pass site, pushnet samples were significantly more diverse than the light-trap samples.

Environmental Variables and Larval and Juvenile Fish Abundances

At GC 18, salinity and temperature were the most useful environmental parameters measured in describing trends in larval and juvenile fish abundances. For plankton net collections, densities of *Cynoscion arenarius*, *Scomberomorus maculatus*, and *Symphurus* spp. were negatively associated with the first environmental canonical variate, which was primarily influenced by salinity (Table 10). Densities of *Auxis* spp., *Caranx crysos*, *C. hippos/latus*, *Pristipomoides aquilonaris*, and *Sciaenops ocellatus* were positively associated with the second environmental canonical variate, which was marginally significant (p=0.068) and primarily influenced by temperature. Densities of *Citharichthys spilopterus* and *Mugil cephalus* were negatively associated with the second environmental variate. For the dominant taxa collected with light-traps, six taxa, primarily benthic species such as *Saurida brasiliensis*, *Microdesmus longipinnis*, *Syacium* spp., and *Symphurus* spp., were positively associated with the first environmental variate, which was negatively correlated with salinity and positively correlated with macrozooplankton biomass (Table 11). Five taxa, comprised mostly of pelagic taxa (i.e., *Auxis* spp., *C. crysos*, *C. hippos/latus*, and *Eucinostomus* spp.) were positively associated with the second environmental variate, which was primarily explained by temperature.

At GI 94, temperature contributed substantially to our model in describing trends in larval and juvenile fish abundances. For plankton net collections, densities of *Euthynnus alletteratus* and *Symphurus* spp. were positively associated with the first environmental variate, which was positively correlated with temperature and negatively correlated with salinity, while *Synodus foetens* was inversely correlated with this variate (Table 12). The second environmental variate was explained primarily by salinity, and was positively associated with the scombrids *Auxis* spp. and *E. alletteratus*. For dominant taxa collected with light-traps, abundances of the blenny *Parablennius marmoreus* and the lizardfishes *S. foetens* and *S. poeyi* were positively associated with the first environmental variate, which was positively correlated with salinity and negatively correlated with temperature (Table 13). A third lizardfish species, *Saurida brasiliensis*, and *E. alletteratus* were negatively associated with the first environmental variate. *Synodus foetens* was also negatively associated with the second environmental variate, which was correlated with low macrozooplankton biomass. The third environmental canonical variate was only marginally significant (p=0.067) and was positively correlated with macrozooplankton biomass. Abundances of *Caranx crysos*, *Pomacentrus* spp., *S. foetens*, and *S. poeyi* were positively associated with this environmental variate.

At ST 54, the seasonal variables temperature and salinity were again the most correlated with the environmental canonical variates. For plankton net collections, densities of the pelagic

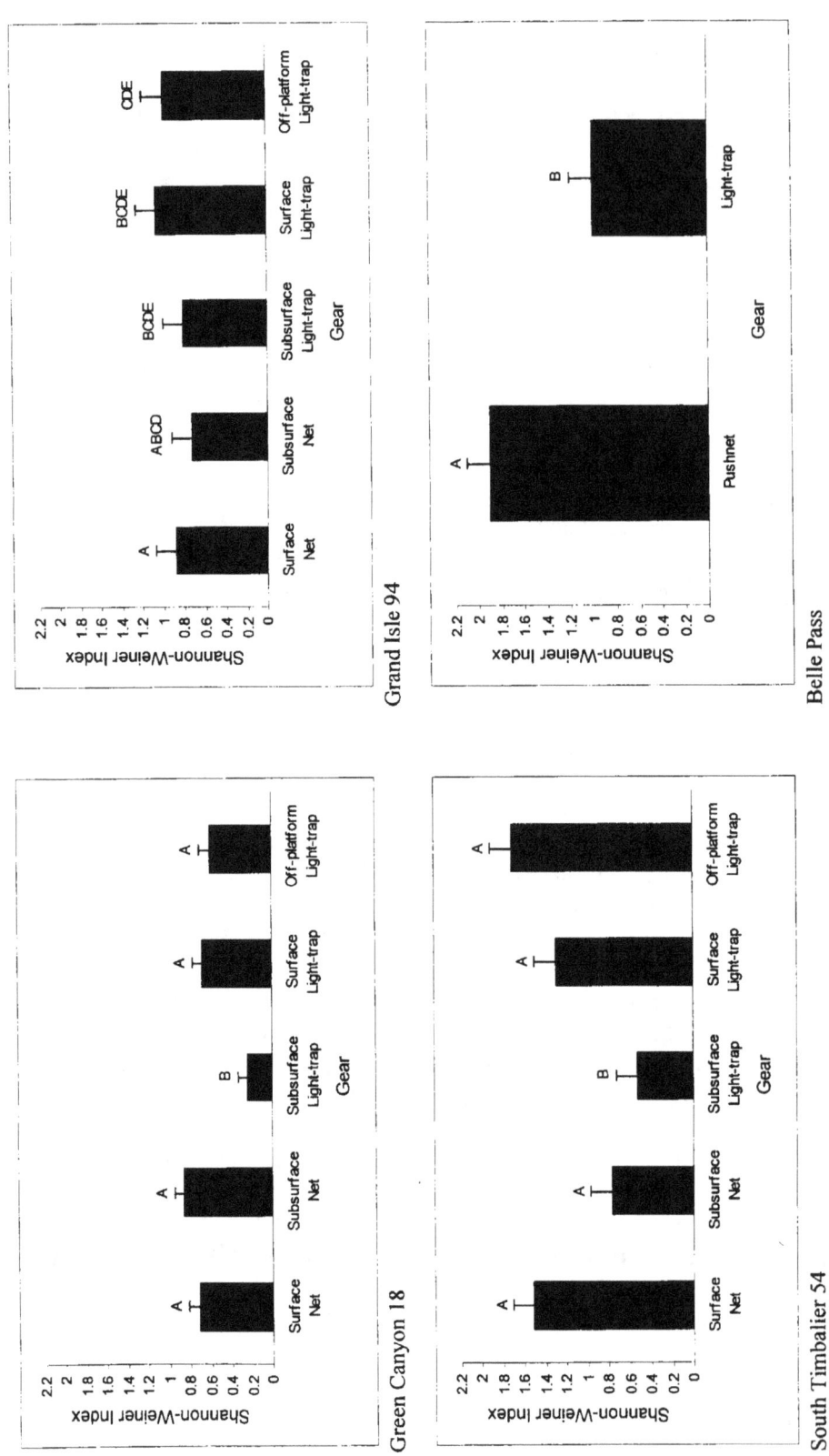

Figure 33. Mean Shannon-Weiner diversity indices (with standard error bars) for each gear type and sampling location for each site. The same letter above each bar indicates no significant difference between the gear types based on Tukey's Studentized Range tests (α=0.05). Different letters indicate significant differences.

Table 10. Results of a canonical correlation analysis on log-transformed plankton net densities (15 most dominant taxa) and environmental variables for Green Canyon 18. Loadings in bold under statistically significant canonical variates V1 and V2 explain at least 15% of the variation for that taxon. Loadings in bold under the environmental canonical variates W1 and W2 indicate the most influential environmental variables.

Canonical Correlation	Likelihood Ratio	Approximate F	Pr > F
1 0.750369	0.26739839	2.8134	0.0001
2 0.502430	0.61197053	1.3766	0.0680

Taxa	Correlations between plankton net densities and their canonical variates	
	V1	V2
Ariomma spp.	0.1426	-0.0114
Auxis spp.	0.0857	**0.5186**
Bregmaceros cantori	0.1748	-0.1150
Caranx crysos	0.2340	**0.6215**
Caranx hippos/latus	0.1016	**0.6166**
Citharichthys spilopterus	0.1724	**-0.4127**
Cyclothone braueri	0.1817	-0.1283
Cynoscion arenarius	**-0.7049**	0.1691
Lepophidium spp.	0.0850	0.0303
Mugil cephalus	0.2068	**-0.4356**
Peprilus burti	0.1115	-0.2048
Pristipomoides aquilonaris	0.1901	**0.4764**
Sciaenops ocellatus	0.0597	**0.4175**
Scomberomorus maculatus	**-0.7415**	0.0507
Symphurus spp.	**-0.7149**	-0.0638

Environmental Variables	Correlations between environmental variables and their canonical variates	
	W1	W2
Zooplankton Biomass	-0.3742	0.1562
Suspended Solids	0.0640	-0.2760
Salinity	**0.9829**	-0.1659
Temperature	-0.5120	**0.8549**

107

Table 11. Results of a canonical correlation analysis on log-transformed light-trap CPUEs (18 most dominant taxa) and environmental variables for Green Canyon 18. Loadings in bold under statistically significant canonical variates V1 and V2 explain at least 15% of the variation for that taxon. Loadings in bold under the environmental canonical variates W1 and W2 indicate the most influential environmental variables.

Canonical Correlation	Likelihood Ratio	Approximate F	Pr > F
1 0.566445	0.50304207	3.1136	0.0001
2 0.413382	0.74070398	1.8532	0.0004

Taxa	Correlations between light-trap CPUEs and their canonical variates	
	V1	V2
Auxis spp.	-0.3640	**0.5669**
Bregmaceros cantori	-0.0579	-0.0234
Caranx crysos	-0.1666	**0.6483**
Caranx hippos/latus	-0.1349	**0.3970**
Cyclothone braueri	0.2205	0.1095
Cynoscion arenarius	0.2667	0.1967
Eucinostomus spp.	-0.1460	**0.3976**
Euthynnus alletteratus	**0.4647**	0.3416
Gobiesox strumosus	0.1569	0.0549
Holocentrus spp.	-0.3507	**0.4954**
Microdesmus longipinnis	**0.3868**	0.1855
Mugil cephalus	-0.1229	-0.3138
Peprilus burti	-0.1153	-0.0422
Pomacentrus spp.	**0.5047**	0.2425
Saurida brasiliensis	**0.4637**	0.2239
Syacium spp.	**0.4087**	0.2510
Symphurus spp.	**0.5289**	0.2751
Trachinocephalus myops	-0.2060	0.2437

Environmental Variables	Correlations between environmental variables and their canonical variates	
	W1	W2
Zooplankton Biomass	**0.5991**	0.3731
Suspended Solids	-0.1026	-0.2868
Salinity	**-0.8725**	-0.4174
Temperature	0.3657	**0.9057**

Table 12. Results of a canonical correlation analysis on log-transformed plankton net densities (15 most dominant taxa) and environmental variables for Grand Isle 94. Loadings in bold under statistically significant canonical variates V1 and V2 explain at least 15% of the variation for that taxon. Loadings in bold under the environmental variates W1 and W2 indicate the most influential physical variables.

Canonical Correlation	Likelihood Ratio	Approximate F	Pr > F
1 0.588892	0.50402811	3.8641	0.0001
2 0.406611	0.77162236	2.0014	0.0002

Taxa	Correlations between plankton net densities and their canonical variates	
	V1	V2
Auxis spp.	0.0642	**0.5517**
Bregmaceros cantori	0.0074	0.0583
Caranx crysos	0.3272	0.0475
Chloroscombrus chrysurus	0.3167	-0.2754
Cynoscion arenarius	0.2667	-0.1755
Etropus crossotus	-0.1902	0.1164
Euthynnus alletteratus	**0.5109**	**0.5440**
Microdesmus lanceolatus	-0.1983	0.3366
Peprilus paru	0.2351	0.0501
Saurida brasiliensis	0.1278	0.0595
Sphraena guachancho	0.3473	0.1880
Syacium spp.	0.2955	-0.0865
Symphurus spp.	**0.7408**	-0.1918
Synodus foetens	**-0.5515**	-0.3527
Synodus poeyi	-0.1838	0.0322

Environmental Variables	Correlations between environmental variables and their canonical variates	
	W1	W2
Zooplankton Biomass	0.0176	-0.3841
Suspended Solids	-0.2643	0.0480
Salinity	-0.7272	**0.6783**
Temperature	**0.9987**	0.0063

Table 13. Results of a canonical correlation analysis on log-transformed light-trap CPUEs (16 most dominant taxa) and environmental variables for Grand Isle 94. Loadings in bold under statistically significant canonical variates V1, V2, and V3 explain at least 15% of the variation for that taxon. Loadings in bold under environmental variates W1, W2, and W3 indicate the most influential environmental variables.

Canonical Correlation	Likelihood Ratio	Approximate F	Pr > F
1 0.727366	0.36024110	8.2854	0.0001
2 0.407126	0.76494371	2.8369	0.0001
3 0.250076	0.91692543	1.4435	0.0647

Taxa	Correlations between light-trap CPUEs and their canonical variates		
	V1	V2	V3
Auxis spp.	0.3411	0.3626	0.0228
Bregmaceros cantori	-0.1958	-0.0774	-0.0539
Caranx crysos	-0.2602	-0.0894	**0.4223**
Caranx hippos/latus	0.3000	-0.2098	-0.1797
Chromis spp.	0.1613	0.3585	0.2160
Euthynnus alletteratus	**-0.4596**	-0.0891	0.2976
Hypsoblennius hentz/ionthas	0.2219	0.2988	0.3527
Hypsoblennius invemar	0.2575	0.2320	0.2696
Parablennius marmoreus	**0.7294**	0.0392	0.1578
Pomacentrus spp.	-0.0228	0.3720	**0.4550**
Rhomboplites aurorubens	-0.1795	0.0404	0.1092
Saurida brasiliensis	**-0.4268**	-0.3509	0.0881
Scartella/Hypleurochilus	0.3028	0.2477	0.1846
Symphurus spp.	-0.2566	0.0372	0.1930
Synodus foetens	**0.4688**	**-0.5865**	**0.4341**
Synodus poeyi	**0.4316**	0.0227	**0.5475**

Environmental Variables	Correlations between environmental variables and their canonical variates		
	W1	W2	W3
Zooplankton Biomass	-0.2046	**-0.5927**	**0.7534**
Suspended Solids	0.2965	0.0269	0.1712
Salinity	**0.8998**	0.3507	0.2520
Temperature	**-0.9412**	0.3281	-0.0758

Table 14. Results of a canonical correlation analysis on log-transformed plankton net densities (15 most dominant taxa) and environmental variables for South Timbalier 54. Loadings in bold under the statistically significant canonical variate V1 explain at least 15% of the variation for that taxon. Loadings in bold under environmental variate W1 indicate the most influential environmental variables.

Canonical Correlation	Likelihood Ratio	Approximate F	Pr > F
1 0.695653	0.29159946	1.3663	0.0552

Taxa	Correlations between plankton net densities and their canonical variates
	V1
Bregmaceros cantori	**-0.4343**
Caranx hippos/latus	0.0448
Chaetodipterus faber	-0.2547
Chloroscombrus chrysurus	**0.7188**
Cynoscion arenarius	0.3017
Etropus crossotus	**-0.5026**
Menticirrhus spp.	-0.1820
Microdesmus lanceolatus	0.2774
Ophidion nocomis/selenops	-0.2217
Peprilus burti	-0.1917
Peprilus paru	0.3096
Scartella/Hypleurochilus	-0.1934
Scomberomorus cavalla	0.1881
Scomberomorus maculatus	**0.4750**
Symphurus spp.	-0.0072

Environmental Variables	Correlations between environmental variables and their canonical variates
	W1
Zooplankton Biomass	0.1809
Suspended Solids	0.4344
Salinity	**0.9623**
Temperature	**0.7410**

Table 15. Results of a canonical correlation analysis on log-transformed light-trap CPUEs (16 most dominant taxa) and environmental variables for South Timbalier 54. Loadings under statistically significant canonical variates V1 and V2 explain at least 15% of the variation for that taxon. Loadings in bold under environmental canonical variates W1 and W2 indicate the most influential environmental variables.

Canonical Correlation	Likelihood Ratio	Approximate F	Pr > F
1 0.667016	0.38618143	2.6350	0.0001
2 0.472763	0.69571078	1.3486	0.0708

Taxa	Correlations between light-trap CPUEs and their canonical variates	
	V1	V2
Caranx crysos	**0.4844**	0.1927
Chloroscombrus chrysurus	**0.3888**	0.3043
Cynoscion arenarius	**-0.4716**	**0.4499**
Etropus crossotus	-0.1215	-0.2264
Euthynnus alletteratus	0.1801	0.0141
Gobiesox strumosus	-0.3192	0.3644
Hypsoblennius hentz/ionthas	-0.2699	0.0054
Hypsoblennius invemar	-0.1376	-0.2595
Peprilus burti	-0.3591	0.1883
Saurida brasiliensis	-0.1630	**-0.4101**
Scartella/Hypleurochilus	-0.1226	-0.1717
Scomberomorus cavalla	0.2114	-0.0868
Scomberomorus maculatus	**-0.4006**	-0.1659
Sphoeroides parvus	-0.0846	-0.1286
Synodus foetens	-0.3693	-0.2336
Trachinocephalus myops	-0.1217	-0.1479

Environmental Variables	Correlations between environmental variables and their canonical variates	
	W1	W2
Zooplankton Biomass	0.3169	0.1424
Suspended Solids	0.2328	-0.2829
Salinity	**0.7209**	**0.6438**
Temperature	**0.9880**	-0.1033

112

Table 16. Results of a canonical correlation analysis on log-transformed pushnet densities (15 most dominant taxa) and environmental variables for Belle Pass. Loadings in bold under the statistically significant canonical variates V1, V2, and V3 explain at least 15% of the variation for that taxon. Loadings in bold under environmental variates W1, W2, and W3 indicate the most influential environmental variables.

Canonical Correlation	Likelihood Ratio	Approximate F	Pr > F
1 0.746141	0.12473748	3.3677	0.0001
2 0.709788	0.28140077	2.6115	0.0001
3 0.553340	0.56711076	1.5750	0.0201

Taxa	Correlations between pushnet densities and their canonical variates		
	V1	V2	V3
Bairdiella chrysoura	-0.1343	0.3102	-0.1418
Citharichthys spp.	-0.0063	**0.6759**	0.0738
Cynoscion arenarius	0.2336	**0.7453**	0.3118
Cynoscion nebulosus	0.1423	**0.4605**	0.1065
Dormitator maculatus	**-0.6133**	0.2318	-0.2055
Gobiesox strumosus	**-0.7488**	0.2128	-0.1829
Gobionellus oceanicus	0.2488	0.2903	0.0099
Gobiosoma bosc	-0.3128	**0.5788**	0.0476
Gobiosoma spp.	-0.2878	-0.1962	**-0.4318**
Hypsoblennius hentz/ionthas	**-0.3878**	-0.1485	0.0130
Membras martinica	-0.2631	-0.3167	**0.7042**
Microgobius spp.	0.2499	-0.3423	-0.2313
Sciaenops ocellatus	0.2969	0.3477	0.2035
Symphurus spp.	-0.1966	0.2238	0.2620
Synodus foetens	-0.1768	0.3649	-0.2772

Environmental Variables	Correlations between environmental variables and their canonical variates		
	W1	W2	W3
Temperature	**0.9097**	0.1977	-0.1327
Salinity	0.0587	-0.0616	**0.9812**
Dissolved Oxygen	-0.0430	**0.8447**	-0.5265
Turbidity	0.3061	**-0.5865**	-0.4929

Table 17. Results of a canonical correlation analysis on log-transformed light-trap CPUEs (15 most dominant taxa) and environmental variables for Belle Pass. Loadings in bold under the statistically significant variate V1 explain at least 15% of the variation for that taxon. Loadings in bold under environmental canonical variate W1 indicate the most influential physical variables.

Canonical Correlation	Likelihood Ratio	Approximate F	Pr > F
1 0.679900	0.33598275	1.56599	0.0032

Taxa	Correlations between light-trap CPUEs and their canonical variates
	V1
Bairdiella chrysoura	0.2172
Chloroscombrus chrysurus	0.1320
Citharichthys spp.	-0.1391
Cynoscion arenarius	-0.2046
Dormitator maculatus	-0.1928
Gobiesox strumosus	**-0.8280**
Gobionellus oceanicus	0.1573
Gobiosoma bosc	-0.1403
Gobiosoma spp.	-0.1859
Hypsoblennius hentz/ionthas	**-0.6848**
Membras martinica	0.2208
Microdesmus longipinnis	0.0841
Sphoeroides parvus	**-0.6076**
Symphurus spp.	0.0819
Synodus foetens	-0.0705

Environmental Variables	Correlations between environmental variables and their canonical variates
	W1
Temperature	**0.7618**
Salinity	0.1838
Dissolved Oxygen	-0.2384
Turbidity	**0.4234**

species *Chloroscombrus chrysurus* and *Scomberomorus maculatus* were positively associated with the first environmental variate, which were marginally significant (p=0.0552) and positively influenced by salinity and temperature (Table 14). *Bregmaceros cantori* and *Etropus crossotus* were negatively associated with the first environmental variate. For light-trap collections, abundances of the carangids *Caranx crysos* and *Chloroscombrus chrysurus* were positively associated with the first environmental variate, which was positively correlated with temperature and salinity (Table 15). *Cynoscion arenarius* and *S. maculatus* were negatively associated with the first environmental variate. A second environmental canonical variate was marginally significant (p=0.0708) and was also influenced by salinity. Abundances of *Cynoscion arenarius* were positively associated with the second environmental variate and *Saurida brasiliensis* was negatively associated with the second environmental variate.

At Belle Pass, temperature, and to some extent salinity, were still influential environmental variables, but turbidity and dissolved oxygen were also important in our models. For pushnet collections, three common coastal taxa (*Dormitator maculatus, Gobiesox strumosus,* and *Hypsoblennius hentz/ionthas*) were negatively associated with the first canonical variate, which was explained primarily by temperature (Table 16). A second environmental variate was positively correlated with dissolved oxygen and negatively correlated with turbidity. Abundances of *Citharichthys* spp., *Cynoscion arenarius, C. nebulosus,* and *Gobiosoma bosc* were positively associated with the second canonical variate. Abundances of *Gobiosoma* spp. were negatively associated with the third environmental variate, which was positively correlated with salinity, while *Membras martinica* was positively associated with this variate. For light-trap collections, three taxa (i. e., *G. strumosus, H. hentz/ionthas,* and *Sphoeroides parvus*) were negatively associated with the first canonical variate, which was positively correlated with temperature, and to a lesser extent, turbidity (Table 17).

Discussion

Overall, reef-dependent taxa (e.g., chaetodontids, pomacentrids, labrids, and scarids) were relatively rare (Table 7). Pomacentrids and chaetodontids were collected only at the shelf slope and mid-shelf sites, while labrids and scarids were also collected at the inshore sites. Our total of 67 families collected at oil and gas platforms throughout the course of this study is comparable with previously published surveys from the Gulf of Mexico (61 families, Ditty et al. 1988; 74 families, Richards et al. 1984), but is generally less than surveys that included more tropical waters (85 families, McGowan 1985; 91 families, Limouzy-Paris et al. 1994; 96 families, Richards 1984; 100 families, Richards et al. 1993). While reef-dependent fish were uncommon, reef-associated fish (e.g., carangids, scombrids, blenniids) were much more common and many times represented a significant component of the community assemblage at each site.

Larval and Juvenile Fish Collected at GC 18

The ichthyoplankton community at GC 18 (230 m depth on the shelf slope, Gallaway's outer shelf zone of > 60 m) was dominated by coastal pelagic species, particularly engraulids and clupeids which accounted for 33% and 25% of the total catch by both gear types, respectively (Table 3). *Opisthonema oglinum* was the dominant species in the mid-to-late summer months, while unidentified engraulids peaked in November. *Engraulis eurystole* was also relatively common throughout the summer and early fall. Another pelagic species, *Mugil cephalus*, was relatively common in the fall-winter months and peaked in November. Larvae of *M. cephalus* are most commonly found over the outer to mid-shelf (Ditty and Shaw 1996), so their presence at our outer shelf sampling station is not surprising. Though the adults are common on the continental shelf and coastally (Hoese and Moore 1977), *M. cephalus* was not collected at the mid- or inner shelf platforms. This is primarily a result of our shortened sampling efforts (April-August or September) at the other platforms, which did not encompass their spawning season (October through March; Leard et al. 1995), so its relative larval abundance at these platforms is unknown. The carangids *Caranx crysos* and *C. hippos/latus* were relatively common, and though they are usually considered pelagic species, they congregate around platform structures (Table 1).

Some of the more abundant demersal taxa included the flatfish *Citharichthys spilopterus*, *Symphurus* spp., and *Syacium* spp., as well as the sciaenid *Sciaenops ocellatus* and bregmacerotid *Bregmaceros cantori*. While not unique to this site, the mesopelagic species, *Cyclothone braueri*, was common in subsurface net collections, and myctophids were present in subsurface light-trap collections. Though not abundant, other outer shelf species of note include *Diplophos taenia*, *Chlorophthalamus agassizi*, *Scopelarchoides* spp., *Paralepis atlantica*, and *Lestrolepis intermedia*. While the adults are seldom observed, the planktonic nature of the early life history stages of these mesopelagic taxa made them a significant component of the outer shelf ichthyoplankton assemblage at GC 18.

The presence of preflexion *S. ocellatus* individuals at this offshore site in September was unexpected, as they are commonly found on the inner shelf and near coastal inlets (Ditty et al. 1988). Ripe adults of this species have been found as far as 4.8 km offshore (Murphy and Taylor 1990) and early larval stages have been collected as far as 17-34 km offshore (Lyczkowski-Shultz et al. 1988), suggesting either some offshore spawning may occur or that periodic offshore transport events may occur. Green Canyon 18 is located approximately 179 km offshore in 230 m of water and it is unlikely that local spawning is occurring at these depths. More likely, the presence of these larvae was related to hydrographic features in the area at the time of sampling. The July and August sampling trips which preceded our collection of *S. ocellatus* were characterized by intrusions of low salinity water (Figure 4). While the mean surface salinity was more typical of offshore waters by September (35 ppt), it is possible that the area was seeded with these larvae (or eggs) when inshore waters were advected offshore. To our knowledge, this is the furthest offshore account of the larval stages of this species in the northern Gulf (Patillo et al. 1997).

The most dominant reef-associated fishes at GC 18 were unidentified gobiids. Second in abundance were serranids, most of which were from the poorly known subfamily Anthiinae. Anthiine adults are residents of rocky reefs on the outer shelf and are not usually found on shallow, inshore reefs (Thresher 1984). Other serranids included *Epinephelus* spp. and *Mycteroperca* spp. Lutjanids were also fairly common among the reef fish taxa, primarily *Pristipomoides aquilonaris*, one of the most common residents of mid- and outer shelf reefs (Hoese and Moore 1977). Other noteworthy taxa included unidentified blennies, *Holocentrus* spp.(reef-associated), and *Pomacentrus* spp. (reef-dependent).

The relatively low abundance of reef fish larvae and juveniles compared to pelagic species at our outer platform site is in contrast to the adult community described by Gallaway (1981). However, the studies cited in Gallaway's (1981) synthesis were primarily visual (SCUBA diver) surveys interested in adult fishes associated with the natural and artificial structures, and not necessarily taxa in the surrounding water column. Pelagic species, therefore, may have been underestimated in those previous studies. Also, reef fish communities are limited, in part, by the supply of pelagic larvae, usually from upstream sources rather than the resident populations (Sponaugle and Cowen 1996; Victor 1986). Reefs and platforms located on the shelf slope would theoretically have significantly fewer upstream sources of potential recruits than those on the mid-shelf, where other natural hard-bottom or reef habitats may be more abundant, or where the density of platforms is orders of magnitude greater. Therefore, the extremely remote location of GC 18 (shelf slope) is probably the limiting factor with regards to the pool of available larvae to be sampled or for recruitment to the platform.

Larval and Juvenile Fish Collected at GI 94

At GI 94 (60 m depth, Gallaway's mid-shelf zone of 20-60 m), pelagic species dominated the catches as well, but there appeared to be a taxonomic shift in dominance. Clupeiforms again dominated the collections, but engraulids became more prominent in abundance (57%) than clupeids (9%). Unidentified engraulids were the most abundant pelagic taxa in the plankton nets, and *Engraulis eurystole* were very common in light-trap collections (Table 4). *Opisthonema oglinum*, which was the most dominant clupeid at GC 18, ranked third in overall abundance. *Caranx crysos* and *C. hippos/latus* were not as dominant at this site as they were at GC 18, but as a family, the carangids had more species richness at GI 94. *Oligoplites saurus, Seriola dumerili/rivoliana, S. fasciata, Trachinotus carolinus*, and *T. falcatus/goodei* were all present at GI 94, but absent at GC 18. Similarly, *Rachycentron canadum*, although not very common, were also collected at GI 94 and not at GC 18. As with the carangids, *R. canadum* is also considered to be a reef-associated species.

Second in abundance to the pelagic forms at GI 94 were demersal taxa, particularly synodontids which comprised 14.7% of the total catch and were approximately equal to the total catch of all perciform fishes combined (15.1%). Unidentified synodontids, *Saurida brasiliensis, Synodus foetens*, and *Synodus poeyi* were very common in the late spring and summer months. Like the carangids, this group was more species rich at GI 94, with seven taxa identified to species as compared to three at GC 18. Other common demersal taxa included *Symphurus* spp., *Syacium* spp., and *Bregmaceros cantori*. Mesopelagic species were not as speciose and abundant as those at GC 18, but some were collected, including *Cyclothone braueri, Vinciguerria nimbaria*, and *Lestrolepis intermedia*.

Overall, there was greater taxonomic richness among reef fish at GI 94 than GC 18. By far the most dominant reef-associated fish taxa at GI 94 were blenniids, particularly *Parablennius marmoreus* and *Hypsoblennius invemar*. These fishes are perhaps one of the most common taxa affiliated with oil and gas platforms, but are probably underestimated in visual surveys due to there small size, cryptic coloration, and tendency to hide in attached barnacle shells. Some blenniids have been found to be rather unusual compared to other common reef-associated taxa in that they have demersal eggs and pelagic, yet fairly competent larvae that

117

appear to be able to feed immediately and are attracted to light (Thresher 1984). If the same early life history attributes are true for the blennies collected at our platform sites, then these traits may combine to form a mechanism by which these taxa are retained and concentrated around platform structures. Other reef taxa that hatch from demersal eggs and have demonstrated photopositive behavior include gobies and pomacentrids, although these larvae are not as competent upon hatching (Thresher 1984). At GI 94, unidentified gobiids and pomacentrids, primarily *Chromis* spp. and *Pomacentrus* spp., ranked next in abundance. Unique to this site was the collection of opisthognathids in surface waters (plankton nets as well as surface and off-platform light-traps) during the spring-early summer. Adult *Opisthognathus aurifrons* are reported to be tropical (south Florida, Bahamas, northern South America) and rarely collected on the mid-to-outer shelf (Hoese and Moore 1977; Robins et al. 1986). Adult *O. lonchurus* are also reported to inhabit the northeast Gulf as well as tropical waters (Robins et al. 1986). The presence of these larvae reinforces the notion that oil and gas platforms may play a role in extending the ranges of more tropical forms that would otherwise be habitat limited in the northcentral Gulf.

Other taxonomic differences in reef-associated fish composition were observed between GI 94 (mid-shelf) and GC 18 (outer shelf). At GI 94, lutjanids were also relatively common, with *Rhomboplites aurorubens* the dominant species, followed by *Lutjanus* spp. While *Pristipomoides aquilonaris* was the primary lutjanid at GC 18, none were collected at this mid-shelf site. With regards to serranids, the dominant group was serraniines (e.g., *Diplectrum* spp., *Centropristis* spp., and *Serranus* spp.), while relatively few anthiines were collected. Also noteworthy was the relatively high abundance of mullids collected at GI 94 (only one individual was collected at GC 18), particularly *Upeneus parvus*, a common species on the mid-to-inner shelf (Hoese and Moore 1977).

Larval and Juvenile Fish Collected at ST 54

At ST 54, clupeiform fishes (mostly clupeids) overwhelmed the plankton net and light-trap collections, and comprised 97% of the total catch (all gears combined). The dominant clupeid was *Opisthonema oglinum*, which alone comprised 94% of the total catch (Table 5). *Harengula jaguana*, though present at GI 94, were more prominent at ST 54. This trend of increasing dominance of clupeiform fishes continued as our sampling efforts moved inshore. In general, it is difficult to discuss the abundances of the other taxa except in very relative terms, since no families of fishes (with the exception of clupeids and engraulids) comprised over 1% of the total catch. Among pelagic fishes, the reef-associated carangids and scombrids were relatively abundant, particularly *Caranx hippos/latus*, *Euthynnus alletteratus*, and *Scomberomorus maculatus*.

Similar to GI 94, the second most abundant group of fishes at ST 54 was composed of demersal species. However, unlike GI 94 where synodontids dominated, sciaenids were the most dominant family, primarily *Cynoscion arenarius*, which was collected throughout the sampling season. Not only did the number of sciaenids increase, but the number of their taxa increased as well, from three at GI 94 to five at ST 54. *Cynoscion arenarius* dominated the plankton net catches, but synodontids, primarily *Synodus foetens,* dominated the light-trap collections. Synodontids were not as prominent at ST 54 as they were at GI 94, and the number of taxa decreased from 7 to 4. Other demersal taxa collected included unidentified myctophiforms, *Trichiurus lepturus*, *Symphurus* spp., and *Etropus crossotus.*

The most abundant reef/structure-associated fishes were blenniids and gobiids. Unlike GI 94, *Parablennius marmoreus* was relatively uncommon. The dominant species at ST 54 were *Scartella/Hypleurochilus* spp., *Hypsoblennius hentz/ionthas,* and *H. invemar.* Difficulties in identification prevent us from confidently separating *H. hentz* from *H. ionthas* and *Scartella* spp. from *Hypleurochilus* spp. but all of these taxa are common in nearshore areas and hard-bottomed habitats, such as oyster reefs and pilings (Hoese and Moore 1977). In general at ST 54, reef fish, although not abundant, were relatively well represented in terms of number of taxa, rivaling that of GI 94. However, other than blenniids and gobiids, abundances of other reef fish were very low (less than a total of 10 individuals collected per taxa) but included *Rhomboplites aurorubens* and unidentified pomacentrids, serranids, and ephippids.

The low reef fish abundances are not surprising, particularly for the more tropical taxa such as haemulids, labrids, and scarids. The adults of these taxa are more typical of the outer shelf assemblages (Table 1). Similarly with regards to reef fish larvae and juveniles, this trend of decreasing taxonomic richness towards the more inshore environments is supported somewhat by our study, particularly with regards to scarids (Tables 3-5). Even though an inner shelf platform would be downstream from potentially more offshore and along-shelf sources of larvae and recruits, perhaps the relatively greater distances involved necessitating extended pelagic larval durations and the potentially less favorable inshore environmental conditions result in increased mortality (Leis 1991).

Larval and Juvenile Fish Collected at the Belle Pass Jetties

The jetty at Belle Pass, though different in its structural complexity, vertical height, and hydrodynamics shared at least one similarity with the platforms in that it was also dominated by clupeiform fishes (74% of total catch). The taxonomic composition of this group was different, however, in that engraulids, particularly *Anchoa mitchilli*, dominated catches (Table 6). The trend of increasing numbers of *Harengula jaguana* and *Brevoortia patronus* as the sampling sites moved progressively inshore continued as well. Another difference was the relatively high abundance of a different pelagic group, the atherinids, particularly *Membras martinica*, a common coastal pelagic species.

By far the most dominant demersal species was *Cynoscion arenarius*, and in general, the number of sciaenid taxa increased from the platform sites. *Bairdiella chrysoura* was also relatively common. *Micropogonias undulatus, Sciaenops ocellatus, Pogonias chromis*, and *C. nebulosus* were all collected as well, none of which were collected at ST 54 and GI 94, although some *M. undulatus* and *S. ocellatus* were collected at GC 18. The jetty site also commonly had the predominantly estuarine species, *Gobiesox stromosus*. The ophichthid eels were most abundant at Belle Pass where they were also the most speciose taxonomic group, with *Myrophis punctatus* being the dominant species. The flatfish *Citharichthys* spp. and *Symphurus* spp. were also very common.

The reef/structure-associated fish group was dominated by small, estuarine/coastal species, primarily *Gobiosoma bosc*, which comprised 75% of the gobiids collected. This species is very common in coastal areas of the northern Gulf, and the adults are typically found in association with weeds and oyster beds in protected bays and estuaries (Hoese and Moore 1977; Robins et al. 1986). The second most abundant gobiid was *Gobionellus oceanicus* (formerly *Gobionellus hastatus*) which comprised 14% of the total catch. Adults of this species are common in estuaries but are also found in deeper waters (22-40 m) on the shelf (Hoese and Moore 1977). Other common gobiid taxa were *Microgobius* spp. and *Gobiosoma* spp. Based on the dominance of estuarine species collected at Belle Pass within this family, it is likely that the individuals in these two genera are also estuarine forms, even though these genera contain tropical forms as well. Taxa from a related group, the eleotrids, were also relatively common in our jetty samples. Blenniids were also a very common group, particularly *Hypsoblennius hentz/ionthas* and *Scartella* spp. Other reef or structure-associated fish taxa collected at Belle Pass include labrids, ephippids, scarids, and sparids.

Lutjanus griseus and *L. synagris* juveniles, though not abundant, were also collected at Belle Pass. *Lutjanus griseus* juveniles are more common along the western Gulf and Florida coasts where they are collected in their preferred habitat, relatively high salinity seagrass beds (Patillo et al. 1997) or mangroves. However, they have been reported (although less frequently) in association with other structures, such as pilings, jetties and rocks (Starck 1971). Young *L. synagris* are also present in coastal areas (Hoese and Moore 1977). The presence of these species at the jetty is noteworthy because it indicates that coastal, artificial structures even in relatively low salinity environments may play a role as nursery areas in absence of other structurally-complex habitats, such as grassbeds in more high-salinity, oligotrophic estuaries. Many species of reef-associated or reef-dependent fish do not settle directly onto reefs but utilize other coastal habitats as nursery grounds prior to moving to offshore reefs. While habitats such as high-salinity seagrass beds are important to many reef related species (Connolly 1994), other structurally-complex habitats have been identified as nurseries (Ferrell and Bell 1991; Bennett 1989; Ross and Moser 1995). Seagrass beds are often the most common form of shelter available in certain settlement areas, but experimental evidence suggests that presettlement larvae of a number of different species select any structurally-complex habitat at the time of settlement (Bell et al. 1987). Due to the overwhelming influence of the Mississippi River and its distributaries, Louisiana estuarine and coastal areas are generally low salinity (18-25 ppt at Belle Pass from April to September), turbid, and lacking in seagrass beds and naturally-occurring hard substrate habitats (except for oyster reefs). Therefore, the role of the artificial habitats such as jetties and breakwaters may be more important as islands of refuge for individuals that would otherwise be lost to unsuitable habitat and, therefore, elevated mortalities.

Taxonomic Similarity Between Sites

In an effort to examine the relative similarity in taxonomic assemblages between the different sites (including the western pilot study sites WC 71D and WC 352) we computed Schoener's Index of Similarity for each site. Since all sites sampled during this study were heavily dominated by a single taxon, for the sake of this discussion we will compare only the similarity values calculated after the dominant taxa were removed. In general, the index values indicate that the sites were not very similar, with the highest similarity value between any two sites being 0.45 for GI 94 and ST 54 (mid- and inner shelf). This is not unexpected since we purposely chose sampling sites in different depth zones across the shelf where there should be some faunal transitions (Gallaway et al. 1980; Gallaway 1981), and indeed there were in many instances. The Belle Pass jetty, which was heavily influenced by the presence of estuarine and coastal pelagic taxa, was very different from the mid-shelf (GI 94) and outer shelf (GC 18) platforms, where mesopelagic and tropical taxa were influential. Similarity indices for GI 94 displayed the expected cross-shelf transitional pattern, with the highest similarity values being for the adjacent sites, ST 54 and GC 18, followed by Belle Pass. The highest similarity index for GC 18, however, was with ST 54, the inner shelf platform, whereas we might have expected GC 18 to most similar to GI 94. This somewhat unexpected result is probably due to the large number of reef taxa collected at GI 94 that were unique to that site (Table 7). Reef fish taxa such as *Chromis* spp., *Abudefduf taurus, Mullus auratus, Ophioblennius atlantica, Pseudopeneus maculatus, Opisthognathus aurifrons*, and *Opisthognathus lonchurus* were collected only at the GI 94 platform. Other taxa (ephippids and scarids) were collected at GC 18 and ST 54, but not at GI 94.

The more westerly, pilot study sampling sites (Figure 1) were also included in these analyses and yielded interesting results. WC 352 (20 m depth) was the least similar to any of the other sites with similarity values ranging from 0.04-0.13 (April, May, and August samples only; Table 8). Within Gallaway's three depth zones, we would have expected this site to be relatively similar to ST 54 (approximately 20 m) in taxonomic composition. Between these two sites, 25 taxa were collected only at WC 352, including relatively large numbers of *Archosargus probatocephalus, Cypselurus cyanopterus, Microdesmus longipinnis*, and *Kyphosis* spp., whereas 41 taxa were collected only at ST54, including large numbers of *Cynoscion arenarius, Scomberomorus maculatus, Harengula jaguana*, and *Peprilus burti*. While all of these fishes are common inner shelf taxa, it would appear that the WC 352 site was influenced much more by its proximity to the Flower Gardens and the influence of the West Texas Current, which flows from Mexican waters northward along the Texas coast and seasonally progresses up along the western coast of Louisiana (Cochrane and Kelly 1986) and may be an additional source of reef or hard-substrate oriented fishes. Differences in local current and salinity and temperature regimes, as well as the timing and location of spawning events along the coast may have also resulted in the observed differences.

Interestingly, WC 71D (12 m) was most similar (0.31) to GC 18 (shelf slope) and least similar to ST 54 and Belle Pass (0.17 and 0.06, respectively; Table 8). This comparison, however, is confounded by July being the only month used for comparisons and by multiple light-trap designs being deployed at WC 71D. The dominant taxa at WC 71D were *Opisthonema oglinum* and *Anchoa* spp. (41% and 12% of total catch, respectively). These taxa were also dominant at GC 18 during July, where *O. oglinum* and *Anchoa* spp. comprised 34% and 19% of the total catch for July, respectively, resulting in a relatively high similarity index (0.52) between the two sites initially. However, this value decreased considerably once *O. oglinum* was removed from the analysis (0.31). The dominance by *Anchoa mitchilli* at Belle Pass (91% of total catch for July) and by other coastal taxa (*Euthynnus alletteratus, Parexocoetus brachypterus*, and *Mentichirrus* spp.) at ST 54 (55% of total catch for July) resulted in very small similarity indices between these sites and WC 71D. Differences between the WC stations (352 and 71D) and Belle Pass and ST 54 indicate that taxonomic assemblages may differ longitudinally along the coast as well as with depth, and point out the need for replicate platform sampling within each depth zone from different geographic areas. Ongoing efforts east of the Mississippi Delta may help resolve these issues and give us a more complete picture of ichthyoplankton assemblages collected at artificial structures across the northcentral Gulf.

While using a similarity index to characterize assemblages helps to synthesize large amounts of information, the analyses are confounded by several problems which can make the results difficult to interpret. First of all, the index is highly influenced by large numbers of individuals of a single taxon and confidence intervals can be quite large (Ricklefs and Lau, 1980). This is why we chose to discuss the values from the analyses without the most dominant taxa from each site, which helped to identify trends that may have otherwise been overwhelmed in the complete data set. Secondly, in any comparison between two sites, we chose only to use samples from each data set where the seasonality overlapped in sampling efforts. In this way, the same species pool would theoretically be available for collection. However, at times this led to large disparities in sampling effort between sites within a comparison. For example, only April, May, and August samples were used to compare WC 352 (n=57, once monthly sampling) and GI 94 (n=331, twice monthly sampling plus the extra May lunar mini-study samples). Finally, taxa utilized in the analyses were limited by our ability to identify the many larval and juvenile forms collected over the course of the study. Since we were trying to analyze the taxonomic assemblage at the lowest level possible, we were forced to eliminate large numbers of fish which could not be identified to genus. Overall, however, we feel the index provides a good idea of the similarity in community assemblages between sites, but should only be discussed in relative terms.

Taxonomic Diversity Between Sites

The mean diversity indices for the plankton net collections taken at the platform sites and the pushnet collections taken at Belle Pass were not significantly different from each other, ranging from 0.73-0.83 (Figure 32). They were, however, slightly higher than those for the light-trap collections, with the exception of GI 94. In general, observed statistical differences in Shannon-Weiner diversity indices between sites were limited to light-trap collections. The similarity between the light-trap diversity indices for ST 54 and Belle Pass is not surprising, since both sites were dominated by large numbers of photopositive clupeiform fishes, which also lowered their diversity indices. Light-trap collections were significantly more diverse at GI 94, a result of being less dominated by clupeiform fishes than ST 54 and Belle Pass, and of collecting more taxa, particularly reef fish species, than GC 18. In general, taxonomic richness in light-traps was highest at GI 94, with 90 taxa identified to genus as compared to 65 taxa at ST 54, the platform with the second highest number light-trap of taxa. Inshore (particularly estuarine) areas are generally characterized as having lower diversity than adjacent shelf waters and are dominated by a few highly abundant taxa (Nybakken 1988). This pattern is generally attributed to the fluctuating nature of the nearshore environment, particularly with regards to salinity and temperature, and the lack of physiological specializations needed to deal with this estuarine environmental variability (Nybakken 1988). This, in part, may explain the relatively low diversity indices for ST 54 and Belle Pass, the two inshore sites. In contrast, species richness and abundance is generally relatively low on the outer shelf, due to the homogeneity of the bottom substrate (Bond 1996). As previously discussed, topographical relief is disjunct throughout the northcentral Gulf (especially west of the Delta) and the sea floor is basically dominated by expanses of mud and silt. Again, this homogeneity and the previously discussed lack of a large amount of upstream supply of larvae may in part explain the low taxonomic diversity observed in the light-trap collections at GC 18.

Environmental Variables and Larval and Juvenile Fish Abundances

Canonical correlation analyses were used to determine the relationship between the dominant taxa collected at our sampling sites and measured environmental/biological parameters, i.e., temperature, salinity, turbidity, dissolved oxygen, and macrozooplankton biomass. At all of our sampling sites, temperature and salinity appeared to explain most of the variation in larval abundances in our models for the dominant taxa. This is not surprising as these physical variables change seasonally, and to some extent across the shelf, as does the availability of larval assemblages. Occasionally, both temperature and salinity were important factors within a single environmental canonical variate, which is probably a reflection of seasonality, i.e., in the northern Gulf as temperatures increase during the late spring through the summer and early fall, salinities tend to increase as well, due to decreased Mississippi/Atchafalaya River runoff and increased evaporation/precipitation ratios.

Many of these relationships (based primarily on the seasonal variables temperature and salinity) were consistent with known information on the seasonal occurrences of the different species. For example at GC 18, where we were able to sample nearly year-round, *Mugil cephalus* was found to be negatively associated with temperature in plankton net samples, which is consistent with their peak periods of abundance (December-February) in the northern Gulf (Table 10; Ditty et al. 1988). Other species collected in plankton nets at GC 18 were positively associated with temperature and represent taxa with peak larval abundances in the spring and summer months, such as *Auxis* spp. (May-September), *Caranx crysos* (June-August), and *C. hippos/latus* (April-August; Ditty et al. 1988). Relationships between seasonal variables (temperature and salinity) and larval peaks in abundance were observed at all sites. For example, positive relationships between abundances and temperature and salinity were found for species with summer peaks in larval abundance, such as *Auxis* spp. (May-September) at GI 94 (Table 12) and *Chloroscombrus chrysurus* (June-September) and *Scomberomorus maculatus* (August-September) at ST 54 (Table 14). Negative relationships for species with spring or winter peaks were found as well, such as previously mentioned *Mugil cephalus* at GC 18 (Table 10) and *Gobiesox strumosus* (March-May) at Belle Pass (Table 16).

While seasonality seems to be an important factor, trends in larval abundances could also reflect the environmental optima and preferences of some species. *Membras martinica*, for example, is found primarily in more saline areas along the coast, as well as offshore areas (Hoese and Moore 1977). At Belle Pass, pushnet densities for this species were positively associated with salinity (Table 16). Larval and juvenile *Caranx crysos* prefer warmer, more saline waters (Patillo et al. 1997), and this species was often positively associated with temperature and salinity in our study (Tables 10-11, 15).

Differences between relationships at the same site between plankton net and light-trap collections may be a reflection of biases towards different life history stages, since the plankton nets collected primarily younger, less competent larvae while light-traps collected larger larvae and juveniles. At ST 54, for example, net collections of *Scomberomorus maculatus* were positively associated with temperature and salinity (Table 14), while light-trap collections were negatively associated with these variables (Table 15). This is consistent with the known early life history preferences for this species, as larval *S. maculatus* require relatively higher temperatures and salinities than juveniles, which are generally more eurythermal and euryhaline (Patillo et al. 1997).

Dissolved oxygen and turbidity were also important variables at Belle Pass for some species, but little is known about these requirements or preferences for the early life history stages of many fishes. Some species which were very photopositive (i.e., *Gobiesox strumosus* and *Hypsoblennius hentz/ionthas*) were also negatively associated with turbidity in our light-trap samples, possibly because of decreased light-trap efficiency in highly turbid waters. Macrozooplankton biomass was influential at GC 18 (Table 11) and GI 94 (Table 13), but only in light-trap collections. This result is not surprising as light-traps tended to collect larger, more competent postlarvae and juveniles which would be more likely to be affected by macrozooplankton prey availability than smaller, less competent larvae. Some of these light-trap taxa that were positively associated with zooplankton biomass also included larval forms such as *Euthynnus alletteratus*, *Saurida brasiliensis*, and *Synodus foetens*, which have well developed mouths and teeth at small sizes and are able to feed on zooplankton.

While canonical correlation analyses were useful in characterizing the environmental correlates for most species, results for others were confounding. At ST 54, for example, *Cynoscion arenarius* was negatively associated with the first environmental variate which related temperature and salinity, but positively associated with the second environmental variate which was positively correlated with salinity alone. In many instances, our models did not explain a large amount of the variation (15%) for many species. One possible reason for some of these discrepancies is that spawning seasons and periods of larval abundances for many species occurred throughout our entire sampling season for many species, particularly at GI 94, ST 54, and Belle Pass where we sampled only from April-September. This is the case for species such as *Citharichthys* spp., *Citharichthys spilopterus*, *Cynoscion nebulosus* and others (Ditty et al. 1988). For other species, particularly small fishes with little economic value such as many of the lizardfishes (*Synodus foetens*, *S. poeyi*, *Saurida brasiliensis*) and blennies (*Hypsoblennius hentz/ionthas*, *H. invemar*, and *Scartella/Hypleurochilus*), little information is available on peak occurrences of these taxa across the shelf. In this respect, our study provides an important contribution to the life history information on these taxa across the shelf.

Gear Selectivity

The most obvious trend observed during this study was the overwhelming presence of engraulids and clupeids at all sites, even on the shelf slope site. Light-trap and plankton net collections (total catch) were dominated by clupeiform fishes at GC 18 (59%), GI 94 (66%), ST 54 (97%), and Belle Pass (74%). The dominance of these taxa in our collections is not unexpected, particularly considering the abundances of these fishes in the northern Gulf and the sampling gears utilized. Clupeiform fishes are often among the most abundant in plankton surveys of the northern Gulf and are present year-round in shelf waters (Ditty 1986; Ditty et al.

1988; Finucane et al. 1979b). Light-traps are selective sampling devices and previous studies have demonstrated that often the catches are dominated by a single taxonomic group (Brogan 1994; Choat et al. 1993; Sponaugle and Cowen 1996; Thorrold 1992). Clupeiform fishes have been shown to be particularly photopositive and have dominated the total catches in several studies utilizing light-aggregating collection techniques (Brogan 1994; Choat et al. 1993; Dennis et al. 1991; Rooker et al. 1996). The bow-mounted, dyed pushnet used in this study was relatively large (1m x 1m) and actively collects fish with a minimum amount of avoidance. It has also been shown to be an effective collector of clupeiforms in previous studies (Herke 1969; Kriete and Loesch 1980; Raynie and Shaw 1994). While the light-trap collects fish based on taxon-specific, photopositive behaviors and the pushnet actively strains the water mass it samples, the dyed plankton nets in our platform study collected fish passively with tidal currents. Even so, it was also very effective in sampling these fishes. This catchability was undoubtedly aided by our nocturnal sampling design.

Even with these sampling efficiency enhancements, these three sampling techniques clearly displayed gear selectivity as evident by differences in taxonomic richness between gear types. Passive plankton nets collected fish from more unique families than light-traps at GC 18 (15 vs. 7) and GI 94 (6 vs. 3), but not ST 54 (8 families unique to each gear). At Belle Pass, the pushnet collected individuals from 20 unique families, as well as fish from all families sampled by light-traps. Previous studies comparing light-traps and plankton nets in marine waters have found similar results (i.e., light-traps collected fewer families than plankton tows) with only a few instances where light-traps collected unique families. Brogan (1994) collected 16 unique families with a diver-steered pushnet and only 4 unique families with light-traps, and the latter 4 families, when combined, comprised a very small proportion (<0.08%) of his total light-trap catch. Likewise, more unique families were collected with a neuston net (10) than with light-traps (4) when fished simultaneously in Onslow Bay, North Carolina, and the unique light-trap families comprising only 10% of the total light-trap catch (Hernandez and Lindquist 1999). These results are similar to ours, where unique light-trap families usually made up less than 1% of the total catch at each platform site. However, whereas the previously cited studies each collected only four unique families with their light-traps, we collected seven (GC 18) and eight (ST 54). Neither Choat et al. (1993) nor Hickford and Schiel (1999) reported any families in light-trap samples that were not present in plankton net samples.

In addition, the large numbers of unique taxa (identified at least to genus) collected by light-traps in our study was also surprising, since this gear is usually considered to be very taxon-specific, and therefore limited in its sampling scope. At the genus level, light-traps collected more unique taxa than plankton nets at GI 94 (31 vs. 26) and ST 54 (27 vs. 19), but not at GC 18 (18 vs. 25). At Belle Pass, however, the light-traps collected far fewer unique taxa (3) than did the pushnet (44). Such large numbers of unique taxa have not been previously reported for light-traps in gear comparison studies. Two studies reported data at the genus level, but found either that all taxa collected by light-traps were collected by nets (Hickford and Schiel 1999), or that there were many more unique taxa in the net collections than light-trap collections (Hernandez and Lindquist 1999). In our study, light-traps proved very useful in sampling available taxa that were not collected by plankton nets.

Trends in taxon selectivity by gear were supported in the similarity indices between the gear types within a given site (Table 9). At GC 18 and GI 94, there was greater similarity between the light-trap samples, regardless of location, than there was between the surface light-trap collections (either off platform or central location) and the surface net collections. Again, this indicates the behavioral or developmental responses of different fish taxa influence their susceptibility to different sampling gears (Hernandez and Lindquist 1999). The trend was not as evident at ST 54, but this is not surprising as 97% of the total catch by both gears was comprised of clupeiform fishes, which are very susceptible to both gear types (Schoener's Similarity Index for total light-trap vs. total net collections = 0.63). There was also a relatively high similarity index value (0.61) for the pushnet vs. light-trap comparison at Belle Pass. Again, this site was dominated by clupeiform fishes (74% of total catch), and light-traps are effective in sampling these taxa.

The diversity indices for the plankton net collections taken at the platform sites and the pushnet collections taken at Belle Pass were not significantly different from each other, but were slightly higher than those for the light-trap collections, with the exception of GI 94 (Figure 32). Several studies have investigated differences in taxonomic richness between different gear types, although few, if any, actually calculated taxonomic diversity indices as a comparison. Choat et al. (1993) collected individuals from more families with a bongo net (63 families), a lighted-seine net (37 families), neuston net (31 families), Tucker trawl (29 families), and purse seine (25 families) than with a light-trap (20 families) in a gear comparison study off Lizard Island, northern Great Barrier Reef, Australia. In the Gulf of California, Brogan (1994) collected more reef fish larvae and juveniles from different families with a diver-steered plankton net (43 families) than with a light-trap (31 families). Hernandez and Lindquist (1999) collected more fish larvae and juveniles from different families with a neuston net (24 families) than with either of the two light-trap designs employed (18 and 21 families) in a study in Onslow Bay, North Carolina. In each of these studies, the authors concluded that the taxonomic assemblage collected in their respective studies was very method-dependent, and the same appears to be true in our study.

Since the three sampling gears operate on different sampling principles, differences may be observed not only between species, but also between different size classes (i.e., developmental stages) of the same species. Of the 35 length-frequency comparisons between passive plankton nets and light-traps involving the dominant taxa, 31 exhibited statistically significant differences (Figures 23-26). In the instances where no significant differences were found, the distributions either overlapped substantially (Figures 23, *Opisthonema oglinum*; Figure 24, *Symphurus* spp.; and Figure 25, *Bregmaceros cantori*) or suffered from too few individuals in the larger size classes for a significant statistical difference to be found (Figure 25, *Chloroscombrus chrysurus*). In general, the light-trap was more effective in sampling larger size classes of the same taxon at each location, depth, or site. In some cases, the light-trap collections did not encompass a significant portion of the plankton net's smaller sizes, but clearly excelled at capturing the larger sizes. This was the case, for example, with *Caranx crysos* and *Scomberomorus maculatus* (Figure 20) and *Euthynnus alletteratus* (Figures 23 and 25). In other instances, the light-trap collections appeared to significantly overlap the smaller sizes of the net collections, but also augmented the size-frequency distribution with much larger sizes, or in some cases, even additional cohorts, as was the case for *C. crysos* (Figure 23), *S. cavalla* (Figure

24), and *O. oglinum* (Figure 24 and 25). These results further illustrate the benefits that multiple gear types can bring to ichthyoplankton studies by sampling a more complete range of size classes, cohorts, ages, and life history/developmental stages (Brogan 1994; Choat et al. 1993; Hernandez and Lindquist 1999).

Although not all taxa are sampled with light-traps, those that are tend to be of the larger size classes and their abundances may be underestimated in more traditional ichthyoplankton studies utilizing only one gear type (Brogan 1994). This size-frequency comparison is strongly influenced by whether the complete size spectrum is available (or supplied to) the sampling site. For example at GC 18, our furthest offshore platform site located on the continental shelf slope, there was no significant difference in the size distribution of *Opisthonema oglinum* between the two gear types , i.e., a near complete overlap in sizes that ranged from 3-20 mm (Figure 23). The larger sizes were found more inshore as evident by the larger individuals (21-50 mm) being collected at GI 94 (Figure 24) and ST 54 (Figure 25), our mid- and inner shelf platform sites. These larger individuals and cohorts were sampled only with the light-traps and, therefore, would have otherwise been underestimated or totally excluded.

Previous studies have demonstrated that pushnets are also effective in sampling larger juveniles and small fishes as well, particularly in coastal areas (Herke 1969; Kriete and Loesch 1980; Raynie and Shaw 1994). Herke (1969) used a pushnet in Louisiana tidal marshes to collect small estuarine fishes, primarily in the 25-100 mm range, and emphasized the maneuverability of the gear and its bow-mounting (free of propeller wash and boat shadow) as major advantages. Kriete and Loesch (1980) used a different design to collect juvenile pelagic fishes in lower Chesapeake Bay and found the gear was easy to deploy and able to fish in a controlled manner within shallow water (minimum depth of 1.2 m). These advantages were traits we considered for the edges of the jetty environment which is structurally complex. We were able to maneuver the boat and pushnet very close to the shallow slope of the rock wall with relative ease. In general, net avoidance is reduced with pushnets compared to towed nets (Raynie and Shaw 1994), and we chose a large mesh size (1000 μm) and net opening (1 m x 1 m) to minimize the pressure wave in front of the net, minimize net clogging, and collect larger larvae and postsettlement juveniles. As a result, many of the size distributions sampled with the pushnet and light-trap at Belle Pass overlapped considerably (Figure 26). Only 7 of the 18 species analyzed exhibited significant size differences between the gear types. In two instances, the pushnet collections clearly had a larger size mode than the light-trap (*Anchoa nasuta/hepsetus, Gobiosoma* spp.; Figure 26). While we were targeting the same size classes with the pushnet, its usefulness was in sampling different taxa. The number of families (41) and taxa identified to the genus level (85) were approximately double that of the light-traps (21 and 42, respectively), which generated a taxon diversity for the pushnet collections that was significantly higher than that for the light-trap (Figure 33). Once again, multiple gear types allowed for the collection of a more complete representation of the ichthyoplankton and juvenile communities at the jetty site as well.

Within and Off-platform Larval and Juvenile Fish Distribution

While our choice of gear types proved to be very beneficial in collecting fish from different taxonomic groups and size classes, our decision to sample within the platform structure

127

at two different depths and to sample away from the structure (downstream) proved interesting as well. Overall, the taxon diversity (Figure 33) and abundance (Figure 15) of fish in light-traps was higher in surface waters, particularly within the platform structure. This result is noteworthy because the ambient light-field from the platform itself could have possibly decreased the effectiveness of our light-aggregating devices in the surface waters. One possible explanation is that the ambient light-field may have already drawn photopositive species to the surface waters prior to sampling, and the surface trap's bright light was able to fish in water with relatively elevated densities of larger and more photopositive fish than the subsurface waters. With regards to differences in plankton net densities, the effect of the ambient light-field may have also increased surface catches of photopositive fish, or may have led to the higher densities in the subsurface collections due to decreased visual avoidance (although dyed nets were used). With the exception of ST 54 where there were only 7 bottom net samples (Table 2), densities were generally higher in the subsurface nets, particularly when clupeiform fishes were removed (Figure 16). If the lights from the platform had the effect of drawing photopositive, and generally larger individuals to the surface waters, then these individuals would be better able to avoid a passively fishing gear at the surface. In contrast, a plankton net at depth would have the advantage of fishing in a less intense light field, resulting in decreased visual net avoidance.

Of the dominant species analyzed, some trends were evident in the distribution of these fishes within and downstream of the platforms, i.e., off platform light-traps (Figures 17-22). *Opisthonema oglinum*, for example, was predominantly collected in surface waters at all of our platform sites, regardless of the gear type utilized. Structure-associated taxa such as *Caranx crysos* and *C. hippos/latus* at GC 18 (Figure 17), and *Euthynnus alletteratus* (Figures 19, 21) at GI 94 and ST 54 were sampled with light-traps in surface waters, generally downstream of the platform. *Synodus foetens*, in contrast, seemed to be common within the platform structure at GI 94 (Figure 19). Relatively few taxa were found only in the off-platform light-trap samples: 4 genera at GC 18, 6 at GI 94, and 12 at ST 54 (Tables 3-5). In all cases, these taxa comprised <1% of the off-platform light-trap total catch, with the exception *of Pomatomus saltatrix* at GC 18 (1.5%). Across all sites, only the mullids were collected solely in off-platform samples. Although fewer in number, some taxa seemed more abundant at depth, including *Mugil cephalus*, *Citharichthys spilopterus*, and *Symphurus* spp. at GC 18 (Figure 18), *Bregmaceros cantori* and *Symphurus* spp. at GI 94 (Figure 20), and *Ariomma* spp. at ST 54 (Figure 22). Several species were collected only in bottom gears, particularly mesopelagic and benthic species such as *Chlorophthalmus agassizi*, *Paralepis atlantica*, and *Lestrolepis intermedia* at GC 18, *Robia legula*, *Ophidion selenops*, and *Priacanthus* spp. at GI 94, and *Ophidion robinsi* and *Rhomboplites aurorubens* at ST 54 (see Tables 3-5). Diversifying our sampling efforts, both with depth and within- and off-platform, ensured that several taxa were not underrepresented or excluded from our analyses.

Lunar Periodicity

We investigated lunar periodicities because there are many hypotheses on larval biology concerning lunar reproductive patterns pertaining to propagule dispersal and predation rates that occur both at the beginning (spawning) and end (settlement) of the planktonic phase (Robertson 1991). Many reef fish, for example, time their spawning events with different lunar cycles (Thresher 1984). Previous studies have also documented higher rates of fish settlement during darker, new moon periods than full moon periods (Victor 1986; Rooker et al. 1996), presumably a response to mortality associated with visual predators. These patterns of spawning, transport, recruitment, and settlement in association with the local physical oceanographic regime, often result in variable larval supply and settlement patterns with distinct lunar periodicities. It should be noted, however, that in the northern Gulf of Mexico tides are dominantly diurnal and their range in tidal height is not often in synchrony with the phase of the moon (i.e., new and full moon maximum tide ranges vs. first quarter and third quarter minimums), but rather the total range is in synchrony with the tropical and equatorial phases of the moon's elevation (i.e., Tropic of Cancer and/or Capricorn crossing maximum tidal ranges vs. equatorial crossing minimums; McLellan 1965). In addition, we wanted to investigate the effects on gear selectivity with respect to ambient light. Since light-traps rely on illumination in the surrounding water mass to attract fish, then theoretically their efficiency should increase when the contrast in trap-generated illumination is greater as during a new moon phase, when there is less ambient light, as opposed to a full moon (all larval and postlarval supply/availability issues being equal).

Few studies utilizing light-aggregating devices have addressed gear efficiency within the framework of lunar periodicities in fish spawning, larval supply (transport) and settlement. Gregory and Powles (1985) observed higher catches during new moon phases in a freshwater system but didn't report a statistical difference. Rooker et al. (1996) used a nightlight lift-net in nearshore habitats in Puerto Rico and reported that new moon abundances of larval fish were four times higher than the next most abundant phase (last quarter) during the summer months, and suggested that ambient light intensities might have played a factor in gear efficiency. The competitive interaction of lunar vs. light-trap illumination may have played a role in the collection of fish at Belle Pass where significantly higher CPUEs were observed during new moons (Figure 30). While some non-clupeiform fishes have life histories with lunar periodicities, clupeiforms generally do not, so the significant difference in the analyses of the whole data set (with clupeiforms) suggests that ambient illumination may have been a factor. Belle Pass pushnet collections also had significantly more fish during new moons, possibly due to decreased visual avoidance under lower ambient light conditions. It is difficult, however, to separate the effects of ambient illumination and gear performance from the supply and/or settlement patterns of the fishes, so lunar periodicity may still play a role in the occurrence of fishes at this site.

In addition, the situation at petroleum platforms may be equally confounded and difficult to definitively discern since the platforms have many bright lights throughout the structure to illuminate the work areas at night and aid ship navigation, which in effect may be attracting fish to the structure. We tried to address this issue by sampling away from the structure (i.e., 20 m downstream), but even these off-platform light-trap collections could still be within the "halo influence" of the platform's light field. Since 97% of the fish collected at ST 54 were clupeiforms, it is not surprising that no clear trend in lunar periodicity is evident (Figure 29). Some of the largest CPUEs observed occurred during the full moon periods at ST 54 which were driven by large catches of *Anchoa nasuta/hepsetus* (June 20-21) and *Opisthonema oglinum* (August 17-20; Figure 11). These large abundances were also evident in the plankton net samples. At GI 94, again the total mean CPUE with clupeiforms was highest during full moon phases (Figure 27). Without clupeiform fishes, however, when significant differences in mean total densities and mean total CPUEs were found between new vs. full moon phases, four out of five instances had greater new moon catches (Figures 27b and d; 29d; and 30b and d). The analysis of the May samples at GI 94 taken over three lunar phases showed very little difference between the lunar phases, with the exception of a relatively high mean density during the first quarter moon (Figure 28). Although these platform results on lunar periodicity are less than conclusive, there may be several explanations for the lack of a consistently strong pattern. First of all, the previously-mentioned, potential competitive interference of the platforms' large ambient light-fields may sometimes over-ride any lunar effect that would otherwise be present. Secondly, some of the species may be responding differently to lunar cues. For example, some peak recruitment events have also been linked to full moon periods (Johannes 1978; Robertson et al. 1988). In addition the light-traps generally caught more larger sized (and presumably older, more competent) larvae, whereas plankton net collections were dominated by smaller sized larvae which could have been displaying different behavioral capabilities. Finally, it is possible that the abundances of these fish are related to more localized factors such as water mass supply. This could be particularly true at the mid- and inner shelf sites where the coastal current regime can dynamically affect salinity, temperature, and food patchiness, and where the geographical concentration of upstream platforms is greatest when compared to the relative isolated shelf slope site.

Belle Pass

Another factor that may affect the efficiency of both gear types is the turbidity of the water masses sampled. Higher turbidity should decrease the effectiveness of the light-trap and increase the effectiveness of the pushnet. As previously mentioned, photopositive taxa such as *Gobiesox strumosus* and *Hypsoblennius hentz/ionthas* were negatively associated with turbidity in our light-trap samples, possibly because of a decrease in the effectiveness of the light-traps in highly turbid waters (Table 17). Differences in turbidity may explain the observed differences between the internal jetty stations versus the external stations (Belle Pass; Figure 31), the estuarine waters potentially being more turbid than shelf waters.

In addition to the environmental factors, the hydrology around the mouth of the inlet may aid in concentrating fish at the outer (i.e., external) jetty stations. Hydrodynamic models describing tidal pass flow patterns often predict the formation of eddies upstream and downstream of inlet mouths (Carter 1988; Crout 1983; Kelly et al. 1982; Murray 1976; Shaw et al. 1985). There is a west-northwest net residual coastal flow along the Louisiana coast that is favorable for this type of eddy formation/setup. While many of these models predict the movement of passive particles, the mechanism may still be a valid explanation for the concentration of postlarval and juvenile fish at the outer stations of the jetty site.

Conclusions

This study represents the first comprehensive look at the ichthyoplankton and juvenile fish assemblages collected within oil and gas platforms in the northern Gulf of Mexico. It is also a first (yet preliminary) attempt at comparing such assemblages across different depth zones and geographical regions. It is apparent that a diverse larval and juvenile fish community is supplied to, and/or inhabits the waters near platforms and that these structures may be important to reef fish feeding or population dynamics. From a management perspective, fish early life history data from a cross-shelf study of petroleum platforms could provide information useful in deciding the future placement of artificial structures (Shinn and Wicklund 1989) and in determining whether or not the platforms serve as nursery areas/refugia for reef species (Steimle and Meier 1997). Based on our results, two obvious conclusions stand out: the peak in taxonomic richness and diversity at our mid-shelf platform (GI 94) and the relatively low abundance of reef-associated and reef-dependent postlarvae and juveniles present at the platforms.

Mid-shelf Peak in Taxonomic Richness and Diversity

In general, while reef-associated and reef-dependent taxa were collected at all platform sites, taxonomic richness and diversity was highest at GI 94 (mid-shelf). Due to the pelagic nature of most reef-dependent eggs and larvae, dispersal in the oceanic environment plays a large role in the eventual settlement and recruitment of postlarvae and juveniles to adult environments. While some studies have determined mechanisms of larval retention in reef environments (Swearer et al. 1999; Cowen et al. 2000), it is widely believed that recruitment is variable and dependent, in part, on the supply from nearby reefs (Sale 1980; Richards and Lindeman 1987; Doherty and Williams 1988; Doherty 1991). Off the coast of Louisiana most oil and gas platforms are concentrated along the inner and mid-shelf within the 200 m isobath (Tolan 2001). At GI 94, the intermediate location, depth, and proximity to a high density of surrounding platforms may create generally favorable conditions for the recruitment of reef taxa. The presence and proximity of upstream reefs and spawning habitats, therefore, may play an important role in the eventual makeup of the pre-adult assemblages.

At GC 18 (shelf slope), the relatively low abundance of reef fish larvae and juveniles may likewise be due to a combination of depth, distance from other natural/artificial reefs, and oligotrophic waters devoid of possible recruits. Similarly, the close proximity of ST 54 (inner shelf) to the coast and hydrologic interactions with the Mississippi River plume may result in fluctuating conditions generally unfavorable for most reef-associated or reef-dependent fishes, but more suitable for estuarine and coastal pelagic taxa, which were dominant in our collections. Previous research on the adult assemblages associated with our sampling sites (Stanley and Wilson 2000) have shown similar results, with the highest taxonomic richness, particularly among reef-dependent taxa, occurring at GI 94. Adult densities were significantly higher at GI 94 as well. Mean adult densities at GI 94 were approximately 15-17 times higher than at ST 54 and GC 18, respectively. On-going research efforts east of the Mississippi River Delta at Santa Fe-Snyder Main Pass (MP) 259A and Murphy Viosca Knoll (VK) 203 (Figure 1) will enable us to both broaden our mid-shelf geographic scale and give us another outer shelf (MP 259 A, 130 m depth) and mid-shelf (VK 203, 30 m depth) site for further comparisons east and west of the Delta.

Rarity of Reef-Associated and Reef-Dependent Juveniles

The fact that we collected relatively few individuals of reef-dependent and reef-associated taxa, particularly lutjanid and serranid specimens, is not surprising for several reasons. First of all, due to the high mortality rates experienced by pelagic larvae prior to settlement (approaching 100%), reef-dependent juveniles are relatively rare in general (Leis 1991). This, coupled with potentially high predation rates at the settlement site itself (see below), may result in a very low abundance of juveniles available for capture. Secondly, recruitment events for these taxa can be extremely episodic (Choat et al. 1993; Rooker et al. 1996), with most of the reef fish replenishment occurring over the course of 1-3 nights (Thorrold et al. 1994; Rooker et al. 1996). Although we targeted peak times of settlement and recruitment (new and full moon periods), it is still very possible that we missed settlement peaks through the course of the study. Finally, although we chose light-traps as a means of collecting larger postlarvae and juveniles, light-aggregation devices can be very taxon-selective. While some reef-dependent taxa, such as pomacentrids, have been collected in large numbers, few research efforts have been able to collect many lutjanids or serranids with light-aggregation devices (Dennis et al. 1991; Choat et al. 1993; Brogan 1994; Rooker et al. 1996; Hernandez and Lindquist 1999). We have recently experimented and deployed different settlement trap designs at MP 259 A and VK 203 in an attempt to address questions concerning size at settlement, habitat selection, and recruitment dynamics.

A popular justification for artificial reefs is that they increase fish populations by improving recruitment (Bohnsack et al. 1994). The occurrence of extremely large numbers of postlarvae and newly-settled juveniles on new reefs suggests that there is a pool of opportunistic surplus larvae (Bohnsack et al. 1994). Numerous observations on the subsequent, rapid disappearance of these newly-settled postlarvae, however, support the "wall of mouths hypothesis" (Emery 1973; Hamner et al. 1988) and the "limited shelter hypothesis" (Shulman 1985; Hixon and Beets 1989), which state that for postlarval reef fish, the time of settlement, especially in the absence of suitable shelter, is characterized by exceedingly high predation-mortality rates by the larger, predominately carnivorous resident population. Thus presettlement postlarvae and postsettlement juveniles may often be displaced from the most favorable reef habitat by this intensive, on-site, adult predation (Frederick 1997).

While much of the evidence for the "wall of mouths" and related hypotheses has been collected from natural reefs, there is some supporting evidence from oil and gas platform studies. Scarborough-Bull and Kendall (1994) studied juvenile recruitment and colonization on three offshore oil and gas platforms that were converted to artificial reefs. Two platforms were explosively toppled and had virtually all of their resident fish community lethally concussed. These sites subsequently served as recruitment sites for juveniles/immature reef fish. A third rig was toppled during a hurricane and experienced minimum impact to its adult fish communities and did not serve as a recruitment site, i.e., virtually all fish observed were adults (Scarborough-Bull and Kendall 1994).

It is with this paradigm in mind (increased production by improving recruitment) that we chose to use light-traps in our sampling protocol in an effort to collect settlement-stage postlarvae and juveniles. The presence of these larger, more competent individuals could provide indirect evidence for the nursery area/refuge function of the petroleum platforms. The adult populations of reef fish at our sites are well-known. Stanley and Wilson (2000) have documented reef-dependent adults at GC 18 (*Epinephelus inermis, Mycteroperca phenax, Paranthias furcifer, Pristipomoides aquilonaris, Balistes capriscus*), GI 94 (*Epinephelus fulvus, E. inermis, Mycteroperca bonaci, M. microlepis, M. phenax, M. venenosa, P. furcifer, Lutjanus campechanus, L. griseus, Rhomboplites aurorubens, B. capriscus*) and ST 54 (*Epinephelus adscensionis, L. campechanus, L. griseus, B. capriscus*). However, we were able to collect few reef-dependent, settlement-size postlarvae and juveniles, mostly pomacentrids and blenniids (Table 7).

The abundance of postlarval and juvenile synodontids and scombrids near the platforms suggests that predation pressure is probably high. This may also contribute to the relatively low numbers of reef-dependent juveniles collected, since most synodontids and scombrids are piscivorous as early as the postlarval stage (Naughton and Saloman 1981; Uchida 1981; Sweatman 1984; Thresher et al. 1986). We frequently collected larvae and juveniles of synodontids in our light-trap samples and observed them preying on other organisms retained in the cod end. Small, cryptic species such as synodontids are often overlooked in surveys and, therefore, their abundances are usually unknown. The presence of a large population of synodontids may have a major impact on fish community dynamics, since they prey directly on postlarvae and juveniles of many commercially- and recreationally-important species (Thresher et al. 1986). Observations on piscivory by a synodontid suggest that new recruits can face a 65% annual chance of predation from just a single species of lizardfish (Sweatman 1984). The high numbers of piscivorous juveniles collected in our study, primarily with light-traps, indicate that predation is important in determining local reef assemblages.

While oil and gas platforms may be very suitable habitat for adult fishes, the physical structure of these artificial reefs may not be ideal for settling postlarvae and juveniles. Previous studies have shown that smaller reefs tend to hold a greater cumulative number of total and resident species, higher fish densities, and more settlers (Bohnsack et al. 1994). The higher carrying capacity and settlement success of smaller reefs is probably a function of their: 1) greater edge effect (higher ratio of perimeter to reef area; Bohnsack et al. 1994); 2) lower vertical relief which often favors juvenile over adult reef fish (West et al. 1994); and 3) greater availability of small shelter holes ($\leq$ a few cm), or porosity, which has been repeatedly shown to be important for post-settlement survival (Shulman 1985; Hixon and Beets 1989; West et al. 1994). Petroleum platforms, in contrast, are large reefs and are generally characterized as having a higher profile (high vertical relief), less complexity, and lower porosity than natural reefs.

Other Potential Oil and Gas Platform Effects

A characteristic often attributed to artificial reefs is that they may increase fish production if they increase the available habitat for adult nesting or spawning (Grossman et al. 1997). While our study did not examine adult spawning activity or pelagic egg densities, we were able to sample smaller, yolk-sac and preflexion larvae with in our plankton net collections. At GC 18, for example, preflexion blenniids, holocentrids, serranids, lutjanids, and scarids were collected, suggesting nearby spawning or local supply. Similarly, reef-dependent/associated, preflexion individuals were collected at GI 94 (pomacentrids, blenniids, holocentrids, lutjanids, and serranids) and ST 54 (blenniids and lutjanids). While our passive plankton net collections do not necessarily reflect platform-association, they do provide an indication of local supply. Since preflexion, reef-dependent larvae were collected, it is likely that they were locally spawned at either natural or artificial habitats nearby. With the limited amount of hard-substrate habitat available in the northcentral Gulf of Mexico, the addition of artificial habitats (platforms) may increase the chances of finding suitable spawning habitat.

133

Another important consideration in artificial reef studies is the degree to which organisms associated with the reef structure interact with pelagic species and contribute to off-reef production (Lindberg 1997). The scombrids, for example, are pelagic but often structure-associated, and the juveniles are competent swimmers and highly predatory. If these juveniles, which were relatively abundant in our collections, are actively feeding in association with the platforms, then they, and similar taxa (e.g., carangids) could serve as an important trophic link between the reef and pelagic environments. Another potentially important link between the production at platforms and pelagic, transient predators may be the blenniids. These fishes are structure-dependent and are attracted to the numerous habitats created by the biofouling community (e.g., barnacles) on the platform legs and cross-members, as well as the associated zooplankton food resources (Gallaway 1981; Bohnsak and Sutherland 1985). Some blennies have been cited as important components of the diets of reef-associated taxa such as *Archosargus probatocephalus* (Gallaway 1980) and *Seriola rivoliana* (Gallaway and Martin 1980). Therefore, predatory taxa such as carangids and scombrids with more generalized habitat requirements may be attracted to the concentrations of zooplankton and forage fish that are dependent on the platforms. For whatever reason, based on the results from this study the oil and gas platforms serve a potentially important function as hard-substrate habitat, and could therefore lead to increased production.

A major problem for managing reef resources is the incomplete understanding of the interactions between recruitment and habitat structure. Although habitat space may ultimately be limiting, many reef fish populations are not at the carrying capacity of their environment and changes in abundance may be controlled by settlement from the plankton or by early postsettlement mortality. Relatively little is known about the relationship between offshore petroleum platforms and the early life history stages of fishes anywhere in the world. Our findings, therefore, represent an important first step towards this aspect of artificial reef research. The additional information from platforms east of the Delta will enable us to develop a larger, more geographically meaningful and comprehensive characterization of the along-shelf and across-shelf ichthyoplankton from continental shelf waters of the northern Gulf.

LITERATURE CITED

Alevizon, W.C., J.C. Gorhan, R. Richardson, and A. McCarthy. 1985. Use of man-made reefs to concentrate snapper (Lutjanidae) and grunts (Haemulidae) in Bahamian waters. Bulletin of Marine Science 37: 3-10.

Bedinger, C.A., J.W. Cooper, A. Kwok, R.E. Childers, and K.T. Kimball. 1980. Ecological investigations of petroleum production platforms in the central Gulf of Mexico. Volume 1: Pollutant fate and effects studies. Draft final report submitted to the Bureau of Land Management, Contract AA551-CT8-17.

Bell, J.D., M. Westoby, and A.S. Steffe. 1987. Fish larvae settling in seagrass: do they discriminate between beds of different leaf density? Journal of Experimental Marine Biology and Ecology 111: 133-144.

Bennett, B.A. 1989. The fish community of a moderately exposed beach on the Southwestern Cape coast of South Africa and an assessment of this habitat as a nursery for juvenile fish. Estuarine, Coastal, and Shelf Science 28: 293-305.

Boesch, D.F., M.N. Josselyn, A.J. Mehta, J.T Morris, W.K. Nuttle, C.A. Simenstad and J.P Swift. 1994. Scientific assessment of coastal wetland loss, restoration and management in Louisiana. Journal of Coastal Research Special Issue 20: 1-102.

Bohnsak, J.A. 1989. Are high densities of fishes at artificial reefs the result of habitat limitations or behavioral preference? Bulletin of Marine Science 44: 632-645.

Bohnsak, J.A. 1991. Habitat structure and the design of artificial reefs. In: Bell, S.S., E.D. McCoy, and H.R. Mushinsky, eds. Habitat Structure: The Physical Structure of Objects in Space. London: Chapman and Hall.

Bohnsak, J.A. and D.L. Sutherland. 1985. Artificial reef research: a review with recommendations for future priorities. Bulletin of Marine Science 37: 11-19.

Bohnsak, J.A., D.E. Harper, D.B. McClellan and M. Hulsbeck. 1994. Effects of reef size on colonization and assemblage structure of fishes at artificial reefs off southeastern Florida, U.S.A. Bulletin of Marine Science 55: 796-823.

Bond, C.E. 1996. Biology of Fishes. Orlando: Saunders College Publishing.

Bortone, S.A. 1998. Resolving the attraction-production dilemma in artificial reef research: Some yeas and nays. Fisheries 23: 6-10.

Bright, T.J., J.W. Tunnell, L.H. Pequegnat, T.E. Burke, C.W. Cashman, D.A. Cropper, J.P. Ray, R.C. Tresslar, J. Teerling, and J.B. Wills. 1974. Biotic zonation on the West Flower Garden Bank. In: Bright, T. J and L.H. Pequegnat, eds. Biota of the West Flower Garden Bank. Houston: Gulf Publication Company.

Brogan, M.W. 1994. Two methods of sampling fish larvae over reefs: a comparison from the Gulf of California. Marine Biology 118: 33-44.

Carter, R.W.G. 1988. Coastal Environments: an Introduction to the Physical, Ecological, and Cultural Systems of Coastlines. San Diego: Academic Press.

CDOP (Committee on Disposition of Offshore Platforms). 1985. Disposal of offshore platforms. Marine Board, Commission on Engineering and Technical Systems, National Research Council. Washington, D.C.: National Academy Press.

Chittenden, M.E. and J.D. McEachran. 1976. Composition, ecology, and dynamics of demersal fish communities on the northwestern Gulf of Mexico continental shelf, with a similar synopsis for the entire gulf. TAMU-SG-76-2008. College Station: Texas A&M University.

Choat, J.H. and D.R. Bellwood. 1991. Reef fishes: their history and evolution. In Sale, P.F., ed. The ecology of fishes on coral reefs. San Diego: Academic Press.

Choat, J.H, P.J. Doherty, B.A. Kerrigan, and J.M. Leis. 1993. A comparison of towed nets, purse seine, and light-aggregation devices for sampling larvae and pelagic juveniles of coral reef fishes. Fishery Bulletin 91: 195-209.

Cochrane, J.D. and F.J. Kelly, Jr. 1986. Low-frequency circulation on the Texas-Louisiana continental shelf. Journal of Geophysical Research 91: 10,645-10,659.

Connolly, R.M. 1994. A comparison of fish assemblages from seagrass and unvegetated areas of a southern Australian estuary. Australian Journal of Marine and Freshwater Research 45: 1033-1044.

Continental Shelf Associates. 1982. Study of the effect of oil and gas activities on reef fish populations in the Gulf of Mexico OCS area. OCS Report/MMS82-010. U.S. Dept. of the Interior, Minerals Management Service, Gulf of Mexico OCS Region, New Orleans.

Cowen, R.K., K.M.M. Lwiza, S. Sponaugle, C.B. Paris and D.B. Olson. 2000. Connectivity of marine populations: open or closed? Science 287: 857-859.

Crout, R.L. 1983. Wind-driven, near-bottom currents over the west Louisiana inner shelf. Doctoral dissertation. Louisiana State University, Baton Rouge.

Defenbaugh, R.E. 1976. A study of the benthic macroinvertebrates of the continental shelf of the northern Gulf of Mexico. Doctoral dissertation. Texas A&M University, College Station.

Dennis, G.D., D. Goulet, and J.R. Rooker. 1991. Ichthyoplankton assemblages sampled by night lighting in nearshore habitats of southwestern Puerto Rico. NOAA/NMFS Technical Report 95: 89-97.

Ditty, J.G. 1986. Ichthyoplankton in neritic waters of the northern Gulf of Mexico off Louisiana: composition, relative abundance and seasonality. Fishery Bulletin 84: 935-946.

Ditty, J.G. and R.F. Shaw. 1996. Spatial and temporal distribution of larval striped mullet (*Mugil cephalus*) and white mullet (*M. curema*, Family: Mugilidae) in the northern Gulf of Mexico, with notes on mountain mullet, *Agonostomus monticola*. Bulletin of Marine Science 59: 271-288.

Ditty, J.G., G.G. Zieske, and R.F. Shaw. 1988. Seasonality and depth distribution of larval fishes in the northern Gulf of Mexico above latitude 26°00'N. Fishery Bulletin 86: 811-823.

Doherty, P.J. 1987. Light-traps: selective but useful devices for quantifying the distribution and abundances of larval fishes. Bulletin of Marine Science 41: 423-431.

Doherty, P.J. 1991. Spatial and temporal patterns in recruitment. In Sale, P.F., ed. The ecology of fishes on coral reefs. San Diego: Academic Press.

Doherty, P.J. and D. McB. Williams. 1988. The replenishment of coral reef fish populations. Oceanography and Marine Biology 26: 487-551.

Emery, A.R. 1973. Comparative ecology and functional osteology of fourteen species of damselfish (Pisces: Pomacentridae) at Alligator Reef, Florida Keys. Bulletin of Marine Science 23: 649-770.

Essig, R.J., J.F. Witzig, and M.C. Holliday. 1991. Marine recreational fishery statistics survey, Atlantic and Gulf coasts, 1987-1989. NOAA/NMFS Current Fisheries Statistics 8904.

Ferrell, D.J. and J.D. Bell. 1991. Differences among assemblages of fish associated with Zostera capricorni and bare sand over a large spatial scale. Marine Ecological Progress Series 72: 15-24.

Finucane, J.H., L.A. Collins, and L.E. Barger. 1979a. Determine the effects of discharges on seasonal abundance, distribution, and composition of ichthyoplankton in the oil field. In: Jackson, W.B., ed. Environmental Assessment of an Active Oil Field in the Northwestern Gulf of Mexico, 1977-1978. NOAA Report to EPA, Contract Number EPA-IAG-D5-E693-EO, NMFS Southeast Fisheries Center, Galveston.

Finucane, J.H., L.A. Collins, L.E. Barger, and J.D. McEachran. 1979b. Ichthyoplankton/mackerel eggs and larvae. In: Jackson, W.B., ed. Environmental Studies of the South Texas Outer Continental Shelf 1976. Contract Number AA550-TA7- 3. NOAA Final Report to BLM, NMFS Southeast Fisheries Center, Galveston.

Floyd, K.B., W.H. Courtenay, and R.D. Holt. 1984. A new larval fish light trap: the quatrefoil trap. Progressive Fish-Culturist 46: 216-219.

Frederick, J.L. 1997. Post-settlement movement of coral reef fishes and bias in survival estimates. Marine Ecology Progress Series 150:65-74.

Gallaway, B.J. 1980. Structure-associated communities, pelagic, reef, demersal fishes and macrocrustaceans. In Jackson, W.B. and P. Wilkens, eds. Environmental assessment of an active oil field in the northwestern Gulf of Mexico. Milestone report to NOAA. EPA project Number EPA-IAG-DS-E693-EO.

Gallaway, B.J. 1981. An ecosystem analysis of oil and gas development on the Texas-Louisiana continental shelf. FWS/OBS-81/27. U.S. Fish & Wildlife Service, Office of Biological Services, Washington, D.C.

Gallaway, B.J. 1998. Cumulative ecological significance of oil and gas structures in the Gulf of Mexico: Information search, synthesis, and ecological modeling: Phase I, Final Report. USGS/BRD/CR-1997-0006. U.S. Geological Survey, Biological Resources Division. Washington, D.C.

Gallaway, B.J. and L.R. Martin. 1980. Volume III-Effects of gas and oil field structures and effluents on pelagic and reef fishes, demersal fishes and macrocrustaceans. In Jackson, W.B. and E.P. Wilkens, eds. Environmental assessment of Buccaneer Gas and Oil Field in the northwestern Gulf of Mexico, 1978-1979. NOAA Technical Memorandum, NMFS-SEFC-37.

Gallaway, B.J., M.F. Johnson, R.L. Howard, L.R. Martin, and G.S. Boland. 1979. A study of the effects of Buccaneer oil field structures and associated effluents on biofouling communities and the Atlantic spadefish (*Chaetodipterus faber*). Annual report of LGL Limited-U.S., Inc., Bryan, Texas to NMFS, Galveston, Texas.

Gallaway, B.J., L.R. Martin, R.L. Howard, G.S. Boland, and G.D. Dennis. 1980. A case study of the effects of gas and oil production on artificial reef and demersal fish and macrocrustacean communities in the northwestern Gulf of Mexico. Expo Chem 1980, Houston, Texas.

George, R.Y. and P.J. Thomas. 1974. Aspects of fouling on offshore oil platforms in Louisiana shelf in relation to environmental impact. Final Report, Offshore Ecological Investigations, Gulf Universities Research Consortium.

Gregory, R.S. and P.M. Powles. 1985. Chronology, distribution, and sizes of larval fish sampled by light traps in macrophytic Chemung lake. Canadian Journal of Zoology 63: 2569-2577.

Gregory, R.S. and P.M. Powles. 1988. Relative selectivities of Miller high-speed samplers and light traps for collecting ichthyoplankton. Canadian Journal of Fisheries and Aquatic Sciences 45: 993-998.

Grossman, G.D., G.P. Jones and W.J. Seaman, Jr. 1997. Do artificial reefs increase regional fish production? A review of existing data. Fisheries 22(4): 17-23.

Hamner, W.M. M.S. Jones, J.H. Carleton, J.R. Hauri and D. McM. Williams. 1988. Zooplankton, planktivorous fish, and water currents on a windward reef face: Great Barrier Reef, Australia. Bulletin of Marine Science 42: 459-479.

Herke, W.H. 1969. A boat-mounted surface push-trawl for sampling juveniles in tidal marshes. Progressive Fish-Culturist 31: 177-179.

Hernandez, F.J., Jr. and D.G. Lindquist. 1999. A comparison of two light-trap designs for sampling larval and presettlement juvenile fish above a reef in Onslow Bay, North Carolina. Bulletin of Marine Science 64: 173-184.

Hickford, M.J.H. and D.R. Schiel. 1999. Evaluation of the performance of light traps for sampling fish larvae in inshore temperate waters. Marine Ecology Progress Series 186: 293-302.

Hixon, M.A. and J.P. Beets. 1989. Shelter characteristics and Caribbean fish assemblages: experiments with artificial reefs. Bulletin of Marine Science 44: 666-680.

Hoese, H.D. and R.H. Moore. 1977. Fishes of the Gulf of Mexico: Texas, Louisiana, and Adjacent Waters. College Station: Texas A&M University Press.

Johannes, R.E. 1978. Reproductive strategies of coastal marine fishes in the tropics. Environmental Biology of Fishes 3: 65-84.

Kelly, F.J., Jr., J.E. Schmitz, R.E. Randall, and J.D. Cochrane. 1982. Physical oceanography. In: Hann, R.W., Jr. and R.E. Randall, eds. Evaluation of brine disposal of the Strategic Petroleum Reserve Program. Final Report of 18 Month Postdisposal Studies, Volume 1. Texas A&M University and Texas A&M Research Foundation, College Station, Texas.

Kriete, W.H., Jr. and J.G. Loesch. 1980. Design and relative efficiency of a bow-mounted pushnet for sampling juvenile pelagic fishes. Transactions of the American Fisheries Society 109: 649-652.

Leard, R., B. Mahmoudi, H. Blanchet, H. Lazuauski, K. Spiller, M. Buchanan, C. Dyer, and W. Keithly. 1995. The striped mullet fishery of the Gulf of Mexico, United States: a regional management plan. Gulf States Marine Fisheries Commission 33.

Leis, J.M. 1991. The pelagic stage of reef fishes: the larval biology of coral reef fishes. In: Sale, P.F., ed. The Ecology of Fishes on Coral Reefs. San Diego: Academic Press.

Limouzy-Paris, C., M.F. McGowan, W.J. Richards, J.P. Umaran and S.S. Cha. 1994. Diversity of fish larvae in the Florida Keys: Results from SEFCAR. Bulletin of Marine Science 54(3): 857-870.

Lindberg, W.J. 1997. Can science resolve the attraction-production issue? Fisheries 22(4): 10-13.

Lyczkowski-Shultz, J., J.P. Steen, Jr., B.H. Comyns. 1988. Early life history of red drum (*Sciaenops ocellatus*) in the northcentral Gulf of Mexico. Technical Report MASGP-88-013, Mississippi-Alabama Sea Grant Program.

Magurran, A.E. 1988. Ecological Diversity and Its Measurement. Princeton: Princeton University Press.

McGowan, M.F. 1985. Ichthyoplankton of the Flower Garden Banks, northwest Gulf of Mexico. Doctoral dissertation. University of Miami, Miami.

McLellan, H.J. 1965. Tides. In: Elements of physical oceanography. Permagon Press, Oxford.

Murphy, M.D. and R.G. Taylor. 1990. Reproduction, growth, and mortality of red drum *Sciaenops ocellatus* in Florida waters. Fishery Bulletin, U.S. 88: 531-542.

Murray, S.P. 1976. Currents and circulation in the coastal waters of Louisiana. Sea Grant Publication LSU-T-76-003, Louisiana State University, Baton Rouge.

Naughton S.P. and C.H. Saloman. 1981. Stomach contents of juveniles of king mackerel (*Scomberomorus cavalla*) and Spanish mackerel (*S. maculatus*). Northeast Gulf Science 5(1): 71-74.

NOAA/NMFS 1993 Fisheries of the United States, 1992. Current Fisheries Statistics 9200.

Nybakken, J.W. 1988. Marine Biology: An Ecological Approach. New York: Harper and Row.

Parker, R.H. 1960. Ecology and distributional pattern of marine invertebrates, northern Gulf of Mexico. In: Shepard, F.P., F.B. Phleger and T.H. van Andel, eds. Recent Sediments, Northwest Gulf of Mexico. American Association of Petroleum Geologists.

Parker, R.O., Jr., D.R. Colby and T.P. Willis. 1983. Estimated amount of reef habitat on a portion of the U.S. South Atlantic and Gulf of Mexico continental shelf. Bulletin of Marine Science 33: 935-940.

Patillo, M.E., T.E. Czapla, D.M. Nelson, and M.E. Monaco. 1997. Distribution and abundance of fishes and invertebrates in Gulf of Mexico estuaries, Volume II: Species life history summaries. ELMR Report Number 11, NOAA/NOS Strategic Environmental Assessments Division, Silver Spring.

Pickering, H. and D. Whitmarsh. 1997. Artificial reefs and fisheries exploitation: A review of the 'attraction versus production' debate, the influence of design and its significance for policy. Fisheries Research 31: 39-59.

Raynie, R.C. and R.F. Shaw. 1994. Ichthyoplankton abundance along a recruitment corridor from offshore spawning to estuarine nursery ground. Estuarine, Coastal and Shelf Science 39: 421-450.

Richards, W.J. 1984. Kinds and abundances of fish larvae in the Caribbean Sea and adjacent areas. NOAA Technical Report NMFS-SSRF-776.

Richards, W.J. and K.C. Lindeman. 1987. Recruitment dynamics of reef fishes: planktonic processes, settlement and demersal ecologies, and fishery analysis. Bulletin of Marine Science 41: 392-410.

Richards, W.J., T. Potthoff, S. Kelley, M.F. McGowan, L. Ejsymont, J.H. Power and R.M Oleva L. 1984. SEAMAP 1982 - Ichthyoplankton. NOAA Technical Memorandum, NMFS-SEFC-144.

Richards, W.J., M.F. McGowan, T. Leming, J.T. Lampkin and S. Kelley. 1993. Larval fish assemblages at the Loop Current boundary in the Gulf of Mexico. Bulletin of Marine Science 53(2): 475-537.

Ricklefs, R.E. and Lau, M. 1980. Bias and dispersion of overlap indices: results of some Monte Carlo simulations. Ecology 61: 1019-1024.

Riley, C.M. and G.J. Holt. 1993. Gut contents of larval fishes from light trap and plankton net collections at Enmedio Reef near Veracruz, Mexico. Revista de Biologia Tropical Suplemento 41: 53-57.

Robertson, D.R. 1991. The role of adult biology in the timing of spawning of tropical reef fishes. In: Sale, P.F., ed. The Ecology of Fishes on Coral Reefs. San Diego: Academic Press.

Robertson, D.R., D.G. Green, and B.C. Victor. 1988. Temporal coupling of production and recruitment of larvae of a Caribbean reef fish. Ecology 69: 370-381.

Robins, C.R., G.C. Ray, and J. Douglass. 1986. A Field Guide to the Atlantic Coast Fishes of North America. Boston: Houghton Mifflin Company.

Robins, C.R., R.M. Bailey, C.E. Bond, J.R. Brooker, E.A. Lachner, R.N. Lea, and W.B. Scott. 1991. Common and scientific names of fishes from the United States and Canada. American Fisheries Society Special Publication 20, American Fisheries Society, Bethesda.

Rooker, J.R., G. D. Dennis, and D. Goulet. 1996. Sampling larval fishes with a nightlight lift-net in tropical inshore waters. Fisheries Research 26: 1-15.

Rooker, J.R., Q.R. Dokken, C.V. Pattengill, and G.J. Holt. 1997. Fish assemblages on artificial and natural reefs in The Flower Garden Banks National Marine Sanctuary, USA. Coral Reefs 16: 83-92.

Ross, S.W. and M.L. Moser. 1995. Life history of juvenile gag, Mycteroperca microlepis, in North Carolina estuaries. Bulletin of Marine Science 56: 222-237.

Sale, P.F. 1980. The ecology of fishes on coral reefs. Oceanography and Marine Biology 18: 367-421.

Sale, P.F. 1991. The ecology of fishes on coral reefs. New York: Academic Press.

SAS Institute, Inc. 1989. SAS/STAT Users Guide, Version 6. Cary: SAS Institute, Inc.

Scarborough-Bull, A. and J.J. Kendall, Jr. 1994. An indication of the process: offshore platforms as artificial reefs in the Gulf of Mexico. Bulletin of Marine Science 55: 1086-1098.

Schoener, T.W. 1970. Non-synchronous spatial overlap of lizards in patchy habitats. Ecology 51: 408-418.

Seaman, W., Jr. and L.M. Sprague. 1992. Artificial habitats for marine and freshwater fisheries. New York: Academic Press.

Secor, D.H., J.M. Dean, and J. Hansbarger. 1993. Modification of the quatrefoil light trap for use in hatchery ponds. Progressive Fish Culturist 54: 202-205.

Shaw, R.F, W.J. Wiseman, Jr., R.E. Turner, L.J. Rouse, Jr., R.E. Condrey, and F.J. Kelly, Jr. 1985. Transport of larval Gulf menhaden Brevoortia patronus in continental shelf waters of western Louisiana: a hypothesis. Transactions of the American Fisheries Society 114: 452-460.

Shinn, E.A. 1974. Oil structures as artificial reefs. In: Marine environmental implications of offshore oil and gas development in the Baltimore Canyon region of the Mid-Atlantic coast. Estuarine Research Federation 75-1.

Shinn, E.A. and R.I. Wicklund. 1989. Artificial reef observations from a manned submersible off southeast Florida. Bulletin of Marine Science 44: 1051-1057.

Shulman, M.J. 1985. Recruitment of coral reef fishes: effects of distribution of predators and shelter. Ecology 66: 1056-1066.

Sokal, R.R. and F.J Rohlf. 1981. Biometry: then principles and practice of statistics in biological research. New York: W.H. Freeman and Co.

Sonnier, F. J. Teerling, and H.D. Hoese. 1976. Observations on the offshore reef and platform fish fauna of Louisiana. Copeia 1976: 15-111.

Sponaugle, S. and R.K. Cowen. 1996. Nearshore patterns of coral reef fish larval supply to Barbados, West Indies. Marine Ecology Progress Series 133: 13-28.

SPSS, Inc. 1999. SYSTAT 9: Getting started. Chicago: SPSS, Inc.

Stanley, D.R. and C.A. Wilson. 1990. A fishery dependent based study of fish species composition and associated catch rates around petroleum platforms off Louisiana. Fishery Bulletin 88: 719-730.

Stanley, D.R. and C.A. Wilson. 2000. Seasonal and spatial variation in the biomass and size frequency distribution of fish associated with oil and gas platforms in the northern Gulf of Mexico. OCS Study MMS 2000-005. U.S. Dept. of the Interior, Minerals Management Service, Gulf of Mexico OCS Region, New Orleans.

Starck, W.A. 1971. Biology of the gray snapper, *Lutjanus griseus* (Linnaeus), in the Florida Keys. In: Starck, W. A. and R.E. Schroeder, eds. Investigations on the gray snapper, *Lutjanus griseus*. Studies in Tropical Oceanography 10.

Steimle, F.W. and M.H. Meier. 1997. What information do artificial reef managers really want from fishery science? Fisheries 22(4): 6-8.

Stephan, C.D., B.G. Dansby, G.C. Matlock, R.K. Rieckers, and R. Rayburn. 1990. Texas artificial reef fishery management plan. Texas Parks and Wildlife Department of Fisheries Management Plan Serial 3.

Stone, R.B., H.L. Pratt, R.O. Parker, and G.E. Davis. 1979. A comparison of fish populations on an artificial and natural reef in the Florida Keys. Marine Fisheries Review 41: 1-11.

Swearer, S.E., J.E. Caselle, D.W. Lea and R.R. Warner. 1999. Larval retention and recruitment in an island population of a coral-reef fish. Nature 402: 799-802.

Sweatman, H.P.A. 1984. A field study of the predatory behavior and feeding rate of a piscivorous coral reef fish, the lizardfish *Synodus englemani*. Copeia 1984: 187-193.

Thorrold, S.R. 1992. Evaluating the performance of light traps for sampling small fish and squid in open waters of the central Great Barrier Reef lagoon. Marine Ecology Progress Series 89: 277-285.

Thorrold, S.R., J.M. Shenker, E. Wishinski, R. Mojica and E.D. Maddox. 1994. Larval supply of shorefishes to nursery habitats around Lee Stocking Island, Bahamas. I. Small-scale distribution patterns. Marine Biology 118: 555-566.

Thresher, R.E. 1984. Reproduction in Reef Fishes. T.F.H. Publications, Inc.

Thresher, R.K., K.L. Sainsbury, J.S. Gunn and A.W. Whitelaw. 1986. Life history strategies and recent changes in population structure in the lizardfish genus *Saurida*, on the Australian northwest shelf. Copeia 1986(1): 876-885.

Tolan, J.M. 2001. Patterns of reef fish larval supply to petroleum platforms in the northern Gulf of Mexico. Doctoral dissertation. Louisiana State University, Baton Rouge.

Uchida, R.N. 1981. Synopsis of biological data on frigate tuna, *Auxis thazard*, and bullet tuna, *A. rochei*. NOAA Technical Report, NMFS Circ. 436.

USDOC (United States Department of Commerce). 1996. Magnuson-Stevens Fishery Conversation and Management Act. NOAA Technical Memorandum, NMFS-F/SPO-23.

Van Guelpen, L., D.F. Markle, and D.J. Duggan. 1982. An evaluation of accuracy, precision, and speed of several zooplankton sampling techniques. Journal du Conseil. Conseil Permanent International pour l'Exploration de la Mer 40: 226-236.

Van Voorhies, D.A., J.F. Witzig, J. F., M.F. Osborn, M.C. Holliday, and R.J. Essig. 1992. Marine recreational fishery statistics survey, Atlantic and Gulf coasts, 1990-1991. NOAA/NMFS Current Fisheries Statistics 9204.

Victor, B.C. 1986. Larval settlement and juvenile mortality in a recruitment-limited coral reef fish population. Ecological Monographs 56: 145-160.

West, J.E., R.M. Buckley and D.C. Doty. 1994. Ecology and habitat use of juvenile rockfishes (*Sebastes* spp.) associated with artificial reefs in Puget Sound, Washington. Bulletin of Marine Science 55: 344-350.

The Department of the Interior Mission

As the Nation's principal conservation agency, the Department of the Interior has responsibility for most of our nationally owned public lands and natural resources. This includes fostering sound use of our land and water resources; protecting our fish, wildlife, and biological diversity; preserving the environmental and cultural values of our national parks and historical places; and providing for the enjoyment of life through outdoor recreation. The Department assesses our energy and mineral resources and works to ensure that their development is in the best interests of all our people by encouraging stewardship and citizen participation in their care. The Department also has a major responsibility for American Indian reservation communities and for people who live in island territories under U.S. administration.

The Minerals Management Service Mission

As a bureau of the Department of the Interior, the Minerals Management Service's (MMS) primary responsibilities are to manage the mineral resources located on the Nation's Outer Continental Shelf (OCS), collect revenue from the Federal OCS and onshore Federal and Indian lands, and distribute those revenues.

Moreover, in working to meet its responsibilities, the **Offshore Minerals Management Program** administers the OCS competitive leasing program and oversees the safe and environmentally sound exploration and production of our Nation's offshore natural gas, oil and other mineral resources. The MMS **Minerals Revenue Management** meets its responsibilities by ensuring the efficient, timely and accurate collection and disbursement of revenue from mineral leasing and production due to Indian tribes and allottees, States and the U.S. Treasury.

The MMS strives to fulfill its responsibilities through the general guiding principles of: (1) being responsive to the public's concerns and interests by maintaining a dialogue with all potentially affected parties and (2) carrying out its programs with an emphasis on working to enhance the quality of life for all Americans by lending MMS assistance and expertise to economic development and environmental protection.